China's Relook at the Neighbourhood Diplomacy DRI

China's Relook at the Neighbourhood Diplomacy DRI

Capt R K Sirohi

PRASHANT PUBLISHING HOUSE
DELHI-110094

Published by :
Prashant Publishing House
C-34, 28 Foota Road, Gali-3,
West Karwal Nagar, Delhi-110094
Phone : 011-22963970, Mob. : 9810396373
e-mail.: prashantpublishinghouse@gmail.com

China's Relook at the Neighbourhood Diplomacy DRI

Reserved
First Published 2018

ISBN 978-81-938012-3-9

PRINTED IN INDIA
Published by Mr. R.K. Jha M/s Prashant Publishing House and Published at H.S. Offset House Press, Delhi.

Contents

Preface

China defines its neighbors broadly. Neighboring countries refer to those who are located east of the Ural Mountains, the Bosporus Strait and the Suez Canal; south of the Caucasus Mountains; and west of the Bering Sea. There are 62 such countries, which implies that China should not, and cannot, conduct an equidistant diplomacy. China needs to sort its 62 neighboring countries then define the level, strength, pattern, and fields of diplomatic policy toward these countries.

Diplomacy is now under rapid evolution. This means ever-widening international contacts by official agencies other than the foreign ministry, the sub-state agencies, and non-state actors; the impact of information and communication revolution; and gradual 'democratisation', via institutional plurality, emerging public-private partnerships and a stronger role of home publics. Most foreign ministries now pursue reform as a continuous activity. China is one such example.

The evolution in China's diplomatic system since 1949 demonstrates how professional expertise challenges ideological commitment, though both criteria remain relevant. On strategic policy issues, this system is highly efficient, and coordinated through the 'leading small group' mechanism operating under the Party Politburo. Yet inter-ministry harmonisation in routine issues is often blocked, thanks to the entrenched old vertical hierarchies. This limits in and out placements of officials, except within set parameters. Political diplomacy is today innovative and supple in its execution.

The practice of economic diplomacy remains low key, with embassies less engaged in 'marketing' projects, compared with Western counterparts. Cultural diplomacy is shifting to high gear, and will be a major theme at the 2008 Olympics. Domestic public diplomacy, outreach to home publics has become a top priority. The foreign ministry makes effective use of think tanks and retired envoys to provide inputs into the policy process, and is far ahead of India in the multiple policy options that this plural process generates, though policy formulation remains tightly guarded and secretive.

Based on Chinese diplomacy in 2015, the first year of OBOR enforcement, the gravity of Chinese diplomacy is turning from great powers, especially the United States, toward neighboring countries. Moving forward, China's diplomacy toward great powers, including the U.S., will decline, relatively . China, now identifying itself as a comprehensive great power, will try to adopt a more balanced approach to great power diplomacy, compared to previously when the U.S. relationship was the "core of the core" of Chinese diplomacy. Now, neighborhood diplomacy is moving to the center of Chinese diplomacy.

China needs to keep in mind that most programs and projects for cooperation should be proposed by Silk Road countries. China should only choose some areas for cooperation; an active China with hundred of project proposals will scare its neighbors and cause many unintended consequences. Besides that, China also needs to conduct diplomacy differently according to the category each country belongs to. China's diplomatic service has unique features— a single class hierarchy; ruthless fast-track implementation that propels the talented to high office at early age; a major problem of attrition, with many quitting in the first few years; an excellent system of language and area specialisation; continuous gender inequality. We may count on continuing refinement and improvement of the Chinese diplomatic process.

This is a reference book. All the matter is just compiled and edited in nature, taken from the various sources which are in public domain.

This book contains the fundamental and basic information of the subject and useful for teachers, students and researchers.

—Editor

1

China's Neighborhood Diplomacy

Under the "One Belt One Road" strategy (OBOR), China has two diplomatic priorities: diplomacy toward great powers and diplomacy toward neighboring countries. Neighboring diplomacy obviously has more potential for improvement than diplomacy toward the United States. During his visit to Singapore in November 2015, President Xi Jinping expounded clearly that neighborhood will be important for China's overall diplomacy, and China will take on the duty of promoting neighboring peace, stability, and development. Xi also declared that neighboring countries will benefit from OBOR and become the chief cooperative partners of China.

Based on Chinese diplomacy in 2015, the first year of OBOR enforcement, the gravity of Chinese diplomacy is turning from great powers, especially the United States, toward neighboring countries. Moving forward, China's diplomacy toward great powers, including the U.S., will decline, relatively . China, now identifying itself as a comprehensive great power, will try to adopt a more balanced approach to great power diplomacy, compared to previously when the U.S. relationship was the "core of the core" of Chinese diplomacy. Now, neighborhood diplomacy is moving to the center of Chinese diplomacy. However, there are huge differences among the large number of neighboring countries. Based on that, China has to work out a conception on how to tackle each of them.

CHINA'S NEIGHBORS

China defines its neighbors broadly. Neighboring countries refer to those who are located east of the Ural Mountains, the Bosporus Strait and the Suez Canal; south of the Caucasus Mountains; and west of the Bering Sea. There are 62 such countries, which implies that China should not, and cannot, conduct an equidistant diplomacy. China needs to sort its 62 neighboring countries then define the level, strength, pattern, and fields of diplomatic policy toward these countries.

China's neighbors can be divided geographically into sub-regions: Northeast Asia (Japan, North Korea, Russia, South Korea and Mongolia), Southeast Asia (divided into two parts: the countries on the Indochina Peninsula, including Vietnam, Laos, Cambodia, Burma, and Thailand and the island countries, including Malaysia, Singapore, Brunei, the Philippines, Indonesia and East Timor), South Asia (India, Pakistan, Bangladesh, Nepal, Bhutan, Sri Lanka, and the Maldives), West Asia (the six countries of the Gulf Cooperation Council, Iran, Iraq, Afghanistan, Turkey, Israel, Palestine, Cyprus, Lebanon, Syria, and Jordan), Central Asia (Kazakhstan, Uzbekistan, Turkmenistan, Tajikistan, and Kyrgyzstan), the South Caucasus (Georgia, Azerbaijan, and Armenia) and Oceania (Australia, New Zealand, Papua New Guinea, and the 11 Pacific Islands countries).

According to their comprehensive power and relations with China, these countries could be divided into four main categories: sub-regional great powers (SGP), sub-regional secondary great powers (SSGP), sub-regional small and middle powers with close relations with China (SSCC), and other sub-regional small and middle powers (SSMP).

Focusing on China's more immediate neighborhood, SGPs include Japan, Indonesia, Vietnam, India, Kazakhstan, and Australia; Russia, the sub-regional great power in North Asia, will be discussed separately later. SSGPs include Thailand, South Korea, Uzbekistan, New Zealand, Malaysia, and Pakistan. North Korea, Papua New Guinea, Turkmenistan, Bangladesh,

Myanmar, Laos, Cambodia, and Singapore should be categorized as SSCCs. The remaining countries belong to the SSMP category.

A BLUEPRINT FOR NEIGHBORHOOD DIPLOMACY

Given the unstable political situation within many Silk Road countries, and the fact that OBOR is a long term strategy, China, besides inter-government relation, must develop ties with various parties in those countries, and pay attention to public diplomacy as well. In this regard, China can learn a lot from Japan, the United States, and European countries.

China needs to keep in mind that most programs and projects for cooperation should be proposed by Silk Road countries. China should only choose some areas for cooperation; an active China with hundred of project proposals will scare its neighbors and cause many unintended consequences. Besides that, China also needs to conduct diplomacy differently according to the category each country belongs to.

The principle for SGP is "cooperation with balance." SGPs are often inclined to become global powers and worry about China's influence in their respective regions. To balance China, they would like to develop close ties with a global power (say, the United States). The United States, as a unique superpower, will be sure to take them as tools for balancing China in Asia.

Acting as a "balancer" is an iron-clad rule practiced by different hegemons in past centuries. Why doesn't China adopt that rule for itself?

China should apply this rule in different ways toward different SGPs according to their relations with China and America respectively. That is, counterbalance supplemented by cooperation toward Japan and India; cooperation supplemented by counterbalance toward Kazakhstan and Indonesia; equal measures of counterbalance and cooperation toward Vietnam and Australia.

For SSGPs, China should offer what could be called "sincere support with a limitation." Facing strategic pressure from SGPs, SSGPs need strategic support from China. China should support these countries sincerely and strongly, with the limitation that these countries are China's partners, not allies.

For SSCCs, China should carry out "whole support without guarantee." A few SSCCs are good at handling their relations with different global powers and finding the most beneficial status for themselves. Most SSCCs do not mind relying heavily on China, especially in regards to economy development and infrastructure building. Besides infrastructure construction, China should place importance on improving their soft capabilities, such as legal systems, medical conditions, and education.

For SSMPs, China needs to conduct "cooperation limited to certain fields and methods." For those states echoing the OBOR positively, China should show sincere support through some projects proposed by the host states, based on careful evaluation. Some of these may become SSCC-like partners in the future. For those whose evaluations of OBOR are not very positive, China should strictly evaluate proposed projects and only choose those that are low-risk. As to those states hostile toward OBOR, China may let it be. OBOR will last for at least eight years; China must have enough patience to see it through. Quality is better than speed.

CHINAS NEW DIPLOMACY AN ADAPTATION TO REALITY

By 2002, China began to make gradual but fundamental changes in its strategic thinking. It decided that it was in its best interests to maintain status quo rather than challenge the world order; integrate itself into the international economic system despite having a political system that was vastly different; recognize US presence in the Asia-Pacific region as a part of its security requirement in its vicinity; and adopt a good neighbourhood policy.

Chinas new diplomacy is multilateralist it enables China to maximize its interests while minimizing its responsibilities. While only a few years ago it had border disputes with most of its neighbours, modern day China has consented to diplomatic engagement and consultation rather than flexing its muscles. Its political dexterity has been accompanied with a complete alteration of its economic image, and China is using its financial clout to counterbalance other superpowers.

Policy reorientation under the peaceful rise strategy:

With regards to the US, China has recognized American might in the Asia-Pacific region. Its policy is more anti-unilateralism than anti-hegemony. With Japan, China has begun to treat it as its Asian neighbour rather than a US ally. In other words, it has delinked US-Japan relations from its own relationship with the island nation. North Korea continues to be one of China's few friends, although this is nothing to brag about. Priorities have now shifted from peace and stability in North Korea to a nuclear free North Korea. The six-party talks hosted by China are an example of this. With regards to Taiwan, since 2004 China has allowed for the existence of an independent-minded Taiwan. It is trying to subtly work on the image that it is for peaceful reunification over the long term, in an effort to address international suspicions that China might still pose a threat to Taiwan. China has signed a treaty with ASEAN nations stating its desire to be non-interventionist and non-confrontational.It has also promoted SCO in an attempt to strengthen border security and counter any threats posed by bordering nation states.

Consequences and Challenges of the Peaceful Rise strategy

Despite its reassurances to the rest of the world that the new China would like to build amicable relationships based on mutual trust and long term bonds, the international community is not entirely convinced of China's new role as a harbinger of peace in Asia and the world.

For starters, any new emerging superpower can be a bit disconcerting. The worry lies not in China's rising, rather what happens after China has risen. The Chinese have had to face some backlash regarding its policies towards Myanmar and

Darfur. With greater participation in the world community, its domestic problems have come to light as well, including but not limited to Tibet and human rights issues. Credibility in the eyes of the international community has become more important than flexibility, something which China did not have to worry about a decade ago.

Chinas military prowess and build up also strike some critics as being in sharp contrast to its message of a peaceful China. The argument is that China, in the long term, will become more opportunistic and abandon its multilateralist approach towards international engagement; in other words, its goodwill will continue only as far as its interests are not threatened. The perception is that Chinese leaders are using economic growth to distract popular opinion and also allow them to monopolize control over China, something which is not possible in a democratic system.

On the other hand, with China's unprecedented growth, it has become a stakeholder in the international order. Other superpowers recognize China's influence, and have accordingly changed their approach. Rather than attempting to contain China, they are hedging against it, using international cooperation and consensus to press China one way or another.

An insecure China from a decade ago has given way to a more assertive China that can not only participate in the game of international politics, but in the very making of the rules of the game itself. In this way, China's global interests have become legitimized.

China however needs to create a greater sense of openness within its own walls in order for the international community to fully accept China's strategy of peaceful rise. Without this, no amount of charm diplomacy is ever going to convince the world otherwise.

CHINA'S DIPLOMACY FOR THE 21ST CENTURY

"Doing our own business well first" – this is one of the admonitions left to the Chinese people by Deng Xiaoping, the designer of the improvement and opening up of the contemporary China. It is also the most direct and the simplest expression of "development demand". The half a century history since the founding of New China has proved that if the domestic economic construction and the improvement of the living of the people do not receive enough attention, the foreign policy of peace and independence would often than not remain empty and powerless, without the social base to last. Only when the domestic economy has developed and the political situation and the relations among all nationalities are kept stable, is it possible for diplomatic work to acquire a solid base. The main threat to China's state security comes not from foreign invasion or other wars, but from within, that is, whether or not China itself can maintain a stable, orderly and healthy development.

The "internal weakness" exhibit by Russia in the Kosovo subject has fully testified to this point. The most profound lesson taught by Russia is: first, a country must first of all manage its own affairs well so as to make it hard for potential or realistic enemy or rival to "penetrate" by exploiting the weakness. It is a common sense that flies hover over only rotten eggs. The fundamental destructive factor to the death of a big country lies not in external sources but the inner problems in the deep layers of the society. It is impossible to wipe out a big country. Its decline often starts from within, from the roots, say national separatism or economic stagnation or political turmoil or social disorder, for if a country were thrown into confusion, it would fall apart without being attacked. The Russian arena over the recent decade has exactly been experiencing every process of "national split—economic stagnation—political upheaval—social disorder". The serious "internal weakness" displayed before the nibbling by NATO is due, essentially, to the "internal war" without the smoke of gunpowder. If asked what we should learn from Russians, it is very simple to answer: it should not be soft toward separatists and, even more important, there should be no internal political strife or social disorder; economic development must not stop and the improvement and institutional improvement should not be interrupted. Stability of a country and growing national strength constitute the corner stone for the security of the country and a major source for having a say externally and exert international influence. "The easiest way to capture a fortress is from within". Without internal security, there would be no defending the state security to speak about, let alone safeguarding it.

It should be stressed here that in spite of the grave negative developments like Kosovo crisis, the relations among big powers have become more dependent upon each other while their relations are growing more complicated and delicate. The globalization process of the economy and science and technology has not been slowing down and the global scientific and technological creation is becoming more active than ever before.

The economic growth of most countries is still strong. The world's economic aggregates are still growing. What is the most important is that the comprehensive judgment from all features shows that a worldwide nuclear war or a world war with the involvement of all major countries in confrontation could be prevented for a considerably long period of time to come. All countries will seize the time to develop their own economies, science and technology and boost their national strength and make great efforts to improve the living of the people and infrastructure facilities.

Recall that during the recent 200 years, China has in most part been in a state of being bullied and humiliated or in an intense period of mobilization for "war and revolution". It did not make any real development and construction until only in the recent 20 years.

But the short span of 20 years has brought about a tremendous leap forward: the country walked out of the shadow of exhaustion in the motive forces for economic development; the GDP has ranked among the first ten in the world if calculated according to the exchange rate; till today, the Chinese people are continuing to realize the most massive economic growth in human history (a country with a population of 1.2 billion has expanded its economy at an annual rate of 8% within 20 years).

To look forward, even in another 20 years, not to say in another 100 years, if China should maintain the speed of the last 20 years and "concentrate its efforts on economic construction", the Chinese people have every reason to expect that the country will reach the level of a middle-developed country in per capita average and secure a place among the top three in the world in total aggregates. By then, China would have a significant say in the international affairs and the new international political and economic order will be most likely to develop toward the direction we expect.

Before talking about a methodical change in the current international relations or about making greater contributions to the external world, the Chinese people must have a sober estimation of themselves. It should be admitted that, after half a century construction, especially the rapid development over the recent 20 years through improvement and opening up, our comprehensive national strength has ascended a new stair and our international status and influence have grown greatly, China remains a developing country, still trailing behind other countries in many areas and still a far cry as compared with developed countries. This manifests itself not only in the "hardware", such as the per capita GNP, the living standards, development of roads, the modernization of educational facilities and means of information, labour productivity and product quality, and the proportion in the global trade and investment, but also in "software", such as institutional creation, comprehensive quality of services, understanding of the external world by the average people, the attractiveness of the whole country to foreign resources (including materials and intelligence), the general level of theoretical studies and the capability of keeping track with the advanced world levels. The strength of software includes the strength in political and social development and in theory and also the following factors: (1) the domestic political, social and economic system arrangements that are open, stable, lasting, and absorbing; (2) powerful culture, political and ethical appeal and rallying power; (3) theoretical guidance; (4) strategic insight and diplomatic skills; (5) effective domestic and international management, including the effective mobilization of domestic and international resources (especially non-military resources; (6) the populace of high educational level and strong cultural awareness; (7) high level of living standards. It is a long way to go for China to acquire such strength. Economic and military strength cannot substitute for the powerful political and social base". Historically, the contemporary China has not and will not possibly have what it used to experience in the heydays of Han and Tang dynasties. Ever since the modern times, it has been in "tight operation" economically, socially and politically. As the changes in the economic structure advance simultaneously with the changes of the whole social and political system, the awareness of opening up grows together with the growth of the awareness of nationalism. The whole country has grown rapidly, but with problems cropping up one after another and a large number of troubles put on the agenda before the problems left from the old system had not be rooted out, such as bankruptcy of enterprises and workers thrown out of jobs, the regional economic and educational disparities, corruption and the so-called "crises in belief, credit and confidence". The problems in themselves have already restricted its power of influencing the world. If no steps are taken to deepen improvement and opening up, no efforts are made to continue the great development, stopping there, rest contented, the prospects of China and the world would not develop toward the direction in our favour. In this sense, the focus of China's diplomacy for a quite a long period of time to come still remains to be on the creation of a neighbouring environment favourable to China's improvement, development and stability and on meeting the major demands of economic construction. Unless major wars break out not to our liking, there would be no reason to change the priority of this demand.

The above essentials show that what is referred to as "development demand" is much richer and much more extensive in content than what we used to construe or disseminate in the past. For instance, economically speaking, the Chinese people have basically realized a "comfortable living". But when measured by fairly comprehensive standards, China needs more profound political democracy and legal construction and needs the synchronization of the development of spiritual civilization (belief, ethics and values) and material civilization, needs more rational and smooth run-in between the stratification of the society and the various interest groups, needs more Chinese people who have broader and more lenient insight on the world, and needs greater development of the strategic thinking and theoretical nature about China's international relations.

The term "Development" covers political development, the development of civilization, social development and development of values. Under the precondition of making economic development the central task, the development in all features mentioned above will greatly help China to raise its status and power of influence internationally in the new millennium and that will naturally provide more solid base for China's diplomacy to display its prowess.

2

China's Challenging Neighborhood Diplomacy

There have been remarkable changes in China's neighborhood diplomacy in recent years. Taking active steps, China has endeavored to guide and shape the environment around it. But it faces increasing risks and challenges.

Over the past two years, China has seen significant fluctuations in its relations with neighboring countries, in particular the Philippines, South Korea and North Korea. The ruling of the South China Sea arbitration in July last year tried to invalidate China's claims in the waters, but Sino-Philippine relations soon saw shifts after Philippine President Rodrigo Duterte took office. China's ties with South Korea deteriorated dramatically after Seoul decided to deploy the Terminal High Altitude Area Defense (THAAD) system on its soil, and forges toward an uncertain future. As Pyongyang conducted missile and nuclear tests regardless of strong international opposition, China has agreed to heighten the sanctions on the regime within the UN framework.

China is forming its style of diplomacy. It is willing to show goodwill, and has no fear of using a big stick when necessary. For instance, it provided economic benefits for the Duterte administration that had been shifting away from the US, and coordinated with his domestic policy.

Nonetheless, China's relationships with the three countries suggest it faces multiple challenges in maintaining security in its neighborhood. China is not sufficiently aware about its security challenges. It often lags behind in taking precautions, and is short in capacity and experience to take the initiative. Hence it often finds itself in a passive position.

After the administration of then Philippine president Benigno Aquino III took the South China Sea dispute to the Permanent Court of Arbitration, China was compelled to put in massive diplomatic resources to cope with the situation, but still failed to turn around international opinion. The ruling came down overwhelmingly in favor of Philippine claims.

China-South Korea ties had been improving after Park Geun-hye held power. She even made an appearance at China's military parade in September to mark the 70th anniversary of the end of WWII, despite pressure from Washington. However, the bilateral relationship plunged to its worst level due to the THAAD deployment. This apparently reflected problems in the two nations' communication and crisis management.

The shift of Duterte's policy on China and political chaos in South Korea have helped improve China's security situation. But this has been achieved due to changes in the politics of other countries and their adjustment in policy focus, such as Duterte's war on corruption and drugs in his country.

In the future, China still faces a number of challenges in its neighborhood. The challenges need to be addressed with a holistic approach if China wants to maintain and prolong its current period of strategic opportunity, promote its domestic economic and political situation, and push forward the implementation of its initiatives and proposals.

Since Indian Prime Minister Narendra Modi came into power, he has adjusted India's policy on China. This year, the China-India border negotiations and the foreign ministers' meeting of China, Russia and India haven't been held. India skipped the Belt and Road Forum for International Cooperation in May as it protested against the China-Pakistan Economic Corridor, and only sent Minister of State for External Affairs Vijay Kumar Singh to attend the meeting of BRICS foreign ministers last month. New Delhi's latest incursion over the

Sino-Indian border is another example of its actions against Beijing.

Washington may put an end to its strategic patience with Pyongyang. Under the circumstances, the North Korean government may launch a new nuclear test and accelerate efforts to miniaturize nuclear warheads to put them on missiles. China's challenges in the South China Sea remain. There is a possibility that Vietnam and other countries will bring their disputes with China to the international community, or that Southeast Asian countries will band together to resist China. As Seoul is set to deploy the THAAD system, the alliance of Japan, the US and South Korea may be strengthened.

Yet the biggest challenge for China lies in Donald Trump's China policy, given Washington's important position in the Asia-Pacific region and the unpredictability of the Trump administration. The anti-establishment president has made it more difficult for China and the US to coordinate their policies. But what's certain is that Washington will adopt an offshore balancing act to intensify the great power strategic competition, whoever the US president is. This definitely hampers China's diplomatic activities in its neighborhood and its strategic rise.

Political changes in China's neighbors will be a big test for China's diplomacy. In response, China needs to make choices and seek opportunities out of chaos for making breakthroughs and reshaping the situation. This entails great diplomatic wisdom and a coherent strategy.

THE CHANGING FACE OF CHINESE DIPLOMACY

One of the most curious and underexamined features of the evolving North Korean nuclear crisis is the active and leading role played by China in the last nine months. Breaking with years of traditional Chinese passivity on global-security challenges, Beijing has helped to walk both Pyongyang and Washington back from the brink, surprising even China's critics.

Chinese diplomats were instrumental in bringing about a first round of tripartite discussions and six-party talks. Since then, senior Chinese officials have shuttled between Pyongyang and Washington to maintain momentum for the next round. Beijing has also used coercive measures such as a reported temporary suspension of oil supplies, an "inspection" of a North Korean ship in a Chinese port and shifting troop deployments on the China-North Korean border.

Beijing's consistent efforts to resolve the North Korean nuclear subject is one of many indications of a broader evolution in China's diplomacy. In recent years, Beijing's foreign policy has begun to reflect a more sophisticated, confident and, at times, constructive and proactive approach toward regional and global affairs.

For many previous decades until the mid-1990s, China regularly criticized the structure of the international system and complained that other powers colluded against its interests. Beijing now increasingly appears to be embracing the current constellation of international institutions, rules and norms as a means through which to promote and pursue its national interests. China is now working within the international system as opposed to criticizing and challenging it.

Evidence of the changes in Chinese diplomacy abound. China has expanded the breadth and depth of its bilateral relations, joined numerous regional and international agreements and increased the quality of its participation in multilateral organizations. Beijing's embrace of multilateral institutions represents one of the most dramatic shifts in its foreign relations. In the early 1990s, China was wary of such forums as venues that would criticize and constrain China. Beijing now views participation as a means to shape international rules, improve relations with neighbouring countries (especially in Southeast Asia) and limit what it perceives as undue U.S. global influence.

In East Asia, China has actively engaged the Association of Southeast Asian Nations and the Asean Regional Forum. Beijing has taken a series of calculated steps to reassure Asean states that China's rise doesn't threaten their economic and security interests. In 2001, China proposed the establishment of a China-Asean Free Trade Area, the first of its kind. To allay regional fears about its territorial ambitions, China also agreed to a Declaration on a Code of Conduct for the island disputes in the South China Sea. And Beijing most recently signed the Treaty of Amity and Cooperation, one of the first non-Asean states to take this step, signaling its acceptance of their norms of conflict resolution.

Elsewhere in the region, China led the establishment of a multilateral organization focused on regional security in Central Asia, known as the Shanghai Cooperation Organization. The group now has six members who cooperate on border demilitarization, counter terrorism and trade.

Beyond Asia, China initiated an annual meeting with the European Union in 1998 and recently approached the North Atlantic Treaty Organization about starting an annual dialogue on strategic perceptions and regional security threats. This effort stands in stark contrast to China's traditionally critical approach to U.S.-led security alliances. In the U.N. Security Council, China voted in favour of the November 2002 U.N. Resolution 1441 on weapons inspections in Iraq. This was only the second time since China joined the U.N. in 1971 that it supported a Security Council resolution under Chapter 7 of the U.N. Charter, which authorizes the use of force. Through the 1990s, while it generally did not block U.N. action, China abstained on similar votes, including during the first Gulf War. More recently, China has voted in support of resolutions relating to the rebuilding of Iraq.

Over the past 10 years, China has sign several key arms control and nonproliferation treaties. Beijing has also subjectd numerous domestic export control laws in an effort to enforce these new nonproliferation commitments. While differences in interpretation of the regimes and problems with implementing controls on sensitive technology exports continue, the overall trend is encouraging.

China has also actively addressed numerous territorial disputes that historically soured its regional relations. Since

1991, it has resolved disputes with Laos, Russia, Vietnam, Kazakhstan, Kyrgyzstan and Tajikistan. In these settlements, China often received less than half of the disputed areas. In addition, China has instituted troop reductions and confidence-building measures on border security with key neighbors such as India and Russia.

Likewise, the execution of China's diplomacy has become more sophisticated, as Beijing seeks to shape world opinion. At an individual level, China's third and fourth generation of leaders have sought to personalize China's diplomacy by traveling abroad far more than previous leaders.

More broadly, China has subjectd well over a dozen "white papers" outlining the government's official position on domestic and international policy subjects. The Foreign Ministry's and State Council's Web pages include an impressive trove of basic data on Chinese positions, new policy developments and official statements. Perhaps most surprising, Chinese officials have started providing the international press with Western-style "background briefings" before and after most important diplomatic events.

Within the last few years, and especially since September 11, 2001, even more dramatic shifts have occurred in China's thinking about its role in the international system. Influential Chinese analysts have begun advocating that China abandon its long-held victim mentality and instead promote the adoption of a "great-power mentality."

An important manifestation of these ideas is that Chinese strategists increasingly see their interests as more akin to most important powers and less associated with those of developing nations. This change alone represents a significant perceptual shift from the 1990s, when many Chinese still viewed their nation as disenfranchised by globalization, the other most important powers, and multilateral forums. Reflecting this change, President Hu Jintao was the first Chinese leader to attend a dialogue meeting of the Group of Eight leading nations this past summer.

Chinese diplomats and political leaders now talk about "shared global responsibilities" and improving cooperation among "great powers" (which includes China) to combat global security threats. This thinking stands in stark contrast to China's previously narrow view of its national interests, its identity as a most important power and its role in the international community.

A final, most important element of China's new thinking is a recent, if grudging, acceptance that the world is for the moment unipolar and that U.S. preponderance will persist for decades. Although Chinese leaders publicly tout multipolarization as the trend of the times (and condemn American unilateralism), Chinese analysts also acknowledge that their country cannot (and will not) challenge U.S. global dominance anytime soon.

While all these trends are important, China still faces serious obstacles to becoming a high-profile, much less a dominant, player in the international community. Even as the country's diplomacy becomes more active, Chinese leaders need to grapple with severe political, social and economic challenges.

China's new diplomacy presents Asian and American leaders with both opportunities and challenges. China's active participation in international institutions creates more chances to elicit its assistance on key subjects. Recent examples of this trend include U.S.-China cooperation on counterterrorism, counternarcotics and nonproliferation.

However, policy makers should remember that even as China becomes more engaged, it is also growing more adept at using its foreign policy and foreign relations to serve Chinese interests. Today's China is certainly smarter and more sophisticated — but not necessarily kinder or gentler.

Beijing's new skills may at times frustrate Washington's objectives, as China is potentially becoming better equipped to challenge the policies of the U.S. and its allies. China's ability to consistently outmaneuver the U.S. at the U.N. Human Rights Commission in recent years should serve as a wake-up call.

China is dissatisfied with some features of the international system, such as U.S. preponderance and especially the status of Taiwan. Washington should remain aware of these frustrations and shape its ties with Asian nations in a way that recognizes the reality of China's expanding regional role. China is rapidly emerging as the engine of growth in Asia, which affords it increasing influence and leverage. Washington needs to pay consistent attention to managing relations with regional friends and allies, if it hopes to maintain its pull.

A longer-term task for the entire international group of people is to ensure that China's new diplomacy is consistent with regional stability and security. China's top political leaders have deemed the next 20 years a strategic opportunity to develop their country. An opening exists for the international community as well, and policy makers should use it wisely, to manage China's emergence as a diplomatic power.

SOUTH ASIA'S MANIFOLD CHALLENGE

The concept of "the international community", if it is to have practical meaning and encapsulate the notion of "solidarity without borders" instead of being an empty slogan, must come to terms with the multitude and gravity of the challenges confronting the peoples and nations of South Asia (Bangladesh, Bhutan, India, Maldives, Nepal, Pakistan and Sri Lanka). The scale of the problems faced in the region and the numbers of people involved are so huge that success or failure in South Asia pose defining challenges to the core mandates of the United Nations as the global arena for problem-solving. South Asia by itself accounts for one-fifth of "We the peoples of the United Nations". Developments in South Asia cut across the major faultlines of the UN system with respect to the challenges of economic development, environmental protection, food and water security, democratic governance and human rights, nuclear war and peace, inter-state and internal conflicts, and new security issues such as AIDS (acquired immune deficiency syndrome) and international terrorism. What happens in South Asia will surely shape the contours of the global community in the decades ahead. Two of the central purposes of the United Nations as expressed in the UN Charter – to maintain international peace and security and to promote social and economic advancement – make it imperative for the organization to address these issues in South Asia.

The United Nations University (UNU), in collaboration with the UN agencies in Japan, organized an international conference in May 2002 on "The United Nations and South Asia". UNU in Tokyo is particularly well suited as a forum for discussing these issues as the major UN agencies are located in its headquarters building in Tokyo, "UN House". The South Asian embassies in Japan offered their support for the conference and collaborated in its organization. The conference was well timed in that 2002 marked the fiftieth anniversary of the establishment of diplomatic relations with Japan by India, Pakistan and Sri Lanka. But it was ill timed in that on that date India and Pakistan were in the middle of the biggest and most tense mobilization of their full military mights along the full length of their border. Yet, by presenting a forum for communication between different actors within the various sectors, the conference helped to alleviate the substantial lack of interaction and thus contributed to improved efforts at addressing the problems in South Asia.

The chapters in this volume are revised versions of the papers presented at that conference. Their emphasis is on discussing issues of particular relevance to the region and exploring the potential for improvement in both domestic and international efforts at alleviating the problems of South Asia. If and where appropriate, the role that the United Nations can play in this respect is also underscored.

One of the more interesting features of this volume is the divergence of cultures and writing styles of the scholars and the practitioners (officials, politicians, generals). Academics are addicted to notes, whereas practitioners are allergic to them. Many academics have to be reined in so that their contributions form chapters in a book instead of mini-tomes in themselves, whereas some practitioners have to be coaxed into extending their brief vignettes to a length and intellectual weight suitable for publication by a university press. Two of the UNU's five mandated tasks are to serve as a bridge between the normally isolated worlds of scholarship and policy and to serve as a platform for dialogue. This volume is testimony to the need for dialogue not only between participants from the different nations and societies of a deeply divided region of the world, but also between the different professional cultures in the modern world.

Former prime minister of India, I. K. Gujral, expresses the hope that the recent international interest in South Asia is not temporary and based solely on the threat of terrorism and nuclearization, but rather reflects a realization that the world community cannot be safe or happy unless it involves the billion-plus people of South Asia in the critical decisions regarding peace, security and development. According to Gujral, the most serious current challenge facing South Asia is terrorism. But the fight against terrorism cannot be won by force alone. It is of course necessary to fight the jihadi culture. But, even without jihad, there would still be manifestations of terrorism in all South Asian countries in the form of insurgency movements. Therefore there is an urgent need to address the root causes of terrorism, such as lack of good governance, low levels of human development, and new threats such as drug trafficking and the spread of AIDS. Although the main responsibility for the problems and their resolution lies with the South Asian countries, the region has not been brought into the global developmental mainstream by the international community. The international community needs a peaceful, cooperative and dynamic South Asia; it is in its interest to facilitate this.

Gujral sees great potential for development in South Asia in the fields of science and technology, as well as in traditional industries such as chemicals, pharmaceuticals, heavy industries, steel and electronics. For this potential to be realized, however, regional cooperation is necessary. India, as the leading power, can afford to be accommodative to promote such cooperation.

Sartaj Aziz, while calling for a comprehensive programme to reduce poverty in South Asia, also asks for UN action to reduce tension between the region's two nuclear powers. There is an urgent need to accelerate the pace of economic and social progress in the region and to meet the challenges of globalization. The United Nations must assume and discharge its responsibility to focus on the inequalities of the globalization process and regain a leadership role in providing a level playing field.

Nor can the international community continue to overlook the security problems in the region. International assistance is needed to fight terrorism and extremism in the region as well as to stabilize Afghanistan. At the same time, Aziz calls for the United Nations to curb "liberal imperialism", that is, the notion that the so-called "postmodern" world can use force, pre-emptive attack or even deception to violate international boundaries with impunity.

Peace and Security

An immediate concern of the international community is the region's impact on international peace and security. South Asia poses many potential threats to regional and global peace and security: it has two nuclear powers engaged in a major territorial dispute; there are several dominant insurgency conflicts here; terrorism is pronounced; and the refugee situation has the potential to be deeply destabilizing. There are also significant cross-regional linkages with respect to relations with China (one of the five permanent members of the UN Security Council), Central Asia (and Russia beyond), the Middle East and South-East Asia. How can domestic and international efforts at resolving conflicts in the region be improved?

Inter-state Conflict

Since the end of the Cold War, the global pattern of conflict has shifted from inter-state to intra-state conflicts (many of which have transnational regional links), yet one of the remaining potential inter-state conflicts is found in South Asia. The situation is aggravated by the fact that the two potential belligerents are armed with nuclear-armed weapons. Whereas the stability of the nuclear deterrence between the superpowers during the Cold War was itself somewhat suspect, the relationship between Pakistan and India is qualitatively different and even more volatile. The two countries share a long border, which allows little time to decide whether to "use or lose" nuclear weapons in response to a perceived threat.

Furthermore, Pakistan and India are involved in a territorial dispute over Kashmir. This dispute has already resulted in two wars between the countries and the possibility of armed conflict has not yet been eliminated. Neither country has second-strike retaliatory capability, which makes both of them more vulnerable to a pre-emptive strike than was the case between the superpowers during the Cold War. South Asia's relationship with and ties to neighbouring countries also have implications for the involvement of the international community in the region. A complicating element is India's disputed border with China, a third nuclear power with tangible interests in the region. Resurgence of Islamic fundamentalism in the region is also a cause for concern for regional stability. The disruptive nature of this potential conflict is exacerbated by domestic political volatility in all South Asian countries. It is imperative for the United Nations to contribute to a de-escalation of this conflict in order to maintain international peace and security. Stephen Cohen cautions that, in light of the failure of past predictions, it is impossible to predict future use of nuclear weapons by India and Pakistan with any confidence. It is likely that the future will look much like the current situation – a stable relationship between China and India and a rocky one between India and Pakistan, but with innate common sense or external mediation preventing an outbreak of nuclear conflict. However, Cohen also acknowledges the large number of political and military variables that might affect possible outcomes with regard to the nuclear future of South Asia, only some of which can be influenced or controlled by outside powers. He offers two suggestions: the international community should assist in managing crises; and security planners in the region should avoid overconfidence in deterrence and keep their arsenals low so as to reduce the scale of the catastrophe if there should be a regional war.

Echoing many of the same themes, Christophe Carle emphasizes that the future security of South Asia depends on the relationship between Pakistan and India; the other security threats of the region pale in comparison. He points to the elements of instability in the subcontinent's nuclear deterrence. Contiguity undermines the development of effective and reliable command and control systems and, with ballistic missiles, decision-making time may be reduced to 5–10 minutes. The nuclearization of South Asia and the inherent volatility of the nuclear equation in the region mean that external actors, particularly the United States, have become increasingly important. Thus South Asian (in)security has been internationalized.

INTRA-STATE CONFLICT AND TRANSNATIONAL LINKAGES

Most of the countries in South Asia have insurgency movements. The level of violence is variable, but several of these conflicts have been classified as high intensity. The separatist Tamil Tiger movement in Sri Lanka is one example, where an ethnic group seeks territorial withdrawal from the state entity. The Kashmir dispute feeds on and exacerbates political instability in both India and Pakistan.

India faces further challenges in its northeastern regions. The Maoist movement in Nepal impedes effective government in a similar way, and over the past few years commentators have expressed concern about the possible Talibanization of Pakistan. With these threats to political stability and territorial integrity, South Asia remains a region with a high potential for violence and conflict. How can the international community contribute to the peaceful settlement of these disputes? And what can be done domestically to defuse these conflicts?

Nepal has been much in the news in the past couple of years or so, in part because of the palace massacre of the royal family, but mainly because of the ferocity and intractability of the Maoist insurgency. Lok Raj Baral's chapter illustrates the close link between intra-state and interstate conflicts. He points to the transnational elements of the conflict in Nepal, noting that India is often dragged into domestic issues in Nepal, a landlocked Himalayan kingdom sandwiched between two Asian giants with porous and open borders. Weakened states and enfeebled political institutions and leaderships are increasingly incapable of dealing with domestic crises in South Asia, which, in turn, breed inter-state conflicts. Cross-country migration and refugee flows, as well as the issue of treatment of one's own nationals in neighbouring countries, have the potential to trigger inter-state conflict. Conflicts occur over the exploitation of natural resources such as Nepal's water, and over transit rights for a poor and small country seeking an outlet to the sea for its products. There are also challenges with respect to new security issues such as trafficking in drugs and women.

The insurgency in Sri Lanka has been going on for much longer and is also more ferocious: it is the Tamil Tigers, after all, who introduced and perfected the gruesome art of suicide terrorism. Kingsley de Silva notes that South Asia's record of violence in public life is unusual even compared with other post-colonial states. One special feature is the high number of public figures assassinated. Rajiv Gandhi was killed on Indian soil but in the context of Sri Lanka's bitter civil war. The Kashmir conflict has clearer external factors in its origin than Sri Lanka's but, once the conflict in Sri Lanka erupted and persisted, it was prolonged largely because of Indian intervention. In the Kashmir conflict, terrorism became a distinctive factor in the mid-1980s. The two principal protagonists remain inflexibly resistant to any change in their attitude on this issue. In Sri Lanka the Tamil movement was transformed from a relatively peaceful one until the 1960s into an extraordinarily violent struggle with regional ramifications in the 1980s. Assassinations and suicide bombings became central means of terror. Once terrorism becomes a major factor in the political struggle, de Silva notes, the prospects of negotiating a settlement become all the more difficult. A similar central trait is the marginalization of the so-called moderates.

It is argued by some that the major locus of international terrorism has shifted to South Asia. Terrorist acts are committed in relation to both internal and inter-state conflicts, and the level of violence is alarming. Allegations are also frequently made that governments may support cross-border terrorism to undermine neighbouring states. The phrase "aid, abet and harbour" terrorists has entered the international policymaking agenda since 11 September 2001. How can terrorism be curbed; how can domestic and international actors work to decrease terrorist violence? Is terrorism a purely security problem with no significant political dimensions? Can the challenge of "political terrorism" be met without addressing the fundamental political issues that may underlie it?

Peacekeeping

If South Asia poses a challenge to international peace and security, it is also true that the region contributes strongly to the UN efforts at peacekeeping. The chapters by Lieutenant General Satish Nambiar and Brigadier-General Syed Roomy must be read in the context of three of the world's top four UN peacekeepers being currently from South Asia: Bangladesh, Pakistan and India. Of the total of 44,715 military observers, civilian police and military troops involved in UN peacekeeping operations (PKOs) in July 2001, 12,590 (28 per cent) were from South Asian countries.

As of March 2002, Bangladesh was the biggest contributor to UN PKOs, Pakistan was in second place, India third and Nepal eleventh. What accounts for their continued commitment to UN peace operations in the light of the marked reluctance of some Western countries to accept the burden of UN peacekeeping? South Asian countries contribute with unique and useful skills, for example the Indian army's experience in counter-insurgency operations. Are there wider lessons to be drawn from their experience in peacekeeping operations? One might be improved cooperation on training and perhaps institutional cooperation in the future. In the light of the contributions by South Asia to the United Nations and the size and importance of the region, one may ask also if South Asia has gained the influence in international forums that it ought to have. The generals call for adherence to recommendations from the Brahimi Report on UN Peace Operations, especially that troopcontributing countries must be involved in decision-making on mandates for missions. In addition, though, should South Asia have permanent representation on the Security Council?

INDIA'S NEW GOVERNMENT AND ITS CHINA POLICY CHALLENGES

India's new government led by the Congress Party, which came into power in the April 2004 General Elections, has until now focused entirely on its relations with Pakistan. The reason for this could be that most of the foreign policy hands in the current policy establishment have been former High Commissioners in Pakistan and therefore at more professional ease to deal with it. However, India's most significant foreign policy challenge is China and not Pakistan. Pakistan despite its nuclear weapons arsenal is not our "strategic competitor"; it is only a, regional 'spoiler state'. But in India's aspirations to rise to an effective regional power status, China is a "strategic competitor" both in the South Asia context and also in the Asian security context.

India's policy making establishment and especially within the Congress Party, with its hangovers of 'Panch Sheel' and non-aligned mindsets, has short memories when it comes to China's policies of strategic destabilization of India. They are still under way. Similarly, the Indian media suffers from a total amnesia of China's perfidious policies in South Asia to the strategic detriment of India. China has adroitly exploited both these vulnerabilities of India. China in its approaches to South Asia in the last fifty-five years, with particular reference to India has relied heavily on "power politics", creation of 'spoiler states' on India's periphery and upsetting the natural balance of power in the Indian sub-continent. The new Indian Government policy establishment may like to consider the following observations when formulating its policy stances towards China:

* "It can be a fundamental and analytically mischievous error to confuse peace with tranquility, certainty or predictability." "To achieve peace, people do not necessarily have to become admirable or gentle." -Prof John Mueller.
* Only when countries have accepted the existence of conflict and sought to manage it through a balance of power have enduring periods of general peace resulted" -Former US President Nixon.
* "Peace therefore cannot be aimed at directly; it is the expression of certain conditions and power relationships. It is to these relationships –not to peace-that diplomacy must address itself" -Former US Secretary of State, Henry Kissinger.

So while India must pursue peace and conflict-avoidance in its relationship with China, the new Indian Government should recognize that the route to peace lies through power relationships and power politics. But first, a look at the Congress Party's "China Baggage". The Congress Party Needs to Jettison its "China Baggage":

The Congress Party comes into power after eight long years, very nearly a decade. A decade is a long time in international relations and power politics. Contemporary Congress Party articulations give an impression that its perspectives remain time-frozen in the Nehruvian-era China politics.

Current international strategic realities dictate that the following main planks of Congress Party's China perspectives are no longer relevant:

* Non-alignment is dead. The concept could operate in a bi-polar world only. Further, both the superpowers gave no credence to this concept. If India was given importance then, it was not because of Nehru and nor for its non-

alignment policies. India was given importance for its intrinsic potential as a power in the making.

* 'Panch Sheel' (five principles of peaceful co-existence) enunciated by Chou-en-lai and Nehru stood negated when China sneakingly occupied Aksai-Chin in the 1950s and later the Sino-Indian War of 1962.
* "Panch Sheel" concept stood further negated in the following years when China in its policies of strategic de-stabilisation of India built-up Pakistan's nuclear weapons arsenal, attempted to make Myanmar a military client state and entered into a Mutual Defence Agreement with Bangladesh.
* Multi-polar world as espoused by China and currently being seconded by the Congress Party Government is an unworkable proposition in today's international strategic realities. Neither China nor France has been able to win concrete support for multi-polarity.

The New Congress Government would be well advised to jettison its above baggage and formulate its approaches to China on the basis of power-politics and in consonance with existing global power relationships. Hans J Morgenthau, the most noted foreign affairs authority has remarked that: " A nation can only take a rational view of its national interests after it has parted company with the crusading spirit of a political creed." The Congress Party Government needs to jettison the crusading missions of the Nehruvian era. It only brought more conflict and contentiousness for India.

India's Build-Up of her Strategic Assets as Part of its China Policy

In this connection two points need to be made, namely:

* China's attitudes towards India changed after the BJP Government's nuclear weapons tests in 1998. After the rabid Chinese reactions for a year or so, China realised that it had to adapt to the new strategic reality, that India had arrived to claim some strategic space in the "power-politics" scene. Hence the flurry of Chinese high

level official visits thereafter and the stupendous growth of two way trade. An argument can therefore be made in terms of China relations that India's power politics has stimulated trade exponentially.

* China's attitudes towards India changed as it dawned on Chinese leaders that India was getting drawn into an increasing strategic partnership with the United States and increasing military-to-military contacts also.

A major deduction from the above is that an essential component of India's policies towards China should also be the building up of her own independent strategies assets to add power to her diplomacy in the form of:

* ICBMs (Inter Continental Ballistic Missiles). At present Indian missiles do not have a reach upto Bijing.
* SLBMs (Sea Launched Ballistic Missiles). The third leg of India's nuclear arsenal triad is overdue.
* Cruise Missiles. With multimode launch capabilities.
* Nuclear Submarines. The project is over 15 years old. It needs to be resuscitated and put on priority.
* Strategic Bombers. These are an essential element of the nuclear triad.

China's missile arsenal is predominantly deployed in Tibet, Sichzuan and Yunnan— all targeted against India and with an inherent element of political coercion. Development of India's strategic assets as given above would make India's foreign policy approaches towards China more strategically equitable and in the process generating equitable responses from China.

India's Power-Relationship Approaches to China

India's national security interests imperatives dictate that any long range formulation of its China policy should deliver the following end-aims:

- China's intrusive influence in the Indian sub-continent in the form of creation of regional 'spoiler states' acting as its proxies is curtailed.
- China's assistance to Pakistan in terms of WMD Proliferation is curtailed, if not ended.

- China's attempt to build a naval presence in the Indian Ocean through Pakistan, Bangladesh or Myanmar is impeded.
- China's strategic nexus with Pakistan and Bangladesh is neutralized.
- China's unobtrusive influence in India's politics through the Communist Parties, a strategically unwise Indian media and India's pseudo-liberal establishment is rendered ineffective.

A quick glance at the above would reveal that except for the last point, India on its own, cannot tackle these challenges. India would have to co-opt or be co-opted in existing global power relationships that are working to constrain China's power politics in their respective regions. To arrive at the answer, a brief look is required at the existing strategic realities and global power equations and these are:

- United States is the only superpower existent today with the strategic, political and economic might to enforce its will globally.
- United States global predominance is estimated to continue well into the major portion of the 21st century.
- Russia is unlikely under existing circumstances to emerge in a resurgent mode for another three to four decades. Its strategic power potential stands shrunk decisively.
- China is a revisionist power. It challenges the status-quo and in the process generates strategic uneasiness in global strategic equations of its intentions and motives.
- China's massive military modernization and expansion of her strategic assets are nowhere near to challenging US supremacy.
- China today stands strategically hemmed-in by the United States on its Western and Eastern flanks.

India therefore has no choice but to be co-opted in the United States scheme of things to protect her national security interests vis-à-vis China. The United States too is not engaged in 'Containment' of China; but only in 'Constrainment' so that its policies do not create strategic turbulence in contiguous areas.

In terms of South Asia alone, India's national security interests dictate that Pakistan needs to be cut to size and accept its asymmetric equation in the Indian sub-continent. India cannot hope that China will assist her in this direction. China is a major part of the problem of Pakistan's intransigence and military adventurism against India. Here again the United States enters into the picture in multiple ways: (1) To control Pakistan directly and coerce it into strategic compliance from desisting from military adventurism. (2) To neutralize China-Pakistan strategic nexus by building strategic counter-pressures against China. (3) United States global naval supremacy is unquestionable and in relation to India's Indian Ocean strategic interests, major convergence exists between India and USA.

Here again, in the South Asian context, the answer is clear, that in relation to China, the national security interests of India are best served by entering the power-relationships of the United States in terms of Asian security. Until India builds up her military and strategic power to levels commensurate with those of China, it has no options in her China policy but to get co-opted with the China policies of the United States.

The new Congress Government has come into power, seemingly obsessed with the conviction that the policies of the previous BJP Government must be changed at all costs. It needs to note that India's foreign and defence policies need to be bi-partisan in character and content. The previous Government adopted the "power politics" approach to China as evident from the nuclear weapons tests and also evolving a strategic partnership with the United States. Both these had an effect on China and its policies towards India and South Asia in general. One could also attribute the Chinese neutrality during the Kargil War 1999 to this approach

The Congress Governments in the past followed ill-conceived and ill-advised policies towards China based on mistaken beliefs. This led to India's national humiliation in 1962. The new

Congress Government in power today should jettison its " China baggage" of the past and adhere to the "power politics" approach towards China. It is not to suggest that India enter into confrontationist stances with China; it is to suggest that while peace must be the quest in India-China relations it does not distract India from the parallel track of foreign policy i.e. To adopt power relationships and build strategic assets so necessary to maintain "real peace". India's new policy establishment needs to be reminded what one Chinese author has observed on China's perspectives on international relations: " Power is the cornerstone of Chinese politics. Chinese politicians and diplomats are often recognized as masters of power politics having inherited a well-spring of experience of power play over the millennium".

INDIA'S CHINA POLICY: IMPORTANCE OF A STRATEGIC FRAMEWORK

According to many political observers, the global political architecture is undergoing a transformation with power increasingly shifting from the West to the East.The two most populous nations on the earth China and India are on their way to becoming economic powerhouses and are shedding their reticence in asserting their global profiles. Japan is gradually flexing its military muscle and the Southeast Asian tigers are roaring again after the 1997 "Asian Flu". Whether it is such hopeful prospects or the challenges ahead in the Korean peninsula, Taiwan, and Kashmir, it is clear that this new century will, in all likelihood, be an Asian century.

The future of this Asian century will to large extent depend upon the relationship between the two regional giants, China and India. According the United States National Intelligence Council Report on emerging global trends, by 2015, international community will have to confront the military, political and economic dimensions of the rise of China and India. The bilateral relationship between China and India will define the contours of the new international political architecture in Asia and the world at large. As of today, however, the trajectory of the Sino-

Indian relationship remains as complex as ever to decipher despite some remarkable positive developments in the last few years.

This article attempts to explore this complex, multi-layered relationship in all its dimensions, largely from the perspective of Indian foreign policy priorities. It mainly focuses on the recent developments in the Sino-Indian relationship. It reviews India's and China's view of each other and their policies. It examines the trends of convergence that have emerged in the past few years. Additionally, it looks at the points of divergence and possible areas of concern in the relationship between Asia's giants.

Divergences and Challenges

The number one priority for China's leadership today is economic growth and social stability. China recently underwent one of the most peaceful and orderly political transformations in its recent history, even though its exact ramifications remain far from clear. Hu Jintao became Communist Party chief in 2002 and President of China in 2003 replacing Jiang Zemin. He also finally ceded the effective control of the armed forces to Hu Jintao in September 2004. Hu Jintao is now formally in command of the vast party, government, and military bureaucracies that rule China. This shift, although important for the smooth working of the Chinese government, is unlikely to produce any radical change in China's foreign policy. China's focus is going to be on maintaining its high rate of economic growth in the coming years. It should be remembered that Hu Jintao is a product of the "evolutionary policies" of Deng Xiao Peng that emphasize economic growth and orderly governance. President Hu Jintao has made it amply clear that Western-style multiparty democracy is something that would not serve the Chinese people well, terming it a "blind alley" for China. Therefore, one can expect China to continue on its current economic trajectory and shaping its foreign policy accordingly.

China has enjoyed average annual rates of real income growth of around 10 percent in the last two decades of the twentieth century, something unprecedented historically. China accounts for about 5 percent of world trade and foreign direct investment (FDI) to China is predicted to reach an annual utilized rate of 100 billion in 2005. After its accession to the WTO, China's already-high global economic profile is set to rise manifold. China will continue to focus on maintaining its high rates of economic growth in the coming years, even as some of the economic challenges China faces will become more acute. The burgeoning income disparities, restructuring of its states owned enterprises and the problem of non-performing loans in its banks are just a few of the economic problems China's economy is likely to face in the coming years. So far China has managed remarkably even though the future remains uncertain.

Broadly speaking, Indians either view China's economic growth as a façade or envy it. While India has achieved some remarkable growth rates in the last few years enjoying average annual rates of real income growth of six percent in the last two decades of the twentieth century, it still lags behind China. India accounts for less than one percent of world trade in goods and services. Currently, China outperforms India in terms of levels of growth, education, health, and living standards of its population, and global integration of its economy. China outpaces India, in sectors where the two compete for third country markets. Sino-Indian competition for these markets is bound to further intensify in the coming years.

Though some argue that the long term economic prospects of India are much better than China's, China remains the undisputed economic powerhouse of the moment driving the Asian and global economy with India somewhere far behind. The fact of the matter is so long as India does not place its own economic house in order; it will remain a second-rate power even in Asia. And China will remain the Asian power that the world will look up to when trying to manage problems in Asia.

What should be equally, if not more, significant for India is the fact that it is China's economic transformation that has given it the capability to become a military power with China spending as much as $65 billion a year on its military. China's military may or may not be able to challenge US supremacy in the next few years but it will surely become the most dominant force in Asia. According to authoritative sources, China is set to overtake Japan in the next decade to become Asia's major regional military power. The US involvement in the global war on terror has put the "containment" of China on the backburner and China has seized on this opportunity to strengthen its armed forces further.

China imbibed the lessons of US military undertakings such as the 1991 Gulf War, war in Afghanistan and the recent operation Iraqi Freedom. These have spurred China's pursuit of the latest Revolution in Military affairs (RMA) manifested in the buying, adopting of latest technologies and weapons systems (particularly from Russia) along with concomitant changes in doctrine and organizational structures. The People's Liberation Army (PLA) has been shedding its manpower since late 1990s to save funds so as to be able to focus on high tech. Despite a western embargo on China preventing transfer of military technologies, China has been able to deftly use US corporations to garner and apply dual-use technologies. China is simultaneously pursuing a qualitative and quantitative transformation of its nuclear infrastructure. China plans to deploy new road-mobile, solid-fuelled, long-range missiles over the next several years possibly to counter US ballistic missile defence.

Overtime, China's enhanced military prowess will lead it to assert its interests more forcefully, thereby, adversely affecting Indian interests. As China becomes more reliant on imported oil for its rapidly growing industrial economy, China will develop and exercise military power projection capabilities to protect the shipping that transports oil from the Persian Gulf to China. The capability to project power would require access to advanced naval bases along the sea lines of communication and forces capable of gaining and sustaining naval and air superiority.

China's assistance to Myanmar in constructing and improving port facilities on two islands in the Bay of Bengal and the Andaman Sea is the first step to securing military base privileges in the Indian Ocean. This can be used as a listening post to gather intelligence on Indian naval operations and a potential forward base for future Chinese naval operations in the Indian Ocean. India's traditional geographic advantages in the Indian Ocean are also increasingly at risk with deepening Chinese involvement in Myanmar. China's increasing naval presence in the Indian Ocean is of tremendous strategic consequence for India. There are also suggestions that the balance of air power in the China-India theatre has shifted in China's favour with it acquiring an inventory of about 1500 modern combat aircraft for deployment in the theatre.

China remains the only major power in the world that refuses to discuss nuclear issues with India for fear that this might imply a de facto recognition of India's status as a nuclear power. It continues to insist on the sanctity of the UN resolution 1172 which calls for India (and Pakistan) to give up its nuclear weapons program and join the Nuclear Non-Proliferation Treaty (NPT) as a non-nuclear weapon state. This was reflected in China's lack of response to the Indian Foreign Minister's proposal of a common nuclear doctrine for China, India, and Pakistan. China would not like to get into any sort of nuclear dialogue with India that might give the impression of China recognizing India as a nuclear power. Moreover, while both India and China have a "no first use" nuclear doctrine, China's doctrine is not applicable to India as it is not a party to the NPT.

China has done its best to maintain a rough balance of power in Indian Subcontinent by preventing India from gaining an upper hand over Pakistan. It has consistently assisted Pakistan's nuclear weapons and ballistic missile programs to counterbalance India's development of new weapons systems. India's preoccupation with Pakistan reduces India to the level of a regional power while China can claim the status of an Asian and world power. China signed a charter to step up bilateral defence cooperation with Pakistan "to help maintain peace and stability in South Asia " even as it professes to improve its relations with India. Moreover, even as India and China share similar concerns regarding Islamic terrorism in Kashmir and Xinjiang respectively, China has been rather unwilling to make a common cause with India against Pakistan. China's use of India's neighbors to curtail Indian influence has not been restricted to Pakistan. China has actively sought to contain India all around its periphery by engaging Nepal, Bangladesh and Myanmar.

Despite resolving most of its border disputes with other countries, China is reluctant to move ahead with India on border issues. India's discussion of border issues with China is seen as a concession. India remains satisfied with the "positive" and "satisfactory" Joint Working Group negotiations on the boundary issue. Despite the need for an expeditious demarcation of the Line of Actual Control, the talks seem to be continuing endlessly and the momentum of the talks itself seems to have flagged.

The momentum of the issue of Tibet seems to have been lost. Tibet has become a platform for the projection of Chinese military power. India's tacit support to Dalai Lama's government-in-exile has failed to have much of an impact either on China or on the international community. Today even Dalai Lama seems ready to talk to the Chinese as he realizes that in a few years Tibet might get overwhelmed with the Han population and Tibetans themselves might become a minority. The proposed opening up of the Nathula trade route that connects Tibet and Sikkim has been much trumpeted by the Indian government as a major achievement of Indian diplomacy. However, this step is fraught with dangers as there is no certainty that internal security threat posed by Chinese infiltration would not get worse with the opening of Nathula. This has probably led to some rethinking in India on this issue.

There were disturbing reports during the Indian Prime Minister's visit to China, that Chinese troops had intruded into the Indian territory along a stretch of the unfenced border with Arunachal Pradesh. China refuses to recognize Arunachal Pradesh as part of the Indian territory, laying claim to 90, 000 sq. km. of its land. If recent reports are to be believed after a two-decade gap, China has resumed the supply of weapons to various insurgent groups fighting in northeastern India. China seems to be getting successful in hemming India in from both, the eastern and the western flanks.

AN ASSESSMENT OF REFORMS IN INDIA AND CHINA AND CHALLENGES AHEAD

The analysis in the preceding sections brings out that there are significant differences in the financial system of India and China. The Indian financial system is reasonably well developed with both the banking system and the capital market playing important roles, even as the financial system is dominated by the banking system. There has been significant improvement in the profitability and health parameters of the banking system as a result of which the financial system, on the whole, has become relatively safe, sound and efficient. The capital market in India has also undergone metamorphic changes in the recent past and is now comparable to the best in the world.

Several improvements have also taken place in the financial system of China. The level of NPAs over the years has declined significantly, even as it continues to be large by international standards. The intermediation cost in China has also declined quite significantly.

The capital market in China has grown rapidly. Empirical evidence also suggests that firms' stock prices do reflect their fundamentals to a significant extent indicating that stock prices play a role in signaling information about issuers' fundamentals. Notwithstanding several initiatives by the Chinese authorities to reform the financial system, there are several areas which merit attention.

- The banking system continues to be characterised by large non-performing loans.
- Financial intermediation in China continues to be largely bank-based with the capital market playing only a peripheral role in the financial system. The share of

capital market funding remains small in comparison with that in developed economies. In the first half of 2004, bank deposits constituted the largest source of funding (83 per cent) for non-financial sector (including households, enterprises and government), followed by treasury bonds (12 per cent), stocks (4.6 per cent) and company bonds (0.4 per cent).

- There is evidence to suggest the prevalence of excess capacity build-up in several manufacturing industries and real estate. One of the major reasons for this has been the large proportion of lending to the SOEs.
- The Chinese financial market is still lacking in product varieties. Financial deepening is still inadequate and there are hardly any innovations.
- China's monetary system is still dominated by direct control measures in the form of credit and interest rate ceiling and reserve requirements.
- The size of the primary capital market is small with limited number of new issuances of debt and equity. Also, the majority of shares (accounting for about two-third of stock market capitalisation) are not traded.
- The Chinese capital market continues to remain fragmented. Apart from segmentation between 'A' and 'B' shares, there is also no fungibility between 'A' and 'H' shares, which impedes arbitrage and efficient pricing in two markets.

It needs to be noted that unlike in India, reforms in the real sector in China preceded reforms in the financial sector. In comparison with the agricultural and industrial reforms, the reforms in the financial sector in China moved at a slow pace. It was perhaps due to this reason that the financial sector remains vulnerable.

In India, on the other hand, financial sector reforms started early in the reform cycle which imparted in a significant way efficiency and stability to the financial sector. The faster reforms in the other sectors of the economy call for quick reforms in the financial sector in China.

Major Challenges faced by the Financial Sector in China

As part of its accession to the WTO, China has promised to open banking business in all places and in all currencies to foreign banks by 2006. After December 2006, foreign and domestic banks should be able to provide products to all customers in China throughout the country. With this, the banking system in China will face serious challenges; First, there is a large stock of NPLs in comparison with the international standards. Secondly, there is still a gap between the management and operational capacity of the wholly state-owned commercial banks and that of the world's leading banks. Third, the regulatory and supervisory system is not yet prepared for the complexities of the new situation.

The key focus of further reforms in the Chinese financial system is on resolution of NPLs problem. This requires concrete action plan on two fronts, *i.e,* to resolve the existing stock of NPLs and to avoid accumulation of further NPLs. The flow problem perhaps could be tackled by further enhancing commercial orientation of the lending operations of banks. Ceiling on interest rates as and when removed could also allow banks to price their products based on their risk-return perception. To overcome the stock problem, the authorities need to keep in view the experience of the four AMCs set up, which has not been satisfactory as their losses are expected to surpass the current financial contributions to the AMCs from both the Ministry of Finance and the PBC. Further improvements in bankruptcy and foreclosures would also enable banks to recover NPLs.

The further development of financial markets apart from imparting market discipline into the system, would have several other advantages. A balanced financial system, where both banks and financial markets play important roles, not only helps in averting crises, but also creates competitive conditions which would benefit both savers and investors. The capital market could help in improving allocative efficiency of resources by putting competitive pressures on the banking system. The financing needs of the Chinese economy appear to be far more than the lending capacity of banks. Those enterprises, which are not able to raise funds from the banking system could finance their requirements from the capital market. The capital market could, thus, help in spurring the growth of the private sector.

In China, ownership of shares is based on the status of the investor as well as of that of the company. There is no transferability between 'A' and 'B' shares, even as they are identical in respect of shareholder rights. Because of segmentation, the Chinese capital market is also not much integrated with other capital markets. Further integration with the international capital market could help China in reaping the benefits. The convertibility of state and legal person shares into 'A' class shares and making them tradable along with 'B' shares could also help in integrating its market further.

Administrative controls over raising of capital perhaps could be phsed out in favour of well defined and objective entry and disclosure norms. Reforms of the capital market in China could also include the development of the private debt market, which could provide the financing choices to the borrowers and the opportunity to diversify risk to the savers.

Challenges Faced by the Financial Sector in India

Financial sector reforms in India have undoubtedly brought about significant improvements in the profitability and health parameters of the banking system. However, some issues in the Indian financial system would have to be addressed in the near future. Furthermore, as a result of deregulation, financial integration and advances in information technology, several new challenges have emerged which merit attention in India.

Notwithstanding some improvements, the intermediation cost in India continues to be high in comparison with the international standards. In fact, intermediation cost of scheduled commercial banks changed only marginally from 3.0 per cent as at end-March 1998 to 2.9 per cent by end-March 2004. In contrast, intermediation cost in China declined significantly from 2.6 per cent in 1998 to 2.0 per cent in 2002. The high intermediation cost in India is a cause of concern and it needs to be brought down. Banks are now exposed to increased market risk. With the increasing financial integration, banks are also exposed to serious asset-liability mismatch with serious implications for interest rate risk, liquidity risk, foreign exchange risk. These risks need to be managed in a proactive manner as they pose a serious challenge for the banks and the regulatory authority.

Distinctions among providers of various financial services are getting increasingly blurred which have the potential to lead regulatory gaps/overlaps. This, along with the emergence of large and complex financial institutions as a result of consolidation could pose a supervisory challenge and call for quick and coordinated responses on the part of all the regulatory authorities.

Although the capital market in India has become modern, safer and more transparent, the lack of interest by the retail investor in the market is a cause for concern. The new capital being raised from the market for the last several years has remained insignificant both in absolute and relative terms. As a result, the relative significance of the primary capital market in the financial system has declined. Although sizeable funds have been raised from the capital market in the current year, it would have to be seen as to whether this trend would be sustained in the coming years. In the secondary market, although there are about 9000 companies listed in the stock exchanges, bulk of the trading is confined to a few large companies. It is estimated that about 50 stocks make up for as much as 75 per cent of the total turnover in the Indian stock exchanges as against 15 each in the case of the US and the UK and 25 per cent in the case of Japan. There has also not been any significant progress in the private corporate debt market. With the major DFIs disappearing from the scene and banks having difficulties to undertake project finance in a big way, a gap has emerged in financing the long-term requirements of funds, especially for the infrastructure sector. This could have serious implications for the real sector in the future.

INDIA'S ENERGY DIPLOMACY: UNDER CHINA'S SHADOW

With an economy that is projected to grow at a rate of 7 to 8 per cent over the next two decades, meeting its rapidly increasing demand for energy is one of the biggest challenges facing India. Burgeoning population, coupled with rapid economic growth and industrialisation, has propelled India into becoming the sixth-largest energy consumer in the world, with the prospect of emerging as the fourth-largest consumer in the next four to five years.

Rising incomes in India, along with generating prosperity, are pushing demand for energy resources even further. India is not only rated as one of the highest energy-intensive economies in the world, energy intensity being a measure of energy required by an economy to produce one unit of GDP growth, but Indians also pay one of the highest prices for energy in purchasing power parity terms. India faces a growing imbalance between the demand for energy and its supply from indigenous sources resulting in increased import dependence.

Though it has the third-largest reserves of coal after China and the United States, dependence on imported oil is India's greatest vulnerability, because it imports about 70 per cent of its oil, and this dependence is likely to increase to around 92 per cent by the year 2020. Hydrocarbons have been viewed as better alternatives to the less efficient and more polluting coal energy. While natural gas is India's most important potential alternative to coal, the effective exploration and distribution infrastructure is yet to develop. And despite some recent attempts to think seriously about nuclear power, oil retains its primacy in India's energy matrix.

The recent fluctuations in global oil prices have been a worrying trend for India. It has been estimated that a sustained 5 per cent rise in the oil prices over a year could dampen India's GDP growth rate by 0.25 per cent and raise the inflation rate by 0.6 per cent. India can only sustain its high rates of economic growth in the long term if it is successfully able to bridge the increasing demand-supply gap. According to the Integrated Energy Policy Report of the Indian Planning Commission, India will have to quadruple its energy supply to sustain an 8 per cent rate of growth for the next twenty-five years, which calls for an energy regime that ensures supply, manages demand, and balances pricing to enable growth. The report goes on to recommend that India pursue all available fuel options and forms of energy.

The Indian government has only recently woken up to the challenge of managing the nation's energy security with the realisation that it has already fallen behind other major players, such as China. Despite this, India continues to lack an overarching energy strategy because of a lack of consensus on crucial choices that the nation needs to make in the domestic political as well as global context. In so far as India's engagement with the outside world is concerned, four schools of thought have been identified: the "self-sufficiency" school; the "cooperation with Asian states" school; the "greater integration into the global energy markets" school; and the "free-for-all" school that calls for India to pursue its interests by all necessary means.

The last school, not surprisingly, seems to have an upper hand at the moment, which is more a result of confusion in Indian policymaking circles than any attempt on the part of the government to evolve a coherent policy framework. India is now trying to work at multiple levels by opening up the domestic energy market to multiple players, thereby making it more competitive; by adopting relatively rational principles for energy pricing; by establishing credible energy pricing regulatory framework; by diversifying beyond oil to access alternative energy sources such as nuclear power and natural gas; and by focusing greater on exploration activities with its borders. India is trying to increase fuel efficiency by slashing state subsidies on all petroleum products. But this is a politically contentious policy issue, and subsidising of household necessities is viewed as essential for supporting the poor in the country. India is also trying to put its emphasis on the import of natural gas. Various proposals are in the offing to import natural gas from Central

Asia, the Middle East, and even from its neighbours such as Bangladesh. India is also trying to promote investment in the exploration and production of domestic oil and gas, and it has had some successes in that regard in the last few years.

But these attempts are aimed at the long-term management of the nation's energy security. India's greatest challenge as of now is to ensure successful diversification of sources for oil procurement to minimise possibilities of disruption in supplies. It is towards this end that India has devoted its diplomatic energies in recent times as it encourages its public sector companies to acquire energy stakes in oil and gas fields abroad. India, like China, is reshaping its diplomacy to serve energy needs, because its booming economy also needs new supplies of oil to ensure its continued growth.

Not surprisingly, perhaps, the focal point of India's energy diplomacy has been the Middle East, because around 65 per cent of its energy requirements are met by this region. India's large and growing energy demand and Iran's pool of energy resources make the two nations natural economic partners. India's search for energy security in a rather volatile energy market makes Iran, with its fourthlargest reservoir of oil and second-largest reserves of natural gas, highly attractive. Iran has described India as one of its best customers and had offered to supply more crude oil to India in case of a disruption caused by an American military attack against Iraq in 2003.

This energy relationship between India and Iran is at the heart of a strong bilateral partnership between the two countries, despite the fact that Indo-Iranian relations have significantly diversified across various sectors in recent years. The proposal to build a gas pipeline between India and Iran has consumed a lot of diplomatic energy. Various options, such as offshore and overland routes, have been under consideration for quite some time now. Both these options have their problems, especially the problem of relying on Pakistan for the security of these pipelines. The United States has also been discouraging the pipeline proposal. Yet, India officially continues to insist that the 1,625-mile-long, $4.16 billion pipeline project intended to carry gas from Iran through Pakistan to energy-starved India remains firmly on track.

India has enjoyed traditional ties with Iran and Iraq for long, partly to meet its energy requirements. However, with Tehran adopting an aggressive anti-Western posture and pursuing an independent nuclear programme in defiance of its obligations under the Nuclear Non-Proliferation Treaty, and the ongoing instability in Iraq, India has been looking to expand its influence beyond the Persian Gulf to the Saudi peninsula.

As with Saudi Arabia's relations with China, energy has become the driving force in its relations with India, with India emerging as Saudi Arabia's fourth-largest destination for oil exports and Riyadh being the largest supplier of oil to India. India's crude oil imports from the Saudi kingdom are projected to double in the next twenty years. During his visit to India last year, the Saudi king emphasized his country's commitment to uninterrupted supplies to a friendly country such as India regardless of global price trends. During the state visit, King Abdullah bin Abdul-Aziz Al Saud and Indian prime minister Manmohan Singh signed an Indo-Saudi "Delhi Declaration," calling for a wide-ranging strategic partnership, putting energy and economic cooperation on overdrive, and committing to cooperate against terrorism.

Reliance, a private Indian energy firm, has decided to invest in a refinery and petrochemicals project in Saudi Arabia, and India's state-owned energy firm, Oil and Energy Gas Corporation (ONGC), is also planning to engage Saudi Arabia as its equity partner for a refinery project in the Indian state of Andhra Pradesh. The recent upheavals in India's relationship with Iran and Iran's decision to renege on some of its oil supply commitments in the aftermath of India's vote against Iran at the IAEA have also alerted India to the importance of having a diversified set of suppliers in the Middle East.

However, the Middle East remains a highly volatile region, forcing India to look beyond its regional confines in search of energy security. Following the disintegration of the Soviet empire, Central Asia has emerged as an important region, where many countries, including the United States and China, have evinced a keen interest, especially since it has emerged as a major oil-producing region. India has also actively nurtured its relations with the Central Asian states. Most notably, it has stationed troops in Tajikistan, provided it with $40 million in aid, and is refurbishing an air base near Dushanbe. The North-South International Transportation Corridor agreement signed in 2000 by India, Iran, and Russia and the Agreement on International Transit of Goods between India, Iran, and Turkmenistan, signed in 1997, are also significant, because they go a long way in cutting time and costs in the transit of goods, thereby giving a boost to India's trade with Iran and other Central Asian nations. Though India has expressed an interest in joining the proposed 1,700-kilometer Turkmenistan-Afghanistan-Pakistan gas-pipeline project as the final destination, it continues to remain non-committal to receiving the 3 billion-cubic-feet-per-day pipeline amid doubts expressed by Afghanistan and Pakistan that Turkmenistan has enough gas to make the venture viable, apart from security issues posed by the passage through Afghanistan.

It is significant that India and Iran have agreed to intensify collaboration on transport projects that could link India with the Persian Gulf, Afghanistan, Central Asia, and Europe. India will cooperate with Iran in the development of a new port complex at Chah Bahar on the coast of Iran that could become India's gateway to Afghanistan and Central Asia. There is also another project that involves linking Chah Bahar port to the Iranian rail network, which is also well connected to Central Asia and Europe. India hopes to make Pakistan marginal to its relationship with the Central Asian region so that India's relations with Central Asia can no longer be hostage to Islamabad's policies.

India's growing interest in the acquisition of energy assets in African states as diverse as Sudan, Congo, Gabon, Cameroon, Nigeria, Chad, Ghana, and Angola has also been very prominent in recent years. India has decided to offer lines of credit up to $1 billion on a government-to-government basis to a number of oil-rich but poor African countries for infrastructure projects in exchange for oil exploration rights. A $6 billion infrastructure investment deal struck in Nigeria by ONGC Mittal Energy, a joint venture between India's state-run Oil and Natural Gas Corporation and the world's largest steel maker, Mittal Steel, is seen as a major breakthrough in this strategy.

Nigeria is India's biggest supplier of oil from Africa and India hopes to source an even greater share of oil from Nigeria in the next few years. India will now look to a group of eight West African countries in a special cooperation model called the Team-9 initiative, under which India offers credit for projects set up by Indian companies through the Export Import Bank of India. Team-9 countries include Burkina Faso, Chad, Ivory Coast, Equatorial Guinea, Ghana, Guinea-Bissau, Mali, and Senegal. India is exploring the possibility of high-level cooperation and investment in oil and gas sectors across various African states with India offering assistance in developing a pipeline network and infrastructure for transportation of the LNG. India's energy diplomacy is also now forcing India to undertake a more substantive engagement with Latin America. ONGC Videsh Ltd. (OVL), the overseas arm of India's state-owned ONGC, has finalised the acquisition of 15 per cent stake in a Brazilian oil company, making its foray into the South American territory. Venezuelan president Hugo Chavez signed various energy related trade deals during his visit to India in 2005. One of these agreements is expected to result in the OVL picking up a 49 per cent stake in a major Venezuelan oil field. Chavez told the representatives of Indian big business that Venezuela had the capacity to meet India's annual requirement of 100 million barrels of crude. He emphasized that Venezuela wanted to become a permanent partner of India in the hydrocarbon sector and invited Indian oil companies to follow the example of their Russian and Chinese counterparts and become more active in Venezuela's oil sector.

India's relations with Russia are also becoming energy focused, with Russia being the world's second-largest oil producer and its leading gas producer. Both sides have expressed their keenness to expand cooperation further in this sector, which is already playing an important role in bilateral relations. India's OVL, in partnership with Exxon-Mobil, a U.S. company, runs a profitable off-shore project in Sakhalin. The public sector company, in one of the biggest oil deals signed in Russia, purchased a 20 per cent share in the Sakhalin-I project with an investment of 1.7 billion. According to the terms of the contract, 40 per cent of the production will belong to the ONGC for the first five to six years.

The Sakhalin venture will tap gas that will then be piped into northern Japan. The Sakhalin group of islands lies just north of Japan. There are an estimated 340 million metric tons of oil and 420 billion cubic meters of gas in the Sakhalin oilfield. India and Russia have also decided to cooperate in the Caspian Sea basin and have identified a few other areas for exploration. Already, OVL has signed a confidentiality agreement to evaluate the data of Sakhalin-III (Kirinsky block). This investment alone is expected to be in the range of $1.5 billion. ONGC and Russia's natural gas monopoly, Gazprom, have signed a memorandum of understanding pledging to explore possibilities for joint ventures in India, Russia, and third countries to produce oil and gas and to build trunk pipelines. The Russian company Gazprom and the Gas Authority of India Limited are also jointly developing a block in the Bay of Bengal.

While India is scouring far and wide to quench its thirst for energy, it is in its immediate neighbourhood that it has been most disappointed. It is embroiled in territorial disputes that prevent the launch of a free-for-all energy foreign policy. While its troubled relationship with Pakistan continues to create problems for its plans to import oil from Iran, its other neighbour, Bangladesh has also reneged on its earlier commitment to the tripartite agreement for transportation of gas from Myanmar to India via a pipeline running through Bangladesh. India wants to pursue this project seriously, because of all the pipeline options to bring natural gas from the Shwe fields in offshore Myanmar, the overland option via Bangladesh is possibly the most economical.

The India-Bangladesh-Myanmar pipeline idea was initially seen as a landmark in Indo-Bangladesh relations, with Bangladesh agreeing to its territory being used for transport of any commodity to the Indian market for the first time in three decades. While India seems willing to pay $125 million as transit fee to Bangladesh, Dhaka also wants transit facility through India for hydroelectric power from Nepal and Bhutan to Bangladesh, a corridor of trade between Nepal and Bhutan, and measures to reduce bilateral trade imbalance before it can conclude this agreement.

The one reality that Indian diplomacy has to confront in its search for nation's energy security is the presence of China almost everywhere and its relative success in achieving desirable outcomes, more often than not, to India's detriment.

Oil and Natural Gas Sector

The oil industry can be divided into three major components: upstream, midstream and downstream. The upstream industry includes exploration and production activities, hence is also referred as the exploration and production (E&P) sector. The midstream industry processes, stores, markets and transports commodities including crude oil, natural gas, natural gas liquids (NGLs) like ethane propane and butane and sulphur. The downstream industry includes oil refineries, petrochemical plants, petroleum products distributors, retail outlets and natural gas distribution companies. The downstream industry provides consumers thousands of products such as gasoline, diesel, jet fuel, heating oil, asphalt, lubricants, synthetic rubber, plastics, fertilizers, antifreeze, pesticides, pharmaceuticals, natural gas and propane.

Both internationally and within India the oil and gas sector is characterised by existence of "integrated" companies, which are present in all these three sectors. The Indian Oil and Gas sector is one of the six core industries in India and has very significant forward linkages with the entire economy. The oil and gas sector meets more than two third of the total primary energy needs in the country.

The sector has been instrumental in putting India on the world map. At present India is the sixth largest crude oil consumer in the world and the ninth largest crude oil importer. The country is also increasing its share in the global refining market.

At present Indian refining sector is the sixth largest in the world. At the end of 2005, India had 0.5 per cent of the Oil and Gas resources of the world and 15 per cent of the world?s population whereas the reserve to production ratio is 20.7. At the end of 1995 India had the 5.5 thousand million barrels of reserves, grown only 1 per cent till the end of 2005 whereas crude oil consumption has grown more than 10 per cent over the last 5 years.

Upstream Sector: Exploration and Production

Upstream sector, oil and gas industry, deals with exploration and production of oil and gas. Oil exploration takes place at oil wells in four stages. The first stage is drilling, act of boring a hole through which oil or gas may be produced if encountered in commercial quantities. The second stage is completion, process in which the well is enabled to produce oil or gas.

The third stage is production, production time of oil and gas and the final stage is abandonment, where the well no longer produces or produces so poorly that it is a liability to its owner and is abandoned. An oil field is a region with an abundance of oil wells extracting petroleum (oil) from below ground.

Because the oil reservoirs typically extend over a large area, possibly several hundred kilometres across, full exploitation entails multiple wells scattered across the area.

There are more than 40,000 oil and gas fields of all sizes in the world and the largest discovered conventional oil field is the Ghawar Field (75-83 billion) is Saudi Arabia.

In tandem with the stagnated reserves, the production of oil has also been sluggish over the last decade, as a matter of fact in last ten years oil production has increased by only 1.6 per cent.

Reserve to Production Ratio

Reserve to Production Ration (R/P Ratio) is the portion of the identified resource from which usable natural resources can be economically and legally extracted out of the ground. Production can be offshore as well as onshore. An offshore system of production is defined with a platform raised above the water to support a number of producing wells whereas onshore is a platform at the sea level. R/P ratio for the world at the end of 2005 is 40.6 implying that natural resources that has been identified subject to pull out till date is about 40 times the amount already taken out of the ground.

Downstream: Refining and Marketing

Refining, oil industry after exploration and production, is related with manufacturing petroleum products by a series of processes that separate crude oil into its major components and blend or convert these components into a wide range of finished products, such as gasoline or Aviation Turbine Fuel. Refining capacity depends on the technology used in refineries, capable of processing crude production into clean fuels.

In the recent age of decreasing oil production refining capacity have to have well supportive technology, which meet increasingly more stringent environmental Standards. With the increase in global oil demand and stagnant reserve, refining capacity deserves new capacity addition to meet demand. But the graph shows slightly increasing trend of refining capacity till date in last decade. Refinery throuput, as opposed to designed capacity, is computed by dividing the number of refined barrels of oil processed by the actual number of days the refinery was in operation.

Onshore and Offshore Oil and Gas Fields in India

In India crude oil is produced in Onshore and Offshore. Onshore fields are in Assam/Nagaland, Arunachal Pradesh, Gujarat, and Tamil Nadu/ Andhra Pradesh. Oil India Limited (OIL) and Oil and Natural Gas Commission (ONGC) have the onshore field for crude oil production. Offshore production occurs at Bombay High run by ONGC and Private/Joint Venture companies. For the natural gas onshore fields are the same for Crude oil in addition with Rajasthan as an onshore field. For the offshore Bombay high is the one for the production.

Exploration Overseas

In keeping with the objectives of the Energy Security section of the National Common Minimum Programme, ONGC Videsh Ltd. (OVL), wholly owned subsidiary of ONGC, as well as other national oil companies such as IOC, OIL and GAIL, have been pursuing the acquisition of equity oil abroad, as well as the acquisition abroad of oil and gas exploration acreages and producing properties. These companies have participating interests in oil and gas projects located in Vietnam, Sudan, Russia, Iraq, Iran, Myanmar, Libya, Syria, Australia, Ivory Coast, Qatar and Egypt. OVL, in association with other oil sector PSUs, is aggressively scouting for E&P opportunities in countries such as Venezuela, Kazakhstan, Kuwait, Yemen, Chad, Niger, Nigeria, Angola, Cuba, Sierra Leone and Ecuador in addition to efforts to acquire more E&P assets in the countries where it is operating currently.

Production

Domestic production of crude oil has been a reason of worry for the Indian economy for some time now. For more than 16 years the total production of crude has stagnated around 32-33 MMT. This has been particularly disturbing given the crude oil consumption in the country implying an increasing dependence on imported crude. At present India?s crude dependence is around 78 per cent. According to TERI estimates, by 2030 India?s import dependency may shoot up to a disturbing 93 per cent. In the current year, the production of crude oil in the country during the first half was 16.14 MMT as against 17.00 MMT during the corresponding period of 2004-05, a shortfall of about 5 per cent.

Refining

Oil refining is a continuous process and the cost of refining of individual petroleum products is not worked out separately because all products are produced together. The cost of refining crude oil depends upon a number of factors including the type of crude oil, size of refinery, refinery configuration, age of equipment, technology used, etc. The technology for producing the petroleum products from the crude oil differs from one refinery to another. The hydro cracker and catalytic hydro cracker technology are the two major technologies through which petroleum products are yielded. There are 18 refineries operating in the country, 17 in the Public Sector and one in the Private Sector, with a total installed capacity of 127.37 million metric tonnes per annum (MMTPA).

Natural Gas

Natural gas is a gaseous fossil fuel consisting primarily of methane. In India production of natural gas has increased over 3 times in the last two decades though the share of the production of natural gas with respect to world natural gas production wais only 0.6 per cent at the end of 2005 and reserve to production ratio of 36.2. Petroleum and Natural Gas Regulatory Board (PNGRB) Act came into force on April 03, 2006 to protect the interest of consumers and entitles engaged in specified activities to ensure uninterrupted and adequate supply of petroleum, petroleum products and natural gas in all parts of the country and promote competitive markets in Oil and Gas sector of India.

3

Directorate of Revenue Intelligence: China and India

The Directorate of Revenue Intelligence (DRI) is an Indian intelligence agency. It is India's chief anti-smuggling intelligence, investigations and operations agency. The Directorate is run by officers from the Central Board of Indirect Taxes and Customs (CBIC) who are posted in its various Zonal Units as well as in Indian embassies abroad as part of the Customs Overseas Intelligence Network. It is headed by a Director General of the rank of Special Secretary to the Government of India.

DRI works to secure India's national and economic security by preventing the outright smuggling of contraband such as firearms, gold, narcotics, Fake Indian Currency notes, antiques, wildlife and environmental products. Moreover, it also works to prevent the proliferation of black money, commercial frauds and trade based money laundering. Though its early days were committed to combating the smuggling in of gold, it now also addresses narcotics and economic crimes. DRI routinely makes fake Indian currency note seizures. In the last 5 years, the DRI has seized more than 540 kg of heroin and 7,409 kg of ephedrine along with other narcotics and psychotropic substances.

Function

DRI is the major intelligence agency which enforces the prohibition of the smuggling of items including drugs, gold, diamonds, electronics, foreign currency, and counterfeit Indian currency. The Directorate of Revenue Intelligence functions under the Central Board of Indirect Taxes and Customs in the Ministry of Finance, Department of Revenue, Government Of India. Headed by Director General (Chief Commissioner Rank) in New Delhi, it is divided into seven zones, each under the charge of an Additional Director General (Commissioner Rank). It is further sub-divided into Regional Units, Sub-Regional Units and Intelligence Cells with a complement of Additional Directors, Joint Directors, Deputy Directors, Assistant Directors, Senior Intelligence Officers and Intelligence Officers.

DIRECTORATE OF REVENUE INTELLIGENCE BUSTS BID TO SMUGGLE 4 CR RED SANDERS TO CHINA

The Directorate of Revenue Intelligence (DRI) recovered 10.1 tonnes of red sanders logs here at Visakhapatnam Container Terminal Private Limited (VCTPL) on March 7. On specific intelligence that the red sanders was being smuggled through containers, a special team of DRI raided and found the offloaded two containers from a vessel bound to China. In fact, the contraband was loaded at Chennai and was supposed to be smuggled to China via Visakhapatnam.

On detailed examination of the containers, the DRI officials recovered and detained 10.1 tonne red sanders along with bentonite powder in the two containers. The officials detained the containers containing the red sanders for violation of the provisions of the Customs Act 1962 and the Foreign Trade Policy. The recovered red sanders is estimated to value Rs 4 crore. The DRI officials said that an investigation is still in progress.

CHINA FAILS TO WIN INDIA ROUND TO BELT AND ROAD INITIATIVE AHEAD OF MODI'S MEETING WITH XI

The scheme is Chinese President Xi Jinping's landmark initiative to build infrastructure to connect China to the rest of Asia and beyond, a giant reworking of the old Silk Road. India has not signed up to the initiative as parts of one key project, the US$57 billion China-Pakistan Economic Corridor, runs through Pakistan-administered Kashmir, which India considers its own territory.

Whether or not China will be able to bring India round to the project is likely to be a key measure of the success of Indian Prime Minister Narendra Modi's trip to China for an informal meeting with Xi on Friday and Saturday.

Modi to visit central China for one-on-one summit with Xi

But India's foreign minister did not express support for Belt and Road in the communique released after the foreign ministers of the China and Russia-led Shanghai Cooperation Organisation met in Beijing. India, along with Pakistan, joined the group last year. All the other foreign ministers – from Kazakhstan, Kyrgyzstan, Pakistan, Russia, Tajikistan and Uzbekistan – "reaffirmed support for China's Belt and Road proposal", the statement read.

It gave no further explanation. The communique otherwise was a broad expression of unity by the ministers on issues ranging from their support for the Iran nuclear deal to the need to combat the spread of extremism. Modi is coming to China as efforts at rapprochement gather pace following a difficult year marked by the Doklam stand-off.

The Asian giants were locked in a 73-day military stand-off in a remote, high-altitude stretch of the Himalayan border last year. At one point, soldiers from the two sides threw stones and punches. The confrontation between the nuclear-armed powers underscored Indian alarm at China's expanding security and economic links in South Asia.

In comments carried on the foreign ministry's website, Chinese Vice Foreign Minister Kong Xuanyou said holding the meeting in an informal way meant the two leaders could have a deep exchange of views in a relaxed, friendly atmosphere to promote cooperation. "This not only will benefit the two countries and two peoples, but will also have an important effect on peaceful development in the region and around the world," the ministry paraphrased Kong as telling Indian media in Beijing. Modi will visit China in June for a summit of the Shanghai Cooperation Organisation. China will also have to tread carefully to avoid giving its close ally Pakistan cause for alarm. China on Monday reassured Pakistan that relations between the two countries were as firm as ever and would "never rust".

CHINESE CRACKERS SMUGGLING RISES BEFORE DIWALI, DRI CEASES CRACKERS WORTH CRORES

Before Diwali a major gang illegally smuggling tonnes of Chinese fireworks, which erupt into a toxic haze over Indian cities every Diwali and leave residents gagging for oxygen, were caught by DRI. Chinese firecrackers, despite being banned in India, are getting smuggled in vast quantities in India through seaports under false declarations in the name of toys or electronic goods.

According to intelligence agency, Chinese cracker gang used to bring crackers through ports and send them across north indian cities. The crackers were exported in the name of cycle manufacturer in Ludhiana. The illegal crackers used to first arrive at Mundra post in Gujarat and then it was shifted to ICD, Tuglakabad. DRI got a tip-off about the vehicle carrying huge illegal crackers on Wednesday. They soon investigated the matter and found heaps of Chinese crackers.

"During the course of operation, various types of Chinese make fire crackers have been recovered having value of Rs 19.48 crore in five cases. In this connection two persons have been arrested. The recovered Chinese-make firecrackers have been seized," said the DRI said. Directorate of Revenue Intelligence (DRI), has also sounded a nation-wide alert to check their sale and take punitive action.

This is not all, in the last month many such gangs and vehicles carrying illegal crackers were nabbed. According to DRI official, almost Rs 76 crore illegal crackers have been ceased. The DRI had last month issued a general alert to sensitize all field officers to check import of fire crackers. The Commerce Ministry has not issued any license to any importer to bring foreign-made fire crackers. Besides harming the domestic industry, fireworks of foreign origin are hazardous in nature and jeopardise public safety and health. On the basis of specific intelligence regarding large scale smuggling of sub-standard, poor quality Chinese-make fire crackers by way of concealment and mis-declaration, strict surveillance was maintained by the DRI.

Chinese cracker throng market during Diwali

Merchants said smuggled fireworks enter the market few days before festival Diwali in the capital and spread across to other parts like North India of the country. Ther are mostly sold by temporary licence holders. DRI officials say the crackers were brought ahead of Diwali festival, when sales are on high demand. The containers of crackers enter the country under the guise of different items like toys or sports goods, the official said. Enforcement agencies including DRI, Customs and state authorities, keep a check on the influx of foreign fireworks at Indian borders.

According to DRI official, every year Chinese crackers worth Rs 1,500 crore are smuggled through seaports in India.

CHINA AND INDIA TODAY: DIPLOMATS JOSTLE, MILITARIES PREPARE

Just as the Indian subcontinental plate has a tendency to constantly rub and push against the Eurasian tectonic plate, causing friction and volatility in the entire Himalayan mountain range, India's bilateral relationship with China is also a subtle, unseen, but ongoing and deeply felt collision, the affects of which have left a convoluted lineage. Tensions between the two powers have come to influence everything from their military and security decisionmaking to their economic and diplomatic maneuvering, with implications for wary neighbours and faraway allies alike. The relationship is complicated by layers of rivalry, mistrust, and occasional cooperation, not to mention actual geographical disputes.

Distant neighbours buffered by Tibet and the Himalayas for millennia, China and India became next-door neighbours with contested frontiers and disputed histories in 1950, following the occupation of Tibet by Mao's People's Liberation Army (PLA). While the rest of the world started taking note of China's rise during the last decade of the twentieth century, India has been warily watching China's rise ever since a territorial dispute erupted in a brief but full-scale war in 1962, followed by skirmishes in 1967 and 1987.

Several rounds of talks held since 1981 have failed to resolve the disputed claims. During his last visit to India, in 2010, Chinese Premier Wen Jiabao dashed any hopes of early border settlement, stating that it would take a very long time to settle the boundary issue—a situation that in many ways works to Beijing's advantage.

An unsettled border provides China the strategic leverage to keep India uncertain about its intentions, and nervous about its capabilities, while exposing India's vulnerabilities and weaknesses, and encouraging New Delhi's "good behavior" on issues of vital concern. Besides, as the ongoing unrest and growing incidents of self-immolations by Buddhist monks in Tibet show, Beijing has not yet succeeded in pacifying and Sinicizing Tibet, as it has Inner Mongolia. The net result is that the 2,520-mile Sino-Indian frontier, one of the longest inter-state boundaries in the world, remains China's only undefined land border. It is also becoming heavily militarized, as tensions rise over China's aggressive patrolling on the line of actual control (LAC) and its military drills, using live ammunition, for a potential air and land campaign to capture high-altitude mountain passes in Tibet.

Over the last decade, the Chinese have put in place a sophisticated military infrastructure in the Tibet Autonomous Region (TAR) adjoining India: five fully operational air bases, several helipads, an extensive rail network, and thirty thousand miles of roads—giving them the ability to rapidly deploy thirty divisions (fifteen thousand soldiers each) along the border, a three-to-one advantage over India. China has not only increased its military presence in Tibet but is also ramping up its nuclear arsenal. In addition, the PLA's strategic options against India are set to multiply as Chinese land and rail links with Pakistan, Nepal, Burma, and Bangladesh improve.

Developments on the disputed Himalayan borders are central to India's internal debate about the credibility of its strategic deterrent and whether to test nuclear weapons again. Being the weaker power, India is far more concerned about the overall military balance tilting to its disadvantage. India sees China everywhere because of Beijing's "hexiao gongda" policy in South Asia: "uniting with the small"—Pakistan, Bangladesh, Nepal, Burma, and Sri Lanka—"to counter the big"—India. When combined with Chinese nuclear and missile transfers to Pakistan and building of port facilities around India's periphery, and a dramatic increase in the PLA's incursions and transgressions across the LAC, the official Indian perception of China has undergone a dramatic shift since 2006, with China now being widely seen as posing a major security threat in the short to medium term rather than over the long term. The Indian military, long preoccupied with war-fighting scenarios against Pakistan, has consequently turned its attention to the China border, and unveiled a massive force modernization program, to cost $100 billion over the next decade, that includes the construction of several strategic roads and the expansion of rail networks, helipads, and airfields all along the LAC. Other measures range from raising a new mountain strike corps and doubling force levels in the eastern sector by one hundred thousand troops to the deployment of Sukhoi Su-30MKI aircraft, spy drones, helicopters, and ballistic and cruise missile squadrons to defend its northeastern state of Arunachal Pradesh, territory three times the size of Taiwan that the Chinese invaded in 1962 and now claim sovereignty over as "Southern Tibet."

Propelled by incidents related to border disputes, Chinese opposition to the US-India nuclear energy deal, India's angst over the growing trade deficit due to perceived Chinese unfair trade practices, potential Chinese plans to dam the Brahmaputra River, and the "war talk" in the official Chinese media in the 2007 to 2009 period (reminding India not to forget "the lessons of 1962"), mutual distrust between the Indian and Chinese peoples is growing. Clearly, China's extraordinary economic performance over the last three decades has changed the dynamics of the relationship. China and India had similar average incomes in the late 1970s, but thirty years later they find themselves at completely different stages of development. China's economic reforms—launched in 1978, nearly thirteen years before India's in 1991—changed their subsequent growth trajectories by putting China far ahead of India in all socioeconomic indices. Both China's gross domestic product and military expenditure are now three times the size of India's; recent surveys conducted by Pew Global Research show a growth in popular distrust, with just twenty-five percent of Indians holding a favorable view of China in 2011, down from thirty-four percent in 2010 and fifty-seven percent in 2005. Likewise, just twenty-seven percent of Chinese hold a favorable view of India in 2011, down from thirty-two percent in 2010, with studies of Internet content showing a large degree of "hostility and contempt for India."

Nor is there much effort to keep these emotions submerged. Reacting to the test launch in mid-April of a long-range Agni-V ballistic missile, dubbed the "China killer" by India's news media, a Chinese daily wryly noted that "India stands no chance in an overall arms race with China," because "China's nuclear power is stronger and more reliable." The unequal strategic equation, in particular the Chinese perception of India as a land of irreconcilable socioreligious cleavages with an inherently unstable polity and weak leadership that is easily contained through proxies, aggravates tensions between the two. In 2008, an official reassessment of China's capabilities and intentions led the Indian military to adopt a "two-front war" doctrine against what is identified as a "collusive threat" posed by two closely aligned nuclear-armed neighbours, Pakistan and China.

This doctrine validates the long-held belief of India's strategic community that China is following a protracted strategy of containing India's rise.

India is also responding by strengthening its strategic links with Afghanistan, Tajikistan, Mongolia, Vietnam, and Burma—countries on China's periphery. In testimony to the US Senate in February, James Clapper, the director of national intelligence, noted that "the Indian military is strengthening its forces in preparation to fight a limited conflict along the disputed border, and is working to balance Chinese power projection in the Indian Ocean." That "balance" includes a strategic tilt toward the United States that has also had a damaging effect on Sino-Indian relations. Although leaders from both countries often repeat the ritualized denials of conflict and emphasize burgeoning trade ties, such platitudes cannot obliterate the trust deficit. Few if any of China's strategic thinkers seem to hold positive views of India for China's future, and vice versa. Chinese strategists keep a wary eye on India's "great power dreams," its military spending and weapons acquisitions, and the developments in India's naval and nuclear doctrines. A dominant theme in Chinese commentary in the last decade is that India's growing strength—backed by the United States—could tip Asia's balance of power away from Beijing.

Not surprisingly, bilateral relations between Asia's giants remain, in the words of Zhang Yan, China's ambassador to India, "very fragile, very easy to be damaged, and very difficult to repair." Both have massive manpower resources, a scientific and industrial base, and million-plus militaries. For the first time in more than fifty years, both are moving upward simultaneously on their relative power trajectories. As the pivotal power in South Asia, India perceives itself much as China has traditionally perceived itself in relation to East Asia. Both desire a peaceful security environment to focus on economic development and avoid overt rivalry or conflict. Still, the volatile agents of nationalism, history, ambition, strength, and size produce a mysterious chemistry. Neither power is comfortable with the rise of the other. Both seek to envelop neighbours with their national economies. Both are nuclear and space powers with growing ambitions. Both yearn for a multipolar world that will provide them the space for growth and freedom of action. Both vie for leadership positions in global and regional organizations and have attempted to establish a sort of Monroe Doctrine in their respective neighbourhoods—without much success.

And both remain suspicious of each other's long-term agenda and intentions. Each perceives the other as pursuing hegemony and entertaining imperial ambitions. Both are non–status quo powers: China in terms of *territory*, power, and influence; India in terms of *status*, power, and influence. Both seek to expand their power and influence in and beyond their regions at each other's expense. China's "Malacca paranoia" is matched by India's "Hormuz dilemma." If China's navy is going south to the Indian Ocean, India's navy is going east to the Pacific Ocean. Both suffer from a siege mentality born out of their elites' acute consciousness of the divisive tendencies that make their countries' present political unity so fragile. After all, much of Chinese and Indian history is made up of long periods of internal disunity and turmoil, when centrifugal forces brought down even the most powerful empires. Each has its vulnerabilities—regional conflicts, poverty, and religious divisions for India; the contradiction between a market economy and Leninist politics for China. Both are plagued with domestic linguistic, ethno-religious, and politico-economic fault lines that could be their undoing if not managed properly.

In other words, China and India are locked in a classic security dilemma: one country sees its actions as defensive, but the same actions appear aggressive to the other. Beijing fears that an unrestrained Indian power—particularly one that is backed by the West and Japan—would not only threaten China's security along its restive southwestern frontiers (Tibet and Xinjiang) but also obstruct China's expansion southwards. Faced with exponential growth in China's power and influence, India feels the need to take counterbalancing measures and launch strategic initiatives to emerge as a great power, but these are perceived as challenging and threatening in China.

China's use of regional and international organizations to institutionalize its power while either denying India access to these organizations or marginalizing India within them has added a new competitive dynamic to the relationship. In the past decade, India has found itself ranged against China at the UN Security Council, East Asia Summit, the Asia-Pacific Economic Cooperation, the Nuclear Suppliers Group, and the Asian Development Bank. In 2009, China vetoed a development plan for India by the latter in the disputed Arunachal Pradesh, thereby internationalizing a bilateral territorial dispute. In a tit-for-tat response, New Delhi has kept Beijing out of India-led multilateral frameworks such as the Bay of Bengal Initiative for Multi-Sectoral Technical and Economic Cooperation, the India-Brazil-South Africa Dialogue, and the Mekong–Ganga Cooperation forums, and rejected China's request to be included as observer or associate member into the 33-member Indian Ocean Naval Symposium, started by India in 2008.

Resource scarcity has added a maritime dimension to this geopolitical rivalry. As China's and India's energy dependence on the Middle East and Africa increases, both are actively seeking to forge closer defence and security ties with resource supplier nations (e.g., Saudi Arabia and Iran), and to develop appropriate naval capabilities to dominate the sea lanes through which the bulk of their commerce flows. Since seventy-seven percent of China's oil comes from the Middle East and Africa, Beijing has increased its activities in the Indian Ocean region by investing in littoral states' economies, building ports and infrastructure, providing weaponry, and acquiring energy resources. Nearly ninety percent of Chinese arms sales go to countries located in the Indian Ocean region. Beijing is investing heavily in developing the Gwadar deep-sea port in Pakistan, and naval bases in Sri Lanka, Bangladesh, and Myanmar. Whether one calls it a "string of pearls" or a series of places at which China's navy can base or simply be resupplied, that navy is setting up support infrastructure in strategic locations along the same sea lanes of communication that could neutralize India's geographical advantage in the Indian Ocean region. A recent commentary from the official Xinhua news outlet called for setting up three lines of navy supply bases in the northern Indian Ocean, the western Indian Ocean, and the southern Indian Ocean. It stated: "China needs to establish overseas strategic support stations for adding ship fuel, re-supply of necessities, staff break time, repairs of equipment, and weapons in Pakistan, Sri Lanka, and Myanmar, which will be the core support bases in the North Indian Ocean supply line; Djibouti, Yemen, Oman, Kenya, Tanzania, and Mozambique, which will be the core support bases in the West Indian Ocean supply line; and Seychelles and Madagascar, which will be the core support bases in the South Indian Ocean supply line."

For its part, New Delhi is pursuing the same strategy as Beijing and creating its own web of relationships with the littoral states, both bilaterally and multilaterally, through the Indian Ocean Naval Symposium, to ensure that if the military need arises, the necessary support infrastructure and network will be in place. India has also stepped up defence cooperation with Oman and Israel in the west, while upgrading military ties with the Maldives, Madagascar, and Myanmar in the Indian Ocean, and with Singapore, Indonesia, Thailand, Vietnam, Taiwan, the Philippines, Australia, Japan, and the United States in the east. In December 2006, Admiral Sureesh Mehta, then India's naval chief, expanded the conceptual construct of India's "greater strategic neighborhood" to include potential sources of oil and gas imports located across the globe—from Venezuela to the Sakhalin Islands in Russia. The Indian navy currently has a stronger naval presence on the Indian Ocean than does China. It is strengthening its port infrastructure with new southern ports, which allow greater projection into the ocean. Taking a leaf out of China's book, the new focus is to develop anti-access and area-denial capabilities that will thwart any Chinese attempt at encirclement or sea-access denial.

In short, maritime competition is intensifying as Indian and Chinese navies show the flag in the Pacific and Indian oceans with greater frequency. This rivalry could spill into the open after a couple of decades, when one Indian aircraft carrier will be deployed in the Pacific Ocean and one Chinese aircraft carrier in the Indian Ocean—ostensibly to safeguard their respective trade and energy routes.

In turn, India's "Look East" policy is a manifestation of its own strategic intent to compete for influence in the wider Asia-Pacific region. Just as China will not concede India's primacy in South Asia and the Indian Ocean region, India seems unwilling to accept Southeast and East Asia as China's sphere of influence. Just as China's rise is viewed positively in the South Asian region among the small countries surrounding India with which New Delhi has had difficult relations, India's rise is viewed in positive-sum terms among China's neighbours throughout East and Southeast Asia. Over the last two decades, India has sought to enhance its economic and security ties with those Northeast and Southeast Asian nations (Mongolia, South Korea, Japan, Taiwan, Vietnam, Singapore, Thailand, Indonesia, and Australia) that worry about China more than any other major power. As China's growing strength creates uneasiness in the region, India's balancing role is welcome within the Association of Southeast Asian Nations (ASEAN) in order to influence China's behavior in cooperative directions. While the Southeast Asian leaders seek to deter China from utilizing its growing strength for coercive purposes and to maintain regional autonomy, Indian strategic analysts favour an Indian naval presence in the South China Sea and the Pacific Ocean to counter Chinese naval presence in the Indian Ocean. On maritime security, Southeast Asians seem more willing to cooperate with India than China, especially in the Strait of Malacca.

A key element of India's Pacific outreach has been regular naval exercises, port calls, security dialogues, and more than a dozen defence cooperation agreements. India has welcomed Vietnam's offer of berthing rights in Na Trang Port in the South China Sea, and news reports suggest that India might offer BrahMos cruise missiles and other military hardware at "friendship prices" to Vietnam. The conclusion of free-trade agreements with Singapore, South Korea, Malaysia, Japan, and the ASEAN, coupled with New Delhi's participation in multilateral forums such as the East Asia Summit and the ASEAN Plus Eight defence ministers' meetings, have also reinforced strategic ties. India's determination to strengthen its strategic partnership with Japan and Vietnam, commitment to pursue joint oil exploration with Hanoi in the South China Sea waters in the face of Chinese opposition, and an emphasis on the freedom of navigation are signs of India maneuvering to be seen as a counterweight to Chinese power in East Asia. New Delhi is also scaling up defence ties with Tokyo, Seoul, and Canberra.

The US-India partnership is also emerging as an important component of India's strategy to balance China's power. India seeks US economic and technological assistance. It helps this relationship that India's longtime security concerns—China and Pakistan—also now happen to be the United States' long-term and immediate strategic concerns as well. Both the Bush and Obama administrations have encouraged India's involvement in a wider Asian security system to balance a rising China and declining Japan. Apparently, US weakness—real or perceived—invites Chinese assertiveness. Since the United States does not wish to see Asia dominated by a single hegemonic power or a coalition of states, India's economic rise is seen as serving Washington's long-term interests by ensuring that there be countervailing powers in Asia—China, Japan, and India, with the United States continuing to act as an "engaged offshore power balancer."

The "India factor" is increasingly entering the ongoing US policy debate over China. Asia-Pacific is now the Indo-Pacific, a term underlining the centrality of India in the new calculus of regional power. The 2010 US Quadrennial Defence Review talked of India's positive role as a "net security provider in the Indian Ocean and beyond."

India's "Look East" policy, which envisions high-level engagement with "China-wary" nations (South Korea, Japan, Taiwan, Vietnam, Thailand, Indonesia, and Australia), dovetails with the US policy of establishing closer ties with countries beyond Washington's traditional treaty partners to maintain US predominance. The US-Indian strategic engagement, coupled with India's expanding naval and nuclear capabilities and huge economic potential, have made India loom larger on China's radar screen.

An editorial in a Shanghai daily last November lamented the fact that "India will not allow itself to stay quietly between the US and China. It wants to play triangle affairs with the duo, and will do anything it can to maximize its benefit out of it. Therefore, China will find it hard to buy India over." The Chinese fear that the Indian-American cooperation in defence, high-tech R&D, nuclear, space, and maritime spheres would prolong US hegemony and prevent the establishment of a post-American, Sino-centric hierarchical regional order in Asia. This tightening relationship, and the possibility that what is presently a tilt on India's part could turn into a full-fledged alignment, is a major reason for recent deterioration in Chinese-Indian relations.

Although these relations remain unstable and competitive, both have sought to reduce tensions. Despite border disputes, denial of market access, and harsh words against the Dalai Lama, leaders in both countries understand the dangers of allowing problems to overwhelm the relationship. Burgeoning economic ties between the world's two fastest-growing economies have become the most salient aspect of their bilateral relationship.

Trade flows have risen rapidly, from a paltry $350 million in 1993 to $70 billion in 2012, and could surpass $100 billion by 2015. Several joint ventures in power generation, consumer goods, steel, chemicals, minerals, mining, transport, infrastructure, info-tech, and telecommunication are in the works. Intensifying trade, commerce, and tourism could eventually raise the stakes for China in its relationship with India. On the positive side, both share common interests in maintaining regional stability (for example, combating Islamist fundamentalists), exploiting economic opportunities, and maintaining access to energy sources, capital, and markets.

Despite ever-increasing trade volumes, however, there is as yet no strategic congruence between China and India. As in the case of Sino-US and Sino-Japanese ties, Sino-Indian competitive tendencies, rooted in geopolitics and nationalism, are unlikely to be easily offset even by growing economic and trade links. In fact, the economic relationship is heavily skewed. The bulk of Indian exports to China consist of iron ore and other raw materials, while India imports mostly manufactured goods from China—a classic example of the dependency model. Most Indians see China as predatory in trade. New Delhi has lodged the largest number of anti-dumping cases against Beijing in the World Trade Organization. India is keener on pursuing mutual economic dependencies with Japan, South Korea, and Southeast Asian nations through increased trade, investment, infrastructure development, and aid to bolster economic and political ties across Asia that will counter Chinese power.

Even as a range of economic and transnational issues draw them closer together, the combination of internal issues of stability (Tibet and Kashmir), disputes over territory, competition over resources (oil, gas, and water), overseas markets and bases, external overlapping spheres of influence, rival alliance relationships, and ever-widening geopolitical horizons forestall the chances for a genuine Sino-Indian accommodation. Given the broad range of negative attitudes and perceptions each country has for the other, it is indeed remarkable that China and India have been able to keep diplomatic relations from fraying. How long this situation can last is more and more uncertain as each country is increasingly active in what would once have been seen as the other's "backyard" and both engage in strategic maneuvers to checkmate each other.

Just as China has become more assertive vis-à-vis the United States, Indian policy toward China is becoming tougher. India's evolving Asia strategy reflects the desire for an arc of partnerships with China's key neighbours—in Southeast Asia and further east along the Asia-Pacific rim—and the United States that would help neutralize the continuing Chinese military assistance and activity around its own territory and develop counter-leverages of its own vis-à-vis China to keep Beijing sober.

THE MODI-XI SUMMIT AND CHINA-INDIA RELATIONS

Chinese President Xi Jinping will travel to India for a three-day visit to meet with Indian Prime Minister Narendra Modi and others there in government and business. The bilateral environment for this trip is better than last year when Chinese Prime Minister Li Keqiang went to India a few weeks after a border standoff and former Prime Minister Manmohan Singh traveled to Beijing in his last few months in office. Mr.

Xi's visit is part of what have been three-plus months of intense Indian activity in the foreign policy realm since Mr. Modi took office in May. It comes a couple of weeks after the Indian prime minister's visit to Japan and the Australian prime minister's trip to India, just after the Indian president visited Vietnam, and less than two weeks before Mr. Modi meets with U.S. President Barack Obama in Washington.

The Chinese president's visit, in particular, involves a country that poses both an opportunity and a challenge for the Modi government. As a result of this, and the fact that the state of China-India relations can potentially affect the situation in Asia and beyond, this visit is being watched closely. This piece looks at where the China-India relationship stands, the backdrop of the Xi visit, what the two sides will be looking for and trying to signal, the trip agenda, as well as what all this means for the United States.

Recently, the Indian foreign minister frankly noted that India's relations with China were currently "good," but involved both "competition and cooperation." Arguably, there is also a potential for conflict. The cooperative elements of the relationship include a burgeoning economic relationship, greater dialogue on issues like Afghanistan and counterterrorism, as well as cooperation in multilateral forums, including BRICS

(Brazil, Russia, India, China and South Africa) and on multilateral issues such as climate change.

The competitive and conflictual elements that will hang over Mr. Xi's visit include the long-standing boundary dispute between the two countries, China's concerns about the presence of the Dalai Lama and other Tibetan leaders in India, as well as India's concerns about Chinese dam construction on its side of the Brahmaputra river and cyber-espionage and cyber-security threats. Each country also has broader concerns about the other's relationships with third countries. In China's case, India's developing relationships with countries in the Asia-Pacific, especially Japan and the U.S., and perhaps Australia and Vietnam. In India's case, particularly China's relationship with Pakistan, but also its overtures to India's smaller neighbours and Beijing's increasing interest in playing a role in the Indian Ocean region.

In addition, the very issue that was supposed to bind the two countries—economic ties—has been a source of trouble. Bilateral trade has actually fallen over the last few years from $74 billion in 2011 to about $65 billion in 2013. From India's perspective, what's also been problematic is its growing trade deficit with China ($31 billion in 2013). Furthermore, bilateral investment has remained limited, with both sides complaining about market access in the other country.

The Backdrop: A New Government in Delhi; A Beijing Looking for Partners

None of these problems is new, but what is new is the government in Delhi. The majority government in India—the first of its kind in two and a half decades—is led by someone who is no stranger to China. Mr. Modi traveled there when he was chief minister of the state of Gujarat in order to seek investments and markets for his state and its companies.

In the past, he has expressed concern about China on the security front. However, he has also stated his admiration for its economic achievements and a desire to do business with that country, especially in order to deliver on his campaign promises of growth and development. Mr. Xi's visit thus offers an opportunity to attract Chinese investment, as well as elevate India's role on the world stage. Furthermore, there will be an underlying hope that the visit (and other recent ones) will encourage competitive courting by the U.S.

Chinese officials, in turn, welcomed Mr. Modi's election, emphasizing that they were ready to work with someone they see as a business-minded leader. The first senior official to visit India from the P-5 was indeed the Chinese foreign minister, sent as Mr. Xi's special envoy. For Mr. Xi, his own visit offers an opportunity to establish a relationship with the new Indian government and especially Mr. Modi. A stable relationship with India could ease pressure on one of China's borders. Furthermore, a good relationship could limit how far Delhi takes things with Tokyo and Washington. Mr. Xi's task, at least on this visit, has been made easier by the fact that he postponed his visit to Pakistan. But he will be cognizant of the fact that he is not the only one wooing India right now, and not the only country that India, on its part, is wooing. Moreover, in the outgoing Indian visits to Japan and Vietnam, China was a publicly unspoken theme and it'll likely be so when Mr. Modi visits the U.S. later this month.

Mr. Xi's Visit

These and other issues provide the backdrop to Mr. Xi's visit and in some cases will be agenda items. Economic issues will be a key focus of the visit. The Chinese government is aware that an imbalanced economic relationship poses a problem for broader ties and is not sustainable, not least because Mr. Modi stressed this point when he met Mr. Xi on the sidelines of the BRICS summit in Brazil. It is also an issue the Indian commerce minister discussed with her Chinese counterparts recently in Beijing. Chinese officials have noted that in order to help address this imbalance, Mr. Xi will take with him investment commitments of over $100 billion over five years. They have suggested that these will especially be targeted towards the infrastructure and manufacturing sectors, which are focus areas for Mr. Modi, and will likely involve the establishment of industrial parks, including one in Mr. Modi's home state. Offers of more Chinese financing for Indian companies are also likely to be on the table. Mr. Xi is also likely to seek Indian participation in Chinese initiatives for regional connectivity, an offer that India will likely consider but not to the exclusion of other such initiatives.

The economic component of the relationship is likely to be one of the main points of focus during Mr. Xi's first stop in Ahmedabad in Gujarat. This leg of the visit will also give Chinese officials a chance to highlight that the bilateral relationship does not just involve the central governments in both countries, but also states and businesses. Overall, the economic dimension is also providing Mr. Xi's government a way to try to one-up Japan, with the Chinese consul general explicitly comparing China's potential economic offers to the recent Japanese commitment of $35 billion over seven years.

Some believe that this moment also offers an opportunity for the two countries to move ahead on border talks, especially transitioning from managing the dispute to trying to solve it. Indeed, a former Indian foreign secretary has urged the Indian government to press this issue at what he sees is an advantageous time when China is courting India. During Mr. Xi's visit, we might see the announcement of the next step on this front.

In addition, there will likely be discussion of a number of global and regional issues, not least the situation in Afghanistan, as well as the Middle East.

This visit, however, is not just about substance, but also about style. Just as Mr. Li did last year, Mr. Xi has been trying to use this visit to (a) signal that China considers India to be important and (b) add a personal dimension to the relationship. An underlying irritant for many in India has been the sense that Beijing has, at best, treated India as irrelevant or peripheral and, at worst, been trying to contain India or prevent India's rise—not least through China's support of Pakistan, as well as its reluctance to endorse a permanent seat for India on the U.N. Security Council and past objections to Indian membership in the Nuclear Suppliers Group (NSG).

In the lead up to the visit, Chinese policymakers have tried to mitigate some of these concerns, indicating support for India's membership in the Shanghai Cooperation Organization and inviting Mr. Modi to the Asia-Pacific Economic Cooperation meeting in Beijing. One thing to watch during Mr. Xi's visit is whether China will take further steps on this front—even if just rhetorical.

On his part, Mr. Modi is going out of his way for Mr. Xi in some respects, sending his national security advisor as his special envoy to Beijing to, among other things, stress the importance the government is placing on the visit. More significantly, he is making a "special gesture," possibly against the advice of a number of his diplomats, since it is a departure from Indian protocol, to greet Mr. Xi in Ahmedabad.

While the Chinese president perhaps can't compete with the personal relationship that Japanese Prime Minister Shinzo Abe has established with Mr. Modi over the last many years, Mr. Xi has tried to inject a personal dimension, saying that when he first met Mr. Modi he "felt like meeting an old friend."

He is also travelling first to the prime minister's home state, and will visit the Sabarmati Ashram that is linked to Mahatma Gandhi and India's struggle for independence.

The Chinese president has tried to emphasize the commonalities not just between the two countries, but particularly between the tasks that lie ahead for Mr. Modi and him.

There are indeed commonalities between Mr. Modi and Mr. Xi, two Asian leaders that have tried to emphasize that they will take "strong economy, strong security" approaches. Yet the contrast in terms of how the two leaders came to be in power couldn't be more different: one was elected democratically; the other was selected by a chosen few. As Dhruva Jaishankar of the German Marshall Fund has noted, the disparity in their backgrounds is also striking: one, a former tea seller; the other, a prince-ling.

Challenges and Questions

For this visit and beyond, challenges and questions lie ahead for the China-India relationship.

There are open questions with regard to China, including: How much can and will Mr. Xi do to assuage Indian concerns, particularly on the border and Pakistan? How will China react if the Modi government follows through with its plans for military modernization, border infrastructure upgradation and the development of India's northeast? What will Beijing do with regard to Tibet, particularly in the event of a transition in Tibetan leadership?

There are also a number of questions with regard to the Indian government:

Can Mr. Modi deliver domestically? A common challenge to all India's key relationships is that they are both motivated by and dependent on domestic transformation in India, especially on the economic side. Chinese capital, companies and attention will come to India if Mr. Modi's government is seen as delivering on his promises of growth, governance and getting things done. If there is a sense that he can't deliver, they might lose interest.

What happens if and when there's a crisis or if China crosses an Indian red line? We haven't seen major Sino-Indian tension or setbacks since Mr. Modi took over, but we have seen in his government's approach to Pakistan that its reaching out is contingent on a sense that the other country is acting in good faith. But the relationships with China and Pakistan aren't equivalent, and many will watch to see how Mr. Modi will respond if and when there's a sense that China hasn't acted in good faith.

Mr. Modi's predecessors have found that even minor crises can derail the bilateral relationship or at least result in a two-steps-forward-one-step-back dynamic. This is partly because the Indian media and public are not inclined to give Beijing the benefit of the doubt. There is still a lack of trust in the relationship, especially in India where narratives related to the 1962 Sino-Indian war continue to resonate. There remain questions in India about Chinese intentions, evidenced from the fact that in the press conference to preview Mr. Xi's visit, the Indian foreign ministry spokesperson found himself fielding skeptical questions about allegations of Chinese border transgressions. This lack of trust is compounded by a lack of (or limited) knowledge of the other on both sides.

Can Mr. Modi's government walk the China-India tightrope effectively, with the fine balance necessary to reconcile competing interests? The Indian diplomatic corps is no stranger to this challenge and we've already seen the new Indian government try to grapple with it. For example, the foreign minister stating that China "should understand and appreciate our sensitivities regarding Arunachal" while the foreign ministry has avoided answering the question of whether Indian minister of state for home affairs Kiren Rijiju (who is from the state of Arunachal Pradesh, which China claims) will attend the dinner for Mr. Xi. Or, the government making clear that the Dalai Lama and Tibetans will continue to be welcome in India while they will likely try to limit Tibetan protests—or at least their visibility—during the Chinese president's visit.

Mr. Modi has a base, a media and, arguably, a population that tends to be skeptical, if not suspicious, of China. It won't be lost on Mr. Modi that he's taking a risk; that some will question the nature of his welcome for the Chinese president, that some will draw comparisons with former Indian Prime Minister Nehru's embrace of the Chinese leadership before Sino-Indian relations turned sour. But Mr. Modi is likely calculating that the opportunity is worth it and that his "strong" credentials will dampen criticism.

The tag line that the Indian government is propagating is that its foreign policy will have a strong face, a sensitive face and a proactive face. And while the "sensitive" face will perhaps be more visible during Mr. Xi's visit, the Modi government has also been finding ways to convey that they will neither be push-overs nor hesitate to express Indian concerns, and will speak from a position of strength. Hence, early on, the invitation to Tibetan leader Lobsang Sangay to attend the government's swearing in. Last week, the Indian foreign minster asserted that her Chinese counterpart has been told, "If we believe in one China policy, you should also believe in one India policy." In Japan, we've seen Mr. Modi criticizethose who encroach on others' lands and seas, and state his preference for countries that emphasize a development-focused rather than an expansionist mindset. While the Indian foreign minister refused to confirm or deny that these were references to China, they only reiterated a sentiment Mr. Modi had explicitly expressed about China in Arunachal Pradesh during the election campaign. The just-concluded Indian presidential visit to Vietnam has, in turn, resulted in a joint communique that expresses support for "freedom of navigation in the East Sea/South China Sea," with India welcoming the chance to host the Vietnamese prime minister in October and the offer of additional oil and gas blocks for exploration by an Indian state-owned company.

The "strong face" is also being signaled through statements and suggestions that India is politically stronger and will be economically so as well. Furthermore, there is an attempt to convey this by taking on any suggestion that China is India's superior in civilizational terms—witness Mr. Modi's statements and tweets on how Buddhism traveled from India to China, a connection that China used to try to downplay. Finally, the government will try to signal this strength through the continued pursuit of a diversification strategy, highlighting that India has options by engaging with a number of countries, including Australia, Japan, Russia, Vietnam and the U.S.

Where Does the U.S. Fit In?

The India-U.S. relationship is partly driven and shaped by the two countries' perceptions of and relationships with China. Delhi and Washington, therefore, watch closely how the other is interacting with Beijing.

It's a complex, dynamic triangle. On the one hand, the U.S. would like to see a stable China-India relationship, especially given other tensions in Asia and the world. Furthermore, it won't necessarily mind if Chinese investment in India leads to a better Indian economy and, particularly, infrastructure that can redound to the benefit of American business as well. On the other hand, the U.S. would not like to see China and India grow too close, China dominate the Indian economy or for the two countries to form a tag team—with Russia possibly in tow as well—in multilateral fora.

Similarly, on the one hand, Indian concerns about a potential G-2 persist—the idea that China and the U.S., which are economically interdependent, will act together in a fashion that will be to India's detriment. A different manifestation of this concern is the assessment that the U.S. is not a reliable partner vis-à-vis China because it will choose China when push comes to shove. On the other hand, Indian officials don't want to see Sino-U.S. tensions that might destabilize the entire region, jeopardizing Indian domestic goals.

In addition, the Indian leadership recognizes that American concerns about Chinese intentions and the nature of the Chinese government are partly what make India important to key constituencies in the U.S.—something Delhi finds useful—but it also doesn't want to be asked to choose between China and the United States. Defense Secretary Hagel indeed recently acknowledged this Indian concern in Delhi.

Another dimension for India is that its officials realize that what is partly driving China's diplomatic and economic interest in India is its relationship with countries like Japan and the U.S. Thus, India will continue to reach out to these countries bilaterally and even in a trilateral context. Furthermore, even if not explicitly, the U.S. is also considered to be part of India's strategic insurance policy. The U.S. can help manage China's rise and assure the kind of Asia that India would like to see. The Indian government does not share what some have outlined as Mr. Xi's vision of Asia, with China the dominant country and with the U.S. playing a minimal role. The fact that India would like to see a different kind of Asia is reflected in the Tokyo declaration that notes that the responsibility that India and Japan share to shape "the character of this region." It is also evident in the repeated statements from Indian officials that they would like to see a continued, effective U.S. role in the Asia-Pacific.

While they have various concerns about each other, however, it's also worth keeping in mind that China, India and the U.S. also share some common concerns—including those related to Afghanistan (and even Pakistan), the Middle East and climate change—and this offers the prospect of cooperation, or at least, consultation in the future.

4

India-China: Looking Back to Re-Imagine the Future

Almost exactly four years ago, the outgoing UPA-I government's Cabinet Committee on Security (CCS) was meeting for the last time before the results of the 2009 general elections were to be announced. The sole item on the agenda: enhancing India's military preparedness against China. According to insiders present at that meeting, some of the members of the CCS wanted to leave the decision to the next government. But better sense prevailed and days before, Prime Minister Manmohan Singh's first UPA government went ahead and sanctioned the raising of two new Mountain Divisions for deployment in India's north-eastern State of Arunachal Pradesh, an area claimed by China as South Tibet. In addition, the Indian Air Force was given the go ahead to reactivate half a dozen Advance Landing Grounds (ALGs) spread all along the Arunachal-Tibet portion of the Line of Actual Control (LAC) between the two countries, and base additional squadrons of Sukhoi-30 combat jets in Assam.

The goal was to plug existing gaps in India's preparedness along the Arunachal Pradesh-China frontier. The two new divisions were to include a squadron of India's armoured spearhead — Soviet-built T-90 tanks — and a regiment of artillery.

Now, four years later, the two mountain divisions have completed their recruitment, equipping and orbiting in the north-east. After being raised in Nagaland's Zakhama area, one of them — the 56 Mountain Division — has been placed at Lekhabali, north of the Brahmaputra, adding teeth to Indian Army's presence in East and Central Arunachal Pradesh. The other new Division–71 — headquartered at Missamari in the plains of Assam, will enhance troop deployment beyond Tawang in West Arunachal Pradesh, in addition to the 5 Mountain Division already stationed at Tenga.

However, one lacunae continues to persist. Road links to forward areas remain tenuous. The China Study Group (CSG), which controls India's policy on China, had sanctioned 72 tactically important roads to be built in the tough, mountainous terrain along the China border in the eastern and the western sectors. The roads are being built by the quasi-military Border Roads Organisation to enhance connectivity. But a combination of lethargic BRO, obstructionist state governments, and the ministry of environment and forests has meant that these roads are nowhere near completion. Similarly, the half a dozen ALGs in Arunachal Pradesh are also stuck in red tape.

The recent incursion by Chinese troops in Ladakh's Depsang area should serve as a timely reminder to the government that timelines for infrastructure development along the Chinese frontier and plans to boost military capability, do not have the luxury of slippages. Diplomacy and timing (cancellation of Chinese Premier's visit over the border standoff would have been a loss of face for Beijing) helped end the face off this time. But New Delhi will do well to remember that such an incident is not going to be a one-off. The Chinese will continue to nibble at the undemarcated border and test India's response as they have done for over 50 years. In this context, it is necessary to take a peep into what happened in the late 1950s in Ladakh and in the first seven months of 1962, the year both sides fought a bloody war in the high Himalaya.

The Past Experience

On December 26, 1959, Peking (as Beijing was then known) sends a note to India talking about Aksai Chin. It says: "This area is the only traffic artery linking Singkiang to Western Tibet because to its north-east lies the great Gobi of Sinkiang through which direct traffic with Tibet is practically impossible...The area all along belonged to China." Any move by India to improve its military posture close to Aksai Chin will always invite Chinese ire, as it has been doing since the late 1950s. As Peking and New Delhi continued to exchange protest notes, 1962 began with fresh tension.

Consider this:

- Feb 22, 1962: India protests to China against advance patrolling by Chinese troops
- March: New Delhi protests against the establishment of a military post by China 6 miles west of Sumdo
- April-May 1962: Chinese troops step up advance patrolling in Chip Chap area
- April 30, 1962: Peking orders patrolling in the sector from Karakoram Pass to Kongka Pass, and demands India withdraw two posts in the area
- May 2, 1962: China-Pakistan announce an agreement to enter into "negotiations to locate and align" the portion of India-China border west of Karakoram Pass in Kashmiri territory under Pakistan's unlawful occupation
- Mid-May, 1962: China sets up a new post in Indian territory, 10 miles south-east of Spanggur

Events of 1962 will repeat themselves, however. Half a century later, the world has changed: India's military capability is far better than it was then, and there is too much at stake for Beijing to launch any overt aggression. However, what has not changed is the Chinese tendency of bullying weaker neighbours and its policy to keep redefining "core" interests according to circumstances. Policy making in China is one continuous process. In India, on the other hand, it varies according to personalities and political parties in power.

While the military in India has overcome the trauma of the 1962 defeat, civilian policy makers appear to be still bogged down by the burdens of the past in dealing with China. Of course, these mandarins get their act together only under pressure of a crisis like they did in the post-1986 Sumdorong Chu faceoff. The 2009 sanction for additional forces and the speeding up of infrastructure development projects also came after increasing reports of Chinese belligerence along the LAC.

Therefore, it is essential to push for another round of capability-enhancing drive. The pending financial clearance for the Mountain Strike Corps must come quickly, even if it means brushing aside the rather silly query from the finance ministry which asked: "would the Chinese threat persist after 2015?"

INDIA'S CHINA POLICY SINCE THE END OF THE COLD WAR

Certain scholars believe that India's China policy has undergone three major phases of adjustment since the end of the Cold War: the pre-1998 phase policy of reconciliation; the 1998–2000 phase policy of hostility; and the 2000 to present phase policy of engagement. The second phase around the time of the 1998 nuclear tests featured harangues from the Indian government regarding the 'China threat' and a brief deadlock in Sino–Indian relations. The author, however, believes that two, rather than three, phases of adjustment are applicable to an explanation of the state of bilateral relations between China and India in the post-Cold War era.

When considering India's overall strategic aims at the time of the 1998 nuclear tests and the implications and specific actions of its subsequent China policy, it is difficult to pinpoint two 180 degree-policy shifts in the course of just two years. Facts demonstrate that India named China as a threat at the time of the 1998 tests as a matter of expedience to acquiesce in the anti-China stance of certain parties in the United States and other Western nations; it was a ploy whose purpose was to divert attention from and rationalize the nuclear tests, thereby dispelling any notion of sanctions.

It should be borne in mind, however, that India's understanding of comprehensive national strength deepened after the Cold War, as did its leaders' belief that nuclear arms and credible nuclear deterrence were hallmarks of a superpower. Entering the nuclear club was consequently a stride towards achieving one of the sub-continent's greatest national aspirations. The Rao government, which pursued a China policy of reconciliation and engagement, had made preparations for nuclear tests but stopped short of carrying them out for fear of the potential burden on the newly recovered economy of international sanctions.

Prime Minister Vajpayee and other political leaders repeatedly and publicly expressed soon after the 1998 tests that India had no wish to hold China as an enemy or a threat, stating, to the contrary, their desire for reinforced friendly relations. At no point during this period did diplomatic engagement between India and China cease. Indian External Affairs Minister Jaswant Singh's visit to China in June 1999 demonstrated that the Sino–Indian relationship had recovered in the space of a year from any damage that the nuclear tests had inflicted upon it. That becoming a nuclear power while maintaining stable relations with China were post-Cold War India's strategic goals was also implied by the sub-continent's explicit moves towards repairing its relationship with China. The 1998 nuclear tests constituted no fundamental change to India's China policy and should, within the scope of Sino–Indian relations, be regarded as a minor episode. Moreover, the shift of India's China policy in 1988 was not prompted by any change of security concept; Prime Minister Rajiv Gandhi's trip to China that year was motivated by the fact of Sino–Soviet reconciliation. Changes in security concept explicitly propelled India's; post-Cold War China policy adjustments. This book, therefore, primarily examines developments and changes in India's China policy after the Cold War. It holds that a substantive change indeed occurred; specifically from one of hostility and antagonism during the Cold War (especially 1962–1988) to reconciliation and engagement thereafter. This policy change, however, was by no means instantaneous but characterized by gradual, phased development. Two, rather than three, phases of adjustment tally with changes in India's post-Cold War security concept.

India's China Policy from the End of the Cold War to 1998

Indian leaders believed after 1962 that hostilities between China and India were inevitable, and viewed China as a major enemy. Prime Minister Indira Gandhi considered Sino–Indian antagonism as going far beyond border disputes, and that China was pursuing the more 'complex' policy of pressing India on all fronts and, moreover, displacing the sub-continent by establishing its own dominant position in the Asian power hierarchy.

The goal of India's China policy during this period, therefore, was to ensure its supremacy over China in Asia and, in the event of armed conflict, to avoid repeating mistakes that had led to its defeat in the 1962 Sino–Indian conflict. India's policy at the time can be so summarized: strengthen military capability and deployment; seek aid from major powers, respectively, the United States, United Kingdom and USSR; and support Chinese separatist forces. After the Cold War ended, however, changes in India's domestic and international situation brought tremendous challenges, and its position as regards China and its related policy goals showed clear adjustments. India considered China as a nation going through a reflective, 'inward looking' period and, as such, had no intention of attacking the sub-continent. In the short-term, therefore, it constituted no threat. The goal of India's new China policy was to maintain stability in Sino–Indian relations, ensure peaceful borders and create conditions suitable for India to gather its resources and restore economic and military strength. The specific policy adjustments were as follows.

Achieve Simultaneous Progress in Solving Border Disputes

For almost two decades after 1962, India made resolution of border disputes a pre-condition for normalizing relations with China. Its insistence in this regard was the main reason for the longstanding chill in Sino–Indian relations. Although the two nations restored ambassadorial-level diplomatic relations in

1976, and in 1981 agreed to begin talks on the border issue, this principled standpoint did not change. Upon meeting with visiting then-External Affairs Minister Vajpayee early in 1979, Comrade Deng Xiaoping proposed an agreement that would provide 'a package solution' for relevant border disputes.

He said that if it were not possible completely to resolve border disputes at an early date, he would consider cooperation in other areas. But it was not until 1988 during Rajiv Gandhi's trip to China that the Indian government accepted this suggestion and formally initiated the process of normalizing bilateral relations which the successive Indian governments pursued and implemented after the Cold War ended. It is notable that during the time the two sides promoted negotiations on border issues they also exchanged high-level visits in which the two nations signed cooperative agreements in such areas as trade, technology, education and culture, and that cooperation between them grew ever greater in depth and breadth.

Shift Strategies on Border Talks

As India needed a peaceful, stable environment in which to concentrate on economic recovery, securing Sino–Indian borders was its primary goal in the early 1990s. Because of India's; pre-1988 insistence on not normalizing Sino–Indian relations until the border issues were settled, there were suspicions that the sub-continent was 'taking improvements in bilateral relations as a bargaining chip through which to force China to yield in border disputes'. India consequently insisted in the talks that began in 1981 on its own position as regards a segmented solution to the issue. India's objective understanding of the complexity of the Sino–Indian border dispute after the Cold War and of realistic strategic considerations and needs prompted an adjusted strategy for these talks. This was manifest in its suggestion of a gradual solution to border disputes: the first step would be to stabilize the Line of Actual Control (LAC) situation and eliminate disagreements over its demarcation; the second to reach agreement on preserving peace and tranquillity along the LAC; and the third to take measures to establish mutual trust along the LAC.

This accomplished, the two nations could then address substantive problems in their border dispute. This tentative plan enabled India and China to approach a consistent position whereby the two sides worked to achieve a solution to Sino–Indian border disputes and create an atmosphere of reasonableness and peace. The two nations made progress, signing in 1993 the Agreement on Maintenance of Peace and Tranquillity along the Line of Actual Control in the Sino– Indian Border Areas, and in 1996 the Agreement Between the Government of the Republic of India and the Government of the People's Republic of China on Confidence-Building Measures in the Military Field Along the Line of Actual Control in the India–China Border Areas. India saw these two agreements as on the one hand ensuring the two sides could resolve border disputes peacefully without resorting to violence, and on the other that border disputes would not inhibit the development of their bilateral relations.

Tibetan Issue and do not Provoke China

Leaders of India's independence movement had at the time of the British Raj followed the British colonialist concept of Tibet as a 'buffer region' between India and China. After winning independence, therefore, the Indian government supported from the very beginning the so-called 'Tibetan independence movement'. At around the time of the founding of the People's Republic of China, India seized the opportunity offered by China's political upheaval to promote the international standing of the local Tibetan government and thwart China's liberation of Tibet. New Delhi continued unremittingly in its efforts to convince China's central government, even during the 1950s heyday of Sino–Indian amity, to give Tibet substantial autonomy and to reduce to the greatest extent possible the size of its garrison there. After the insurrection of 1959 the Indian government was more overt in its support of Tibet, giving asylum to fugitive rebels and propping up the so-called 'Tibetan Government in Exile' established by the Dalai Lama in 1960 in the Indian city of Dharamsala. India further incited and encouraged Tibetan independence activities after the Sino–

Indian conflict of 1962.In truth, Indian leaders considered their support for exiled Tibetans' separatist activities as an effective containment against China. But when Prime Minister Rajiv Gandhi visited China in 1988 he issued the statement: 'The Indian side reiterates the long-standing and consistent policy of the Government of India that Tibet is an autonomous region of China and that anti-China political activities by Tibetan elements are not permitted on Indian soil,' which implied India's change of approach from that of support for Tibetan independence. Indian leaders reiterated this pledge after the Cold War ended and imposed limits on Tibetan fugitives' anti-China political activities. For instance, Indian officials would generally contact the Dalai Lama and leaders of the so-called Tibetan government in exile before a visit by Chinese leaders to India, requesting that they refrain from Tibetan protests, demonstrations or other anti-Chinese behaviour.

Yet, differences still exist between China and India on the issue of Tibetan autonomy. Although, proceeding from the requirement of preserving stable Sino–Indian relations, the post-Cold War Indian government has been low-key in its support of the Dalai Lama and other Tibetan fugitives, this does not signify a substantial change in its strategic treatment of the Tibetan issue.

Changes in India's China Policy from 1999 to Present

Achieving recovery, contending for the status of global power had been India's ambition for decades. The growth of the sub-continent's comprehensive strength and improvements in the international environment in the late 1990s presented to it a real possibility of realizing this ambition, as well as a number of other unprecedented strategic opportunities. Against this backdrop, reconciliation with China and the unchanged overall direction of the relationship produced several new adjustments to the positions and goals of India's China policy. At this stage, India saw China neither as enemy nor friend, believing that cooperation could coexist with competition between the two nations. India still considered China as constituting no threat in the short term, but began focusing on long-term trends in the balance of power. The emphasis of the goals of its new China policy are on ensuring that future Sino–Indian relations are of benefit to India by making China a positive factor in the process of its rise. Maintaining the stability of Sino–Indian relations remains fundamental. The new policy adjustments are as follows.

Expand Economic Cooperation with China

Trade between the two nations ceased after the 1962 Sino–Indian Border Conflict, and did not resume until 1977. The volume of trade between the two sides in the 1980s wavered at around roughly Us." million. But after the Cold War ended, Sino–Indian trade experienced a seemingly spontaneous phase of rapid development. The trade volume between China and India increased from $264 million in 1991 to $1.988 billion in 1999—a yearly average of 31.2%—or an increase factor of 6.5 over eight years. Indian leaders' concerns about India's economic recovery nonetheless maintained at this point the China policy focus on stabilizing political relations and establishing tranquil borders. Indian leaders' understanding of economic strength and security having becoming more profound since 1999, their enthusiasm for developing bilateral trade soared. As China and India were the world's two most rapidly developing nations, Indian leaders could see the obvious potential for trade between them and that strengthening bilateral trade would be of great mutual benefit. Also that close economic ties could have a stabilizing influence on their political relationship. Statistics show that bilateral trade since 1999 has entered into a new period of growth. The average yearly growth to 2006 was 44.4%—a rate which exceeded that of the preceeding period and which is being achieved on an ever-stronger numerical foundation. The volume of Sino–Indian trade reached US$24.8 billion in 2006, having increased by a factor of 11.5 over 1999 and one of 93 over 1991. China became India's second largest trading partner in 2006, and India China's tenth largest. It may be said that the role of Sino–Indian trade has grown from one unworthy of mention to a decisive aspect of the overall bilateral relationship.

INDIA'S SECURITY CONCEPT ON ITS CHINA POLICY

India's post-Cold War security concept and adjustments to its China policy. In the process of this discussion, we have distinguished two phases of adjustment to both the post-Cold War India security concept and China policy, and established that these changes were more or less simultaneous. We have also found that India's China policy reflects its security concept; in other words that adjustments to the content of India's China policy correspond to continuities and discontinuities in India's security concept. It may be said that this consistency demonstrates the important influence India's security concept has had on its China policy. Policy-making, in any event, is the linking of concepts and policy; in other words, concepts, through government policy-making, crystallize into policy. Exploring the evolution of the Indian policy-making class and mechanisms, therefore, also benefits understanding of the manner in which security concepts of different eras and phases have influenced India's China policy.

India's foreign policy behaviour during the Cold War was largely determined by a few predominant personalities, both its foreign and security policies having long been dominated by Nehru and Indira Gandhi. The two leader's views on China had decisive influence on India's China policy. When considering India's defeat in the 1962 Sino–Indian Border Conflict and the open wound it represented to both the Nehru family and the INC, their adoption of an unyielding tack toward China was the sole political means of saving face. Sino–Indian relations consequently remained in stalemate for nearly 30 years. When Rajiv Gandhi replaced his mother in 1985, he seemed at first to follow her line on foreign policy. The rapidly changing international situation, however, forced him to veer from it, and specific improvements in Sino–Soviet relations compelled his adjustments to India's China policy. Soviet leader Mikhail Gorbachev urged Rajiv Gandhi during a visit to India in 1986 to improve relations with China, saying it would suit Soviet interests, and hinting at a press conference that the USSR would no longer be willing to provide support to India in the event of Sino–Indian conflict. In this situation, Rajiv Gandhi considered that India on its own would be powerless against a threat on two fronts. He was hence forced to change his preparations for a two-front war, as it was apparent that dispelling tensions along the eastern front through reconciliation with China would allow him to concentrate India's energies on the western front with Pakistan.

The Nehru family's stately bearing was absent after the Cold War, and the INC's power had declined. The insularity that had characterized India's foreign policy-making process since independence, however, did not change. The nation's foreign and security policy stayed in the hands of the prime minister and cabinet from 1991 to 1996, during which time the views of Prime Minister Rao and leaders of the INC government on security and foreign policy matters were decisive, and the influence of parliament, think tanks and academic institutions was negligible. It is notable, however, that Rao's background as home minister, defence minister and external affairs minister throughout the 1980s, as well as his status as the Congress Party's elder statesman, signified that he was a loyal adherent of Nehruvianism, and unrepresentative of any new type of thinking. The transformation of India's security concept during the Rao administration, therefore, can be understood as entirely the result of external forces.

As earlier mentioned, changes in the international and domestic situation compelled Rao to change his understanding of national strength. He began emphasizing the strategic influence of economic strength and promoting restoration of the economy as a matter of urgency in withstanding security threats in the aftermath of the Cold War. This passive reaction to a complex situation gave the impression of India's overall foreign policy as passive and defensive. India adopted a focused approach to diplomacy during this period, directing its energies towards restoring the economy but maintaining a low profile in international affairs, as expressed in its China policy. Rao continued and furthered Rajiv Gandhi's adjustments by focusing on stabilization of Sino–Indian political relations and establishing tranquil borders as means to ensuring the recovery of India's domestic economy.

Two major changes occurred in India's foreign policy-making process during 1998. The first was the BJP's assumption of office that ended the long-standing INC power monopoly, and established foundations for a clean break with the traditional security concept. Although the BJP's domestic policies had a relatively ideological slant and promoted a Hinduist revival, the party was pragmatic as regards foreign policy.

In contrast to the Congress Party, it dared to confront history, criticise India's previous foreign policy and introduce new thinking. Jaswant Singh, successively the Vajpayee government's External Affairs Minister and Finance Minister, published early in 1999 a book entitled *Defending India* in which he systematically describes his new security concept. Various views were thereafter expressed in government-issued articles.

The BJP was obviously preparing to move on from the passive security concept of the Rao era. The second major change was India's refinement of its foreign policy-making mechanism. The November 1998 establishment of the National Security Council symbolized India's casting off of the influence and control of personality-based policy-making in favour of scientific research, inquiry and decision-making, and comprehensive long-term planning. The introduction by National Security Advisory Board subordinated to the National Security Council of scholarly authorities, reporters and former government and military officials demonstrated how much more open India's foreign policy-making process had become.

The BJP differed in its approach to China policy from both that of the Cold War era Nehru family, with its 1962 complex, and the early 1990s Rao government, which had been wearied and bound hand and foot by domestic and international pressure. The BJP's seizing of this historic opportunity confirmed India's rise as the nation's long-term strategic goal and placed its relationship with China on the strategic level. In other words, the BJP saw the Sino–Indian relationship as an important influence on India's rise. Although the two nations would be dealing with historically significant problems, they could be seen as a starting point.

The gradual opening of India's foreign policy-making process, moreover, made way for a vibrant exchange of ideas regarding China policy, which fell roughly into three groups: the first held that Sino–Indian cooperation suits both sides' interests and that post-Cold War China has no intention of making an enemy of India, desiring instead friendly relations and strategic partnership; the second that China is a long-term strategic threat to India because China's strategic objectives lie in establishing hegemony over Asia, which necessitates India's containment and, therefore, limitation of Indian influence. India, therefore, should adopt diametrically opposed policies; and the third group, situated between the two, held that the two nations could simultaneously rise to become main Asian powers and that competition and cooperation could coexist. Discussions on how to evaluate and understand China by Indian scholars and strategic circles are ongoing. After frequent debates among Indian National Security Council groups, the third, middle-ground viewpoint seems to be gaining acceptance.

When the INC regained power in 2004, a variety of factors led the new government to carry on with the previous administration's security concept. The new INC government's China policy was its predecessor's legacy, because the rise of India's international status during the BJP coalition government left the INC powerless to dispute the success of the previous government's foreign policy. The INC's democratized and more youthful leadership team was also willing to jettison historical baggage and look to the future. Although the Nehru family's leadership role within the Congress Party remained uncontested, the influence of Prime Minister Manmohan Singh and Foreign Minister Mukherjee on foreign and security policy could not be disregarded. Moreover, the liberalization of India's foreign policy-making process was superimposed against a long-standing civil service system which ensured continuity of policy. In other words, many masterminds of BJP foreign policy still active in the external affairs ministry, defence ministry and other relevant functional departments under the INC, as well as in consultative committees, the media, think tanks and other non-functional departments, continued to exert influence.

Substantial changes occurred in India's China policy after the end of the Cold War whereby the nation's long-standing (1962–1988) antagonistic approach became one of reconciliation and engagement. These adjustments originated to a great extent in changes in the sub-continent's post-Cold War security concept, manifest in two major shifts which effected two major phases of adjustment in India's China policy. The new post-Cold War China policy nonetheless retained traces of the former, programme, imbuing it with a duality that reflected the overlap of India's old and new security concepts.

A change in India's security concept first became apparent during the period from the end of the Cold War to 1998. The first phase of adjustments this change triggered in India's China policy was evident in the sub-continent's extended concept of military might as national strength to one encompassing economic factors, and acknowledgement of the strategic value of economic strength in countering what it perceived as the looming threat of marginalization within the international community. Restoration of the domestic economy hence became a main measure through which to resist security threats in the post-Cold War era. Having made this shift in foreign policy objectives towards economic recovery, India set about creating a favourable environment within which to achieve this goal. Overall implementation of a China policy of preserving stable Sino–Indian relations by guaranteeing border tranquillity was vital to achieving this strategic objective. India consequently focused on the feasibility of reconciliation and, in view of China's reflective, inward-looking mood, no longer viewed China as an enemy. As regards India's specific policies, while focusing on the establishment of a progressive means to guaranteeing tranquil borders, thereby stabilizing Sino–Indian relations, India at the same time sought communication and cooperation in other areas. To avoid provoking China, the Indian government made tactical adjustments to its approach to Tibet from that of exploiting the issue and causing uproar to handling the matter in a low-key manner.

The new developments apparent in India's security concept in 1999 brought with it the second phase of adjustments to India's China policy. Indian leaders considered that the nation's security environment had improved to the extent that it constituted a strategic opportunity for India to rise to global-power status. This change in thinking and understanding caused the second shift of objective in India's foreign policy from that of improving the economy to the grand goal of global-power status. It corresponded to India's acknowledgement of the crucial nature of the Sino–Indian relationship and change of focus from border tranquillity and stable political relations to comprehensive considerations of how the two nations' relationship would strategically affect India's; rise. These insights compelled a shift of objective in India's China policy towards making China a positive factor in the sub-continent's rise; also recognition that this objective could be accomplished only by maintaining a stable basis for Sino–Indian relations. Official introduction during this phase of a comprehensive security concept signalled India's adoption of a more pragmatic, comprehensive handling of its relations with China. The specific steps it adopted were: increasing economic cooperation with China, thus benefiting India's economic development and stabilizing bilateral political relations; strengthening military communication and security dialogue, thus deepening understanding of China's strategic intentions towards India, increasing mutual trust, minimizing misunderstandings and avoiding conflict; and seeking Chinese support in its quest for a permanent seat on the UN Security Council, which would expand India's political power and international prestige.

In the course of research, however, it became apparent to the author that India's security concept did not undergo a thoroughgoing change after the Cold War ended, as elements of the Cold War approach remained in place. Although India's security concept extended after 1988 to include both military and economic security, the ultimate purpose of national defence as regards a fundamental guarantee of security nonetheless remained that of increased military strength to safeguard national unity and territorial integrity. India abandoned its strategy of pursuing security through alliances, yet still viewed parity and the principle of checks and balances as hallmarks of its national defence. Influenced as it was by traditional concepts, post-Cold War India's China policy was imbued with vigilance. Even though India did not perceive China as a threat in the short term, it was nevertheless concerned that the swing in balance of power between the two was not in its favour, and that China constituted a potential obstacle to India's rise. Indian leaders consequently embarked on a race against China to expand comprehensive national strength, particularly military force, including India's nuclear capability, as the means to a balance of power. India at the same time sought to offset Chinese influence both regionally and globally through development of strategic relationships with the United States, Japan and other nations. The sub-continent also remained vigilant in the long-standing issues of border disputes and Sino–Pakistani relations, and maintained pressure on China in this regard.

Changes in post-Cold War India's security concept were thus the result of both domestic and foreign factors. The first change during the early post-Cold War period was triggered by passive reactions to transformations in the nation's domestic and international situation that, in turn, prompted a passive transformation of thinking and understanding, manifest in passive defensiveness of India's foreign policy, specifically its China policy. The security concept that appeared during the late 1990s was comparatively proactive. The expanded strength of India's domestic economy and improvement of its external environment compelled a new understanding of security issues, as expressed in the proactive change in its security concept. This assertiveness was manifest in strategy and in an active, enterprising foreign policy. Seizing the historic opportunity to realize India's rise had become the common security objective of both major Indian political parties. Decentralization of political power and expanded openness of the foreign policy-making process, however, caused India's old and new security concepts to bind into one, and the resultant duality of India's hybrid security concept since the Cold War's end is reflected in its China policy. As India's dual security concept will continue into the foreseeable future, the duality of its China policy will be difficult to change.

CHINA AND INDIA : THE 'EMERGING GIANTS' AND GROWTH

The economic performance of China and India is critical. This holds the key to global progress. China and India have been relatively 'closed' economies with limited dependence on trade. But they have been opening up. This is particularly so in the case of China.

Trade as a % of GDP has been 32% in China compared to 25% in India. This should be seen against a backdrop of relatively open East and South Asian economies: Malaysia (206%), Korea (Republic) (72%), Thailand (82 %), Pakistan (36%) and Bangladesh (35%). India's import duties as a % of imports, a key measure of openness, have also been declining in China and India. But it is lower in China compared to India: 3% in the former and 24% in the latter.

Foreign Direct Investment (FDI) can enable access to resources and increase productivity. There are two types: one by the transnationals from industrialized countries and the other by overseas Chinese and Non Resident Indians. In China overseas Chinese have been primarily responsible for Chinese FDI while India's FDI has been channeled through the Transnationals. Net flows of FDI as a % of GDP in China have been 12% in contrast to India's 0.61%.

Both countries have been growing fast over the last 25 years: China by 21 fold and India by 8 fold. The growth rate in China has been over 9% per annum making it possibly the fastest growing world economy while India's, too, has been impressive with over 8% per annum. The % living below the poverty line (1 $ a day) has also been appreciably reduced in both though it is more impressive in China compared to India: 12% in the former and 26% in the latter.

The major effect of China's and India's economic advance is evidenced by their contribution to global output: China's and India's share being 20% and 7% respectively in 2004. Both, moreover, have rising demand for energy, raw materials and commodities. This has a positive impact on increasing the exports of developing countries, improving their terms of trade, and initiating shifts in their pattern of trade and investment.

Liberalisation policies have enhanced the economic prowess of both nations. China, moreover, as a recent member of the World Trade Organization (2001), could firmly influence global trade negotiations, possibly joining forces with India, and champion the rights of poor nations. They could establish a 'level playing field' in world trade. Indeed the combined efforts of China and India could ensure that the Uruguay Round (1986-93) to accelerate trade liberalization can be successful. They could pressurize the developed nations to fulfil their promise of opening up their markets to developing country agricultural and non agricultural exports.

Liberalisation emerged much earlier in China, in 1978, while it was initiated in India in 1991 though initial steps were taken in the 1980's. Pre-reform or pre-liberalisation forces laid the basis on which such measures were evolved. China's policies unfolded in the context of bold economic policies in the East Asia region between 1960-1990 emphasizing agricultural development, primary education, macroeconomic stability, firm public policies to support markets, and regional dynamism. China's liberalization has been embodied in market based thrusts in agriculture, industry and services, state owned enterprises, and deregulation of product prices. These have been backed by measures to induce labour mobility, and formation of Special Economic Zones.

On the domestic front, in the pre reform era in China, the savings level was high with significant capital formation (30%) and investment in infrastructure, irrigation and land development. Literacy and primary health care, too, have been impressive with virtual elimination of landlessness. It has also shed surplus labour-a move which has been inhibited in India possibly due to strong trade unions to safeguard the interest of workers. On the external front China's integration with the world economy, as mentioned earlier, has been advanced through its trade and FDI policies. This has made a significant contribution to China's growth and productivity.

India's growth rates have been relatively low in the pre-liberalisation period-4%-5% per annum compared to East Asia's 7%-8% per annum. The level of savings, too, has been lower than in China and East Asia; the levels of literacy and health care, too, have been lower, coupled with the presence of significant landlessness, and marked poverty and inequality between and within regions, sectors and socio-economic groups.

Liberalisation was initiated in India in the 1980's with a shift in attitude towards the private sector. Its momentum was increased from 1991 onwards. The high growth rate (8% per annum) in the post liberalization period and the future targets (9%-10%) are necessary but not sufficient.

The structure of the economy has to be transformed. In this respect, though the % contribution of agriculture to GDP has been reduced to about 25% it still absorbs over 60% of the employed, while manufacturing and services contribute 28% and 55 % respectively to GDP. Over 62% of India's growth over 1990-2003 has been in services but it has been employment inelastic. Hence, the pace of industrialization has to be reinforced.

Though poverty in India has been reduced to about 26% it is critical to widen participation by the poor in development programmes. This can ensure that high growth rates are sustained. This calls for the use of labour intensive techniques, investment in human and physical capital, and infrastructure, enhanced flexibility in labour laws, and supporting institutions to meet socio-economic goals. The state has to play an active role to fulfil such goals though market forces may guide policies. This could enable the poor to be lifted from poverty.

No doubt China has grown faster and sharply reduced the % of people below the poverty line compared to India. However, inter regional and inter group inequalities in China have increased.

China and India need to persist with their integration with the international economy to sustain growth. This should encompass incorporating the poor in the process, particularly in India, and reducing regional and inter-group disparities in China. Such goals are intertwined with maintaining peace within the respective regions. This is exemplified in India by efforts to minimize conflicts with neighbouring Pakistan, curbing terrorism from within and outside the state, resolving historical border disputes between India and China, and meeting the needs of dissatisfied groups within the state. In China it is essential to respect human rights.

China-India co-operation

Enhanced economic cooperation between India and China could bolster their economic power in spite of differing positions on politics and international affairs. Thus, it emerges that the economic relationship between China and India has taken place against a backdrop of tensions.

This is exemplified by China's past political, military and economic support for Pakistan, and China's claim to Arunachal Pradesh which has been vehemently challenged by India. Leaving aside such differences China and India are seen as contributors rather than competitors to each other's development. This is welcomed by India which has adopted a 'Look East' policy to expand trade and investment links with East Asia and forge strong ties with regional institutions (eg. Association of South East Asian Nations, Asia Pacific Economic Cooperation).

The recent visit of the Chinese President Hu Jintao to Delhi is a significant move in initiating a platform on development, peace and stability in Asia and the world. This was underscored by the Chinese President. He perceived the relationship between China and India as being between 'old and close brothers' citing the vision of Rabindranath Tagore the Nobel Indian poet. The President's visit culminated in a pledge to double trade between the two nations to $ 40 billion by 2010. This contrasts with $ 250 million in the 1990's.

China and India have been competing for resources in Asia and Africa. China has been the winner in virtually all the sectors excepting technology. However, the two nations could devise policies to complement each other's need. Thus, India could meet China's growing appetite for raw materials (iron ore, steel and plastics) fuelling its massive manufacturing sector.

China in turn could furnish manufacturing expertise and investment for Indian infrastructure. Indian critics of Chinese policies have expressed concern over the lack of transparency exemplified by their high level of subsidies.

They are also anxious over the sharply increasing Indian imports from China of clothes, electronic goods and even fireworks.

The Chinese have responded by highlighting India's blocking of their investments in ports and telecommunications. This has been justified by India on grounds of security. Overall, though, as the Chinese President reaffirmed, the relationship between China and India was "an opportunity and not a threat." This could pave the way for cooperation between China and India and enhance the nature and pace of globalization.

THEORETICAL SUPPORT OF CHINESE DIPLOMACY

Surly there are some typical resources in terms of which China lays its diplomatic philosophy on the foundation—pluralism. Due to the diversity of resources, not only the practical and objective factors but also the historical and subjective ones should be taken into account. In general, the resources or roots of pluralism as Chinese diplomatic philosophy are in relations with Chinese traditional culture with tolerance, its modernization in the making, nation-state system it faces and particular development routine since 1980s.

Chinese Traditional Culture's Deep Power

It's self-evident that a country's diplomatic features are absolutely influenced by its national culture which not only provides a potential model of the diplomatic practice but also influences the decision-makers who are in charge of national diplomacy. As one country with five thousand years' continuity of statehood and civilization, China's diplomatic philosophy of course should be shaped inescapably by its national traditional cultures. It's very complicated to sort the contents of a culture with a long history, and to examine the influence of each factor of the culture on national diplomatic features, yet it's easy to examine the potential influence of only one factor of the culture on diplomacy. As for China, tolerance as one outstanding factor or feature of Chinese culture has powerful influence on China's foreign affairs.

If tracing back to 2000 B.C., a kingdom called Xia Dynasty ruled one small part of today's China in Yellow River region. After Xia was ended then Shang (also called Yin) Dynasty followed. In that time, Shang kingdom long-drawn-out its territory and created the most primitive Chinese words based on which the recorded history of Chinese civilization was emerged. Shang classified the people living in the world (all under the heaven) into two kinds and five sections, the Chinese (living in Shang, the world centre) and the barbarians which consisted of four ethnics—Yi (in the East), Rong (in the West), Di (in the North) and Man (in the South). When the political legitimacy of the last king of Shang Dynasty was suspected by his people due to his cruelty and inability, one Rong's tribe led by Gi Fa then in the name of the Heaven *(Ban)* called all the people under the heaven to fight against Shang king's ruling. Finally this tribe from western barbarians defeated Shang and built a new dynasty called Zhou, a kingdom that influenced Chinese culture strongly, especially on morality very deeply. It can be concluded that the early Chinese history mirrors one outstanding feature of Chinese culture—openness—not only Chinese living in "world centre" but those Barbarians could govern China, then the feature was consolidated by the following centuries. For example, as one kingdom located in the China's periphery, Qin was recognized by other Chinese kingdoms as one barbarian-like regime in the Rong district. Yet finally this kingdom unified all parts of China and erected a powerful empire—Qin Dynasty which influenced and shaped Chinese cultures deeply, especially in fields of bureaucratic politics and social systems. Generally saying, the openness and incorporation of Chinese culture is due to the helps of the communication and even marriages among different ethnics. In Chinese history, there are several times in which the minority of Chinese ethnics becomes the ruling people, all of whom inescapably not only accepted the core of Chinese culture but also contributed some typical cultures of their own into Chinese civilization.

In accordance with this constant incorporation of diverse ethnics' cultures, the openness of Chinese culture was kept very well and finally made this culture become one of important and famous cultures in the world. Clearly, this honesty directly leads to emergence of tolerance which doesn't permit those extreme and fundamentalist ideologies to grow and boom in China. For this reason, it's hard to find the persecution within different religions as well as the authority's terrible persecution on religious groups in China. The terrible conflicts between two most influential religions, Buddhism and Daoism, never happened. In reality, some Buddhists were Daoists at the same time. In one famous Chinese classic master, Journey to the West (*Xi You Ji*), recorded one interesting story in which the Buddha had helped the Y u Emperor, one God of Daoism, to defeat one monkey monster, that is, the Buddha and Yu Emperor are friends.

Then how was this tolerance functioned in ancient China's foreign affairs? This question could be answered by the example of tributary system which had been run for almost fifteen hundred years in East Asia.

The China-centered tributary system was the overriding international system in which although China was the dominant power, those neighbouring countries as China's vassals could keep their domestic systems well and would not be interfered by China if they could showed their respects for China by visiting Chinese emperor's court regularly. Only those that were invaded by foreigners or suffered from serious civil conflicts would be intervened by Chinese officials or militaries in order to restore their domestic orders and regional stability. In a sum, Chinese influence on its neighbouring vassals' inner affairs not by political and military approaches but simply by Chinese cultural charm.

At present, after a terrible so-called immense Cultural Revolution (1966-1976) which damaged traditional culture badly, and after a new round westernization since 1979 which faded the influence of Marxist ideologies on public daily lives, the renaissance of Chinese traditional culture in the beginning of the 21 century seems become a tendency that is firstly emerged in civil society and gradually supported by Chinese government. In terms of the restoration of traditional culture, Chinese diplomacy will be partly shaped by those ideas including tolerance.

China's Modern Statehood is in the Creation

As a state on the road to modernization, China must defend its sovereign independence, and the idea of pluralism just can legitimize the sovereign independence. Strictly speaking, China started modernization in each facet in 1912 when the Republic of China (ROC) was built in Nanjing city. Perhaps the idea of modernity was emerged in China in the late of 19 century when a Westernization movement for China's richness and strength was taken place by top-down approach and on the one hand, a vacillating political democratization and de-feudalization was also happened before the building of ROC. However, the most influential enlightenment movement was the "May 4" which deeply impressed Chinese common people by the idea of democracy and the spirit of science or rationality.

Unfortunately, this enlightenment group was broken off by Japan's invasion of China in period of 1931-1945. Then, after three years' terrible civil war (1946-1949) between Kuo Min tang (KMT) and Chinese Communist Party (CCP), the People's

Republic of China (PRC) was built in 1949, and since this year, a new enlightenment movement started, based not on liberalism such as electoral democracy and capitalist economy but on Marxism. When leaders started the reform and openness policy in 1979, Chinese government never forsakes the political slogan—Four Modernizations (in fields of industry, agriculture, national defence and science & technology).

Up to now, China is still addressing to two tasks—nation-building and state-building. For a very long time, Chinese as a nation is not a traditional idea for Chinese people. In Chinese traditional culture, to be a Chinese was not a difficult thing if one got ready to accept Chinese culture and Chinese identity, although the person was a barbarian or had very different blood from that of most of other Chinese people. "Before the nineteenth century, when China was still an empire, nationalism did not exist. The Chinese political elite begin to embrace modern nationalist doctrines for China's defence and regeneration only after China's disastrous defeat by British troops in the 1840-1842 Opium War, which led not only to the eventual disintegration of the Chinese empire but also to the loss of national sovereignty to imperialist powers". There are many different ethnics in ancient China, yet after the building of ROC, all these ethnics were grouped into one nation—Chinese *(Zhonghua Minzu)*. Within about 100 years (1912-2009), Chinese as a integrated modern nation is still in problem. Some ethnics living in Northwest and Southwest China don't have the strong Chinese identity. The policy towards almost all minority ethnics is actually undermining the Chinese identity and consolidating those minority ethnics' identity, though this policy is somehow necessary for some reasons. Simultaneously, China's political reform is still not foreseeable in recent years, which means democratic transition is not finished although to some degree it has begun with two typical processes—so-called "inner party's democratization" and "grassroots democratization". In economic field, a capitalist market's construction was started in 1980s and accelerated in 1990s after Deng Xiaoping visited South China in Spring of 1992, and most importantly, China as one big economy has entered the World Trade Organization (WTO) in 2001. However, an integrated national economic market is still a myth rather than a reality by virtue of the imbalance of regional development and the unclear role of government in economic field.

Meanwhile, citizenship authorized by the Constitution always cannot be safeguarded for the immatureness of rule of law. Social justice in some cases cannot be defended and restored well when some citizens are bullied by some others. Citizenship is abased by the societal stratification especially in 21 century when political corruption and the combination of officials and capitalists become more and more serious social problems. Additionally, because of Taiwan's separation from Mainland, Chinese territory is not unified and some people of Tibetan and Uygur at the same time request for their independence. Clearly, a territory-divided country is hard to be recognized as a nation- or modern state. The state-building is also still in the making.

Westphalia System and result of the Cold War in East Asia

In East Asia, after the collapse of China-centric tributary system in the late of 19 century, the international relations were suffered from the unrest situation. After the end of the World War II, the Cold War followed. After the Cold War was finished, potential regional conflicts were still there. It can be said so far as to now, Westphalia system is the dominant international system in East and Northeast Asia where each country doesn't have the power and legitimacy to dominate other countries and keep regional stability by hegemonic approaches. All of them have to protect national interests and prevent sovereign independence by self-helps, except for Japan and South Korea which can resort to allies with US to defend their security. China's potential conflicts with its neighbouring countries such as Indonesia, the Philippines, Vietnam, Japan and North Korea are only under the surface and seem very difficult to be solved. Although the Taiwan Cross Strait relations look alleviated after Ma Ying-jeou came to power in Taiwan, no one can makes sure that this good relations between two sides can be kept perpetually. National security of China is not better than we imagine and China's defence power has to be enhanced partly for these potential conflicts.

Additionally, the aftermath of the Cold War isn't disappeared in East and Northeast Asia because of the US military presence in Japan and South Korea and the existence of so-called North Korea's nuclear issue. It were surprised that US-led military and supporting allies with Japan and South Korea don't collapse but ironically are strengthened after the end of the Cold War in 1990s. It's well known these allies were resulted from the Cold War and their roles were to prevent Japan and

South Korea from being attacked and invaded by their imaginary enemies—China, Soviet Union and North Korea. After the end of the Cold War, NATO in Europe gradually changed its roles from preventing Europe from Soviet's invasion to functionalist responsibility for European security. But both the aim and role of these two allies in East and Northeast Asia are not changed at all. By virtue of the presence of Westphalia-like system and influential aftermath of the Cold War in East and Northeast Asia, to defend national security is a key task for China's government. Self-help is available and not obsolete for China even in the age of economic interdependence and globalization. Under this condition, it's very significant for China to adhere sovereign independence and non-intervention.

China is to Some Degree an Exceptional State

This conception is rooted in typical Chinese history and complicated reality. Historically, CCP in its early time had considered China as a very typical country whose revolution for democracy ought not to be similar to that of Russia. For CCP, Chinese revolution could be successful as long as it was relied upon a road of "cities should be enclosed by countryside and power should be seized by weapons", which is thoroughly different from Lenin's road in Russia. After People's Republic as a socialist country was built, Chinese government smartly used nationalism as one of dominant ideologies to start social mobilization and as one useful ideological weapon to fight against Soviet Union's Chauvinism in 1960s-1970s and against western liberalism in 1980s-1990s.

As regards of practice of Chinese foreign policy, especially after 1979, China's government initiated the reform and openness policy aiming at building socialism with Chinese characteristic, a very particular socialism differed from any others in the world. From the mid-1990s, China started to build market economy in the name of socialism, although for many scholars, the market economy should only depend on capitalism. Moreover, in accordance with long human being's stories, the rising of any power in the world always was accompanied with regional or global conflicts, yet Chinese government argued that China will select a way of peaceful rising or peaceful development, fighting against hegemonim.

When Washington Consensus was scolded when Asian monetary crisis was broken out in 1998, Joshua Cooper Ramo published his famous reporter on Chinese typical experience which was concluded by him to be one term—Beijing Consensus. Although this idea was debated hotly in academic cycle but Chinese government kept silent. Exactly to say, Beijing Consensus was not accepted by Chinese government since this term or idea indicates China could be a model for other developing countries on the road to modernization. For Chinese government, China is an exceptional country whose road of rising cannot be copied by others. In general, the particular continuity of Chinese civilization in last five thousand years, the success of typical road to revolution for neo-democracy in 1920s-1950s, and the recent rising relied on an exceptional approach that only Chinese uses in the world encourage the Chinese and its government to consider China as an particular country.

FUTURE SCENARIOS FOR CHINA AND INDIA AND THEIR IMPLICATIONS

In the country studies for China and India, analysis was undertaken using the Global Trade Analysis Project (GTAP) model and projections of future growth were made to the year 2020. Through this exercise the implications of rapid growth for production and consumption of agricultural products and trading opportunities for other countries in the region and the world have been assessed, based on certain assumptions.

Prospects for Growth and Domestic Implications

The analysis conducted in the China case study projects average annual growth in GDP of 8 percent in 2006 to 2010 gradually slowing to 6-7 percent in the following decade. Several factors favour this strong growth performance, including macroeconomic stability, high domestic savings, increased spending on research and development, continued high levels of FDI, improved market environment and trade liberalization, and the commitment to greater equity — granting higher purchasing power to lower income groups. Also noted are obstacles that will tend to reduce growth particularly in the long run — a decline in the domestic savings rate, an ageing population and pressures on the natural resource base for sustained agricultural production.

While China's growth rate is projected to decline somewhat in the near future, the India study suggests that GDP growth could be rising from the current levels of 6-7 percent to 7-8 percent. It should be noted that these growth projections apply to two economies of considerably different size. Nevertheless, how does one explain the divergence? Part of the explanation is related to the incremental capital output ratio (ICOR). In India it is currently about 4 and expected to decline. In China while the ICOR was 4 in the early 1980s it has steadily risen since then and in 2002 was 5.4. In short, despite reforms in state-owned industries in China, India uses capital more efficiently. Also favouring India is the demographic dividend, with the percentage of the population in the 15 to 59 age group increasing from 59 percent in 2001 to over 63 percent in 2011 which could add 1 percent to GDP growth. In China, by contrast, the ageing population and sharp decline in population growth due to the one child policy will eventually slow overall economic growth.

The picture for agriculture is somewhat mixed. The land area used in crop production is gradually shrinking due to urbanization and in some instances environmental degradation. Thus for staple crops, production growth depends on an increase in yields. China has already achieved high yields in staple crops, and further gains will depend on technological breakthroughs. Indian crop yields are low by comparison with China and other countries. This is attributed in part to the neglect of investments in research and extension beyond the early Green Revolution years. In both China and India the yields for the principal Green Revolution crops, rice and wheat, have plateaued, due in part to falling groundwater tables and environmental degradation. However, if priority can be given to investment in research and development and infrastructure, there appears to be ample scope, particularly in India, for increasing yields and agricultural productivity.

As a result of continued rapid economic growth and increase in income per capita, demand for high income elasticity products, like milk, livestock and horticultural products will continue to grow. China and India are committed to maintaining cereal grain self-sufficiency. The projections for both economies indicate that food security can be maintained at a national level without resorting to significant imports.

The baseline scenario presented in the China study, for example, indicates that in 2020 China will maintain or surpass self-sufficiency in rice, horticulture, pork and poultry, fish and processed foods, and come close to self-sufficiency in wheat, fibre and beef and mutton.

In the case of India, despite low current growth rates of output for many crops, the expectation is that self-sufficiency can be maintained in rice, wheat, coarse grains, sugar, cattle and meat, fish and other foods. The country should also come close to self-sufficiency in other crops (although the model predicts significant decline in both production and consumption of these crops) and milk. However, both countries will need to adopt policies that ensure food security at a regional and household level where hunger and poverty still persist.

China's agricultural production structure is expected to shift more towards labour-intensive products such as vegetables, fruit, fish and processed foods, while self-sufficiency in land-intensive products such as oilseed, fibres and coarse grains is predicted to fall further from current levels.

The largest increases in Indian agricultural production are predicted for oilseed, sugar, fibres, milk, fish, other agricultural products and other foods, while negative or low growth rates are expected in cattle and meat, rice, wheat, coarse grains and other crops. Nevertheless, for some of the high growth products India will continue to require significant imports, especially of oilseed, fibres and other agricultural products.

The dollar-a-day-poverty index had fallen to 16 percent in China in 2002 while it was 34 percent in India. Poverty is projected to continue to decline in India. With a GDP growth rate of 8 percent or more the poverty rate should fall from 26 percent in 1999-2000 to 14 percent in 2010 and then to 8 percent in 2015.

There appears to be an implicit assumption in these figures that the reduction in poverty will come largely from growth in employment in the non-farm sector. The analysis of the Chinese experience suggests that the impact of rapid economic growth on poverty reduction tends to slacken eventually if the rural sector does not grow hand in hand. As incomes have grown, the impact and effectiveness of general economic growth on poverty reduction have weakened.

Implications for Asia and the Greater Pacific Region

Trade liberalization, globalization, and pressures to meet WTO and FTA agreements are generating a substantial growth in trade. China will have the largest impact on Asia and the Pacific region because China's economy is two-and-a-half times larger than that of India, it is growing faster and it is more integrated with the rest of the world. For example, China received some US$60 billion of FDI last year while India received only US$5 billion. FDI and multinational investments are a means of importing technology and entrepreneurial and management skills. By 2020 China is projected to be the world's second largest importer and exporter.

At the level of the overall economy, both China and India will be major importers of energy and minerals principally from Australia, the Russian Federation and the Middle East.

China is projected to drop from 92 percent self-sufficiency in energy in 2001 to 67 percent in 2020. Recognizing this as a potential constraint to growth, China is taking steps to improve efficiency in the use of energy.

The high total factor productivity (TFP) growth projection in the China country report indicates that reliance on energy imports can be reduced by as much as 60 percent and minerals by 50 percent. Aided by FDI and information technologies, China and India along with other developing countries are finding it increasingly easy to transfer technology from developed countries to exercise their comparative advantage in manufacturing. However, both countries have historically made low use of external resources, relative to their economic size, and national initiatives will continue to play an important role in determining their growth paths.

As noted previously, both China and India are projected to be self-sufficient in cereal grains and do not provide a serious threat to global food security. India is projected to continue its current role as a major net exporter of rice. Both China and India will be major importers of oilseed, plant-based fibre and forestry products.

Soybean meal, for example, will come from destinations as distant as Brazil. In China there is already a trend in trade away from land-intensive crops such as food and feedgrains and sugar, and towards export of labour-intensive, high value commodities — horticultural crops, livestock, and aquaculture products. The predictions of the two country reports with regard to net exports and imports in 2020. The use of different scenarios in the China report indicates that China presents considerable opportunities for other agricultural exporters under the baseline and high GDP growth scenarios, but these opportunities are significantly reduced under the high TFP growth scenario. The Indian data, on the other hand, under-represent opportunities for catching up in productivity via technological change.

The China report examines changes in the patterns of agriculture and food trade that are likely to emerge by 2020. Interestingly, Chinese exports to India are predicted to increase by 1 179 percent over their 2001 level, while Indian exports to China are predicted to grow by only 79 percent. The Indian study did not undertake a comparable analysis, but the figures presented in the China report tend to reflect the relatively narrow range of India's net agricultural exports at present — mainly rice, followed by wheat and sugar.

5

Neighboring Countries and China's Increasing Influence

ADVANCING DIPLOMATIC INFLUENCE

China's ideological support of African despots lends them international legitimacy and influence in the United Nations and other international arenas that help to blunt pressure from the Western democracies on human rights, economic openness, and political freedoms. At the same time, when it serves Chinese interests, Beijing succours would-be junta leaders and illiberal rebels who want power and would roll back political reforms in immature democracies. These rebels seem to believe that if they want to overthrow a legitimate government, China will work to bolster their international legitimacy in the United Nations and other international fora.

As China's power and influence grows, Beijing is becoming more willing to challenge the United States, EU nations, and others in international arenas to protect its interests in Africa. Over time, differences between China and democracies over human rights and basic political and civil rights will sharpen. For example, in September 2004, the U.N. Security Council passed Resolution 1564, which condemned the mass killing of civilians in the Darfur region, but stopped short of imposing oil sanctions if Khartoum did not act to stop the killing. China abstained from the vote and threatened to veto any further move to impose sanctions.

In July 2005, Britain, backed by the United States and seven other countries, led a Security Council briefing on Zimbabwe's slum demolition campaign in an effort to organize a formal debate in the General Assembly and possibly generate a punitive Security Council resolution. Meanwhile, Zimbabwean President Robert Mugabe visited Beijing, seeking financial assistance for his failing economy. Because of Beijing's strong support for Mugabe and opposition to Security Council action, the U.N. was unable to reach a consensus.

Another significant Chinese objective in Africa is to isolate Taiwan diplomatically in an effort to pressure Taipei toward unification. Seven African countries-Burkina Faso, Chad, Gambia, Malawi, Sao Tome and Principe, Senegal, and Swaziland-currently maintain official diplomatic relations with Taiwan.

Curtailing Taiwan's diplomatic influence was not a high priority on China's Africa policy agenda until the early 1990s, when the competition between China and Taiwan to win diplomatic recognition from individual African countries escalated drastically. Now, through offers of massive economic assistance, Beijing has secured recognition from six additional African countries at Taiwan's expense.

Lesotho and Niger switched their diplomatic recognition to the PRC in 1994 and 1996, respectively. The Central African Republic, Guinea-Bissau, and South Africa switched their recognition from Taipei to Beijing in 1998, and Liberia switched recognition to Beijing in 2003 shortly before China dispatched PLA troops to assist with Liberian water-supply projects. In addition to ongoing efforts to sever Taiwan's few remaining connections in Africa, China has also sought repeatedly to maintain the support of its African partners for its "one China" policy via diplomatic attention, economic investment, and other assistance.

What the United States Should Do?

China's broad energy, trade, political, diplomatic, and even military interests in Africa threaten to undermine American and European efforts to promote peaceful, pluralistic, and prosperous societies in the region. To protect and advance American interests and influence in Africa, the United States should:

- Develop a coordinated, comprehensive strategy. Appropriate U.S. agencies should develop a comprehensive and coordinated strategy based on a review of the challenges and obstacles in each country and the available American resources. Consistent, constant, and coherent American engagement in Africa will help to counter the illiberal forces that stunt African development.
- Increase the U.S. diplomatic profile in Africa. The United States has demonstrated considerable commitment to promoting economic growth and development, representative government, health, and human rights in Africa. Since 1960, Washington has provided $51.2 billion (in 2003 dollars) in official bilateral development assistance to sub-Saharan Africa. The United States is the largest humanitarian aid donor ($3.3 billion in 2003) and also the largest source of bilateral and multilateral support to combat HIV /AIDS, malaria, and other infectious diseases.

Secretary of State Condoleezza Rice's reorganization and expansion of diplomatic posts, combined with extensive public diplomacy to publicize U.S. assistance efforts in Africa and shared interests between the two regions, will help to change the pervasive African perception that the United States cares little for the region. To further these efforts, President George W. Bush should go on an extended trip to Africa to strengthen relations with Africa.

- Encourage human rights, democratic principles, and good governance. Atrocious human rights violations in Sudan, Zimbabwe, and some West African nations remain a primary concern. The United States should make a more consistent effort to moderate the conduct of repressive African regimes and to help young African democracies lay the institutional foundations for a free, open, stable, and prosperous society in their individual countries and throughout the region.

To this end, the United States has made "good governance" a requirement to qualify for Millennium Challenge Account aid. Washington should go a step further by denying bilateral economic assistance to countries that consistently violate human rights or resist the transition to representative government and by promoting this policy in both international financial institutions and the United Nations.

- Increase trade and economic relations with Africa. Although U.S.-Africa trade accounts for only about 1 percent of total U.S. trade, it has grown rapidly since passage of the African Growth and Opportunity Act (AGOA) in 2000. AGOA significantly lowers, through 2015, trade barriers to goods exported from African countries, provided that they have established or are making progress toward market-based economies, enhancing the rule of law, representative governance, lowering barriers to U.S. trade and investment, improving human rights, and other goals.

While AGOA is a positive step, the United States should continue to press the region and individual countries for permanent free trade agreements that liberalize trade in goods and services, lower investment barriers, and strengthen property rights. Such agreements would encourage stronger economic growth and increase economic ties between the United States and trade partners in Africa. Charity and international aid will not solve Africa's problems, but economic reform and growth can.

- Encourage development of energy resources. Africa is an increasingly important oil supplier for the United States, providing 15 percent of total U.S. oil imports, which is forecast to increase to 25 percent within the next decade. Given America's desire to diversify its energy supplies, the United States should press countries in Africa to open their oil and gas sectors to foreign investment and remove regulatory and other barriers that constrain economic development of those resources.

- Increase security engagement. The American military is the world's premier fighting force, making many nations eager to gain access to U.S. military training and facilities. Security engagement, including the International Military Education and Training program (IMET), will increase the likelihood of advancing U.S. goals, such as civilian control of the military and counterterrorism and peacekeeping capabilities.
- Seek new international partners. International cooperation is a "force multiplier," and Washington should look beyond traditional partners in Europe to the democratic nations of Asia and Latin America to help advance these important issues.

PAKISTAN

One of the biggest OBOR projects is in Pakistan referred to as CPEC (China Pakistan Economic Corridor). China has promised to invest $60 billion into developing rail lines, roads, power plants & development of the strategically located Gwadar port. The official stated goal of this biggest ever foreign investment in Pakistan is to "rapidly modernize Pakistani infrastructure and strengthen its economy by the construction of modern transportation networks, numerous energy projects, and special economic zones". But as they say the devil is in the details. Recently "The Dawn" a newspaper in Pakistan reported that 91% of the income generated by the Gwadar port with go to China while the Gwadar Port Authority will get a measly 9%. With such a low return from the project it begs the question as to how the loan from this project will be repaid eventually. So called "debt trap" where countries are unable to pay back the loan to China either due to insufficient returns or onerous terms of the loan. Many in Pakistan have slowly realizing that the terms of these loans from their so called "iron brother" & "all weather friend" are not in the best interests of Pakistan. This was demonstrated late last year when Pakistan asked

China to exclude the $14 billion Diamer-Bhasha Dam from CPEC . They were reportedly unhappy with the strict conditions laid down for the project by China. Inspite of multiple Chinese denials, for India the worry is that Gwadar port will be eventually converted into a facility for docking Chinese naval ships which will give it strategic advantage overlooking not only the Strait of Hormuz but also open a new front against India from the west in the Arabian Sea.

Chinese is also looking to build gas/oil pipeline from Gwadar up north running through the length of Pakistan through Pakistan Occupied Kashmir (POK) & into the western Chinese province of Xinjiang. This is to have insurance against any closure of Malacca Straits by India or other adversaries where they could bring the gas/oil to Gwadar & transport it by pipeline thus passing the chokepoint Malacca Straits. However many believe that this option is beset with difficulties because of geographical, economic and security problems plus cost of this land based route vs maritime shipping . Due to the poor relations between India & Pakistan India doesn't have much leverage here.

SRI LANKA

Sri Lanka since its independence in 1948 has had close relations with India. The Tamil population (who were in minority) were feeling marginalized by the majority Sinhalese. Groups were formed to protest this & some of these groups eventually morphed into the LTTE militant group. India intervened in Sri Lanka in 1987 when it sent troops to SL as part of the Indian Peace Keeping Force (IPKF) which was withdrawn few years later after disastrous results. India mostly abandoned support for the LTTE once it came to light that they were responsible for the assassination of former PM Rajiv Gandhi who had sent the IPKF to Sri Lanka. The seminal event in modern Sri Lankan history came in 2005 when Mahinda Rajapaksa came to power. Over the next few years he led a hard fought campaign to finally suppress the LTTE for once & all. This bruising campaign where there were allegations of human rights violation meant that Rajapaksa became a pariah in the West who now refused to sell weapons to SL for the war effort. When Sri Lanka turned to India as always for help back then the UPA-I coalition government was in power in New Delhi. The ruling Congress party elite & the bureaucrats were not averse to helping Sri Lanka but were caught up in a bind due to domestic compulsions as openly supporting Rajapaksa meant angering it's its coalition partner DMK. The threat perception of DMK chief Karunanidhi possibly bringing down the UPA government meant New Delhi helped Sri Lanka with mostly intelligence gathering & sale of some non-offensive defense equipment mostly under the radar. This meant that for its offensive weapons needs Sri Lanka turned mostly to China. Thus began the Sri Lanka's phase of drawing closer to China. Once the war ended Rajapaksa wanted to move the country forward after decades of civil war by turning to infrastructure building towards achieving higher economic growth & prosperity. The goal was to improve the infrastructure in Sri Lanka via construction of new roads, airports, ports, container terminals, railways etc. Already at odds with the Western countries over the handling of the civil war, he found a willing partner in China who was more than eager to dole out vast sums of money to Sri Lanka. By some estimates it was found that Sri Lanka had tripled its national debt with these projects financed by China. Later on it was found that many of these deals had very high costs associated with it & there are allegations of wide scale corruption when these deals were awarded to various Chinese groups & banks.

One of these multiple infrastructure projects was in Hambantota, a small costal village in the south of Sri Lanka & also the hometown of Mahinda Rajapaksa. His dream was to construct a new modern city which also sits strategically in the south of the country along the sea lanes between West Asia & South East Asia. Chinese companies were given contracts to build a new deep sea port, airport, conference center, housing developments, and hotels and (since SL a cricket playing nation why not) an international cricket stadium. However once the projects were finished Sri Lankans soon realized that it was as a complete disaster with hardly any ships coming to the port & flights coming to the airport. This affected the revenue stream which meant that there wasn't money to cover the payment for the $1.4 billion loans. By 2015 Sri Lanka owed to China $8 billion for Hambantota & other projects. The foreign debt to China & other countries was equal to 94% of Sri Lanka's GDP while payments to all these loans were accounting for 95% for all revenues generated by the country.

Staring at this financial nightmare the new government (Rajapaksa lost power in 2015) last year did a debt for equity swap for Hanbantota port where Sri Lankan Ports Authority gave up 80% equity to China Merchants Port Holdings Company in a 99 year lease in exchange for $1.1billion dollars which will help facilitate the loan payments. Further 50sq km was to be given to Chinese companies to create LPG plant, factories, refinery to create a sort of an SEZ (Special Economic Zone). India which already had been alarmed by Chinese submarines showing up in Colombo port in the past few years was now up in arms.

The worry was that once China controlled Hambantota they would establish a naval base from where they would now a strong foothold to operate in the Indian Ocean Region exercising control over the vital sea lanes passing south of Sri Lanka. Sri Lanka has on multiple occasions has maintained that it will never allow Hanbantota port to be used by military vessels of foreign nations. Many in India still doubt that when "push comes to shove" & the Chinese dock naval vessels at Hambantota if the Sri Lankans will be able to prevent it from happening. The airport at Hambantota has been ridiculed in the press as being the "world's most emptiest airport" which has just couple of daily flights. To counter China the Indian government last year has proposed buying out the Chinese loans for the airport from Sri Lanka in exchange for a 40 year lease of the airport at cost of $300 million. This will give it capability to do aerial surveillance of the port area to keep an eye on the Chinese activities & discourage China from converting it to a naval base in future. India was basically forced because of its strategic interests to spend $300 million on the "world's emptiest airport". To counter Chinese influence Modi government in 2017 had proposed to develop Trincomalee port in the north of the country, railways lines & power plants (while the Japanese had sought to develop the Colombo port). Sri Lanka's new president Maithripala Sirisena when got elected in 2015 promised to relook at these shady infrastructure deals with the Chinese & cancel the ones where there was corruption or were not in best interests of the country. But the debt for equity sale in Hambantota shows that Sri Lanka is unable extricate from the mess of the Chinese debt. The new regime in Colombo has managed to stabilize the situation with the debt for equity swap & getting an IMF loan but it could again quickly go downhill in the future if either economic condition deteriorates & more loans go sour.

MALDIVES

Maldives is a small littoral state just south of Lakshadweep islands in the India Ocean. They sit just south of the crucial shipping lanes in the India Ocean. Traditionally it has been in the Indian sphere of influence till recently. In 1988 when a coup d'état attempted by hired mercenaries overthrew President Gayoom then Indian PM Rajiv Gandhi dispatched 1,600 troops to restore the status quo in Maldives. India received gratitude & praise from both Maldivians & Western powers alike for this quick & prompt military action.

In 2008 in the first ever democratically held elections Gayoom was defeated by Mohamed Nasheed. Nasheed was later forced to resign in controversial circumstance in 2012 which he claims was at gunpoint. In the subsequent elections in 2013 current president Abdulla Yameen defeated Nasheed. Yameen has slowly turned his rule into more of a dictatorship where he crushed dissent & jailed opponents. This reached its climax in Jan 2018 when Supreme Court removed terrorism charges against opposition figures & Yameen in turn declared emergency arresting two Supreme Court justices. He even went to the extent of arresting his own half-brother & former president Gayoom. Nasheed who was in exile abroad escaped incarceration. USA, India & several other countries have issued strong statements for the "respect of the rule of the law". Indian unlike 1988 can't just simply launch a military operation to restore order because the situation has changed partly due to presence of China. China has issued a veiled warning against foreign intervention in Maldives (implied threat against Indian military operation). For the past few years be it the cancelling of Male airport project ($500 million) & awarding it to the Chinese or singing of a free trade agreement in complete secrecy & rushing it through parliament in middle of night, Chinese influence has grown in Maldives. With the military option off the table India is hamstrung with a lack of good options. India & the western countries can impose hard hitting sanctions but Maldives depends on China & also Saudi Arabia for funds which means the sanctions would lack any real bite unless enforced simultaneously by Saudi Arabia & China.

Yameen is no friend of India & is not going to change his behavior anytime soon. Nasheed has claimed that China has already taken over 16 islands & has been quoted as saying "Without firing a single shot, China has grabbed more land than the East India Company at the height of the 19th century".

Last month it was reported that China was going to setup an oceanic station on a northern Maldives island close to India. This means that they can track movement of surface ships & submarines passing just south of Indian peninsula thus further eroding India's advantage in this region.

Modi has made it a point to visit all SAARC countries except Maldives (even Pakistan was visited on brief stopover on Nawaz Sharif's birthday in 2015 Dec) as snub to the regime being anti-India. India to punish Maldives has decided to switch its vote for a non-permanent member of the UN Security council from Maldives to Indonesia in a upcoming session of the Security Council. However it is yet to be seen if any of the sanctions, diplomatic pressure & change of the UN Security Council vote can bring any substantial change in Yamen's behavior. The only advantage India have is the geographical proximity to

Maldives which means India can land troops if necessary in Male within a couple of hours while Chinese ships while sailing from mainland China would take more than a week.

NEPAL & BHUTAN

Nepal suffered greatly during a civil insurgency by the Maoists from 1996 onwards. The civil war ended 10 years later when they signed a peace accord & joined mainstream politics. A couple of years later the monarchy which ruled Nepal for 240 years was abolished & Nepal became a republic. Modi did visit Nepal twice early in his term & promised $ 1 Billion worth of India investment much of which is yet to come to fruition. India also received praise for the speedy help during the 2015 earthquake which devastated the countryside. The main complaint which many in India's neighborhood have is that India makes tall promises but don't deliver. When Nepal was working on a new constitution in 2015, India tried to pressure Nepali elite living in the hills to accommodate the demands of the Madhesi population living in the plains & adjoining the border with India (who are considered close to India).

When the demands were not met the people in the southern plains blocked transportation of crucial supplies from India (including petrol) to landlocked Nepal as a form of protest. Many living in the northern hills believe that this protest had the tacit support of India government. Eventually the blockade was lifted without any major concessions which resulted in the people in the plains not getting most of their demands while driving up anti India sentiment among the hill folk. In the ensuing election communist leader K.P. Oli who is pro-China came to power replacing the former PM who was seen to be more pro India. Nepal like many countries in Asia is desperately looking for infrastructure building & has seen a huge spurt of Chinese investments which accelerated after Oli took power. Nepalese often complain that India tries to interfere in the inner working of Nepal, a leftover mentality they say from the days of the British Raj. Nepal sandwiched between two Asian giants does try to balance out influences from both neighbors but the blockade fiasco simply drove up the anti-India sentiment in Nepal causing India to lose influence in Kathmandu. Nepal in short has been a failure for the current government as it has drifted out of India's orbit for now.

Bhutan after the annexation of Tibet by China signed a Friendship Treaty which established very close relations with India. Bhutan is required to consult with India in matters of defense & security. Bhutan is only neighbor of China with which it has not established close relations. The Dolam plateau episode as I explained last year was to drive a wedge between India & Bhutan. China is desperate to get a foothold in Bhutan to move it away from Indian sphere of influence but Bhutan has uptill now under great duress avoided all Chinese overtures. After the Dolam episode Indian government quickly reworked the hydropower agreement at higher tariffs (which had been Bhutan's demand from some time) to keep it happy in face of renewed Chinese pressure on Bhutan. Foreign Secretary Vijay Gokhale, National Security Advisor Ajit Doval & Chief of Army Staff Bipin Rawat made quiet trips to Bhutan just this February to send a firm message that India stands with its ally Bhutan. Bhutan to this day remains India's best friend in the neighborhood a fact not lost on PM Modi who made Bhutan his first foreign visit after being sworn in 2014. PM Modi pushed for the BBIN (Bangladesh Bhutan India Nepal) MVA Motor Vehicles Agreement that will allow easy transit of personal & cargo motor vehicles with help of electronic tracking & online permitting sent to all land based ports. This will allow seamless transport of goods across all countries to improve l connectivity, cross border trade & regional integration. Even though Bhutan has opted out the hope is for rest 3 countries to start operation this coming April.

BANGLADESH & MYANMAR

Bangladesh & Myanmar are two of India's eastern neighbors connected to India's North East. Both of these countries have multiple OBOR infrastructure projects ongoing in their countries. Kyaukphyu a port being developed as part of OBOR in Myanmar is part of the concern for India as it could become another Hambantota or Gwadar giving China a foothold in the Bay of Bengal. India always has had connectivity issues with the North East (which now due to tensions with China especially at border has become of vital importance) due to terrain & geographic issues like the Siliguri corridor. It is of strategic interest that India open alternate routes to connect North East via ports in from Myanmar & Bangladesh. Bhutan whose main export is hydropower is always looking for new avenues to export more electricity. India could facilitate extending the transmission lines through the North East to both Bangladesh & Nepal thus creating a win-win situation where Bangladesh can fulfil her power supply needs while Bhutan can generate more export revenue plus not to mention goodwill for India. As part of the Act East policy by the Modi government India speeded up work on the 1360km (India Myanmar Thailand) Trilateral Highway to improve connectivity & boost trade between India & Myanmar &. The goal is to complete the highway by December 2019.

Currently to transport goods from West Bengal to Mizoram in North East one has go through the narrow & congested Siliguri corridor. The Kaladan Multi-Modal Transit Transport Project being undertaken by India is to connect Kolkata by sea route to Sittwe in Myanmar & then by land to Mizoram in the North East which will significantly reduce time & cost. However like many of India's infrastructure projects in the neighborhood this too has been beset by delays & is yet to be completed.

India has enjoyed good relations with Bangladesh with current PM Sheikh Hasina (daughter of the founder of the nation). The land boundary agreement signed in 2015 (which has been in limbo for decades) helped further improve relations. India late last year gave Bangladesh a $4.5 billion dollar credit at a very low 1% rate to be paid back in 20 years (with a 5 year grace period if needed) to develop infrastructure in 17 pre identified projects such as power , railways roads & ports & help move Bangladesh away from Chinese funding. There was a $500 million line of credit for military hardware purchases, to steer Bangladesh away from relying on China for defense purchases. India in an unprecedented move has joined hands with Russia to setup a civilian nuclear reactor facility in Bangladesh.

CHINA'S PRESENCE IN AFRICA: WHAT ARE THE RISKS FOR THE CONTINENT?

Africa's resource-driven growth may be hampered by drastic shift in factors affecting the Chinese economy. These factors include geopolitical issues, the slowdown of the Chinese economy and idiosyncratic risks.

Geopolitical factors: A recently released Chinese policy document highlighted the country's plan to strengthen the relationship with Africa: large in scale, broad in scope and deeper in levels. This expansionary policy has raised concerns among Africa's traditional western partners. For instance, recently the USA accused China of 'securing oil at the sources'. China's relationship with African regimes perceived as undemocratic has specially been the major source of this criticism. For instance, Chinese commitments in Sudan and Zimbabwe are among the most controversial. The Sino-African partnership should therefore be fully explained in order to assuage growing concerns by western scholars and officials.

Risk of a Chinese economic slowdown: Africa has benefited from the Chinese economic boom through increased trade and investment, mainly in natural resource sectors. Thus, Africa is particularly vulnerable to economic shocks hitting the Chinese economy. Recent estimates by the IMF indicate that China's GDP growth is projected to slow to 8.2% and 8.8% in 2012 and 2013, respectively from an average of more than 9% over the past three decades.

Since Chinese economic ties with Africa are largely resource based, a fall in China's demand for Africa's commodities could create tensions in the current account and fiscal positions of these countries. Lower growth in China could also result in contraction of credit lines from major Chinese banks to Africa.

In recent years, Chinese banks have funded large infrastructure projects. Currently, funding to Africa accounts for a third of China EXIM bank's total global assets. Some of the large Chinese financial deals include USD13 billion to Ghana and USD6 billion to Congo.

Idiosyncratic risks: A growing number of small-scale Chinese private firms are making business in Africa without the direct endorsement of the Chinese government. Growth in Chinese private investment in sectors outside traditional natural resources has however fuelled resentment among local investors and the people. For instance, Ethiopian and Zambian farmers have complained of Chinese acquisition of large tracts of land at their expense. At a recent World Bank organized conference, China was identified as the biggest land grabber in the world and in Africa. Chinese companies have also been accused of unfair competition without forging strong links with local firms. This has resulted in lack of transfer of skills and technology to the locals. These issues have perpetuated dissent towards Chinese investments in Africa.

Leveraging the benefits from China's engagement with Africa

Despite the obstacles and the associated potential risks of China's engagement with Africa, Sino-Africa partnerships can play an important role in fostering growth and development of African economies. Economic diversification based on high competitiveness through skills and technology transfer would be the main catalyst of China's contribution to Africa's transformation. Thus, the infrastructure renaissance brought about by Chinese investment provides expanded opportunities for accelerated economic diversification in Africa.

Thus, building bridges with African firms by promoting their presence in China could be an opportunity for Africans to extend their activities towards new markets. Political and economic governance are as important for Africa as they are for China in fostering inclusiveness. The synergies that may be created from collaboration in these areas could benefit both regions as the world is steadily moving toward a more inclusive approach of economic development.

African countries should also adopt policies aimed at diversifying the future financing of economic growth. A possible slowdown in the Chinese economy could unravel Africa's growth momentum by constricting financial viability of major projects due to potential tightening trade and investment credit from Chinese banks actively involved in Africa. In this regard, intra-Africa trade and investment financing from regional financial institutions including the African Development Bank may offer an option to stable long-term finance.

CHINA LOOKS TO BRITISH EXPERIENCE FOR AFRICAN EXPANSION

China has embarked on a series of joint projects with Britain in Africa, with the aim of avoiding the abuses and mistakes committed by former colonial powers as it rapidly increases its economic role on the continent.

China invested $4.5bn in infrastructure in Africa in 2007, more than the G8 countries combined, and much of the investment has been private. The number of Chinese companies operating in Africa has more than doubled in just two years to 2,000, with about 400 operating in Nigeria alone, according to new research.

In contrast to the "one-dimensional" stereotype of state-owned enterprises extracting natural resources, most of the investment is from privately-owned firms and many are involved in manufacturing.

However, many of the business practices followed by those companies, such as a preference for using Chinese workers, coupled with Beijing's belief that human rights are the preserve of host country governments, have led to claims that the rapid rise in Chinese influence in Africa has not helped its human rights.

"The Chinese firms that are moving are building infrastructure, they are building roads, they are providing jobs for people, but at the same time: what they are not doing, neither the Chinese government nor the companies, is raising any issues about how the population are being treated," Irene Khan, Amnesty International's secretary general, said today.

"Therefore we find that the Chinese presence is not helping the human rights situation. It might be aggravating it when revenues and resources are being paid into coffers of hugely corrupt and oppressive governments."

In an apparent reflection of Chinese anxiety over its reputation in Africa, both embassies and companies have been urged by Beijing to forge closer links to local communities.

China has also entered into a partnership with Britain's department for international development, (Dfid)intended to monitor and control the social and environmental impact of Chinese investment.

In the Democratic Republic of Congo, for example, Dfid is working with the government and Chinese companies to fund the drafting of social and environmental standards that road building projects will have to adhere to, and to carry out assessments of the impact of the new roads.

Until now, most attention has focused on the multibillion-pound infrastructure-for-resources deals which China has signed with African governments.

The problem facing such government-to-government programmes is that the projects are no longer being carried out by central planners, but by a plethora of Chinese firms.

Evidence from more than 100 interviews with businesspeople and officials in both China and Africa indicates that more than 80% of the companies operating on the continent are privately owned. In 2006, the Chinese EXIM Bank estimated that there were only about 800 Chinese companies in Africa.

"These entrepreneurs have an agenda of their own, which they have been left free to pursue by the Chinese government. It is the usual one of the pursuit of profit and the exploitation of business and market opportunity," said dr Jing Gu, a research fellow at Sussex University's Institute of Development Studies, which carried out the research.

She said Chinese businesses were well placed to tap into what some called "the last golden land" because of similarities to the Chinese market of the 1980s and 90s, and because there was so much competition domestically.

"The Chinese private entrepreneur... is willing to take a long view and endure tough contemporary conditions and relatively low returns to be able to entrench himself locally," she argued.

Plummeting exports to Europe and America – with trade hit by both the appreciating renminbi and the global economic crisis – have increased the keenness to move into new markets. One Chinese newspaper described Africa as "the best refuge for sunstroke prevention from the financial crisis".

While Beijing has encouraged businesses to move into overseas markets, officials monitor activity so loosely that many of the firms Gu studied have not even registered their investments.

According to official figures, only 4% of China's foreign direct investment went to Africa in 2006, compared to 26% to Latin America and 64% to Asia. But Gu said the pace of growth has been rapid.

While some firms employ significant amounts of local labour in Africa, Gu said resentment was building up in some places.

"Specific problems do arise because of the tendency of Chinese to behave quite ethno-centrically. They prefer to employ their own people; not so much Chinese nationals, as people from the same regions or even extended families as themselves, whom they know and are used to.

"Also, the Chinese work ethic is to work very hard, long hours for little money, hoping eventually to establish themselves in an area, to be able to replace others. Some of them even import some labour illegally to get around local immigration restrictions. This does produce some social tension and even violence between Chinese and Africans in such countries as Nigeria, Ghana and Madagascar," she said.

"But there is also recognition of the actual and potential benefits of China's involvement."

CHINA IN AFRICA: A DIFFERENT KIND OF MILITARY THEATER

China has been trying to show the world just how militarily capable it is by expanding operations. This time, it's focused on Africa. With much fanfare, Chinese military personnel set sail July 11 from the port at Zhanjiang for Djibouti, where they will help set up China's first permanent overseas military base. China says the base will provide support for peacekeeping, anti-piracy and humanitarian operations. But media and military analysts have claimed that the Djibouti base is part of China's so-called "string of pearls" strategy, which is meant to develop a network of military and commercial assets and relationships along the India Ocean to project power abroad. The base, however, is not an example of China's military prowess but rather an attempt to boost China's image at home and abroad.

China chose Djibouti as the location for its base because Beijing has an interest in ensuring the flow of trade from the Persian Gulf to China. Eighty percent of China's seaborne oil imports pass through this route through the India Ocean, so it's a vital part of keeping the country running.

And the need to ensure access to this route is the motivation behind the "string of pearls" strategy. China figures it can secure access to the Indian Ocean and through various chokepoints by building military and commercial facilities throughout the South China Sea, the Bay of Bengal and, to a lesser degree, the Arabian Sea. Facilities have already been developed in Bangladesh, Myanmar, Pakistan and Sri Lanka.

But these efforts are more a case of grandstanding than effective protection of Chinese interests. With a relatively weak navy, at least compared to the U.S. Navy, China lacks the ability to secure this route militarily. So instead, it is trying to portray an image of strength to distract from its actual weakness.

Few details about the facility have been made public, and what little is known suggests that the base has no military significance. Reports indicate that navy warships have been sent to the base, but there is no available information on the number of personnel to be stationed there, the length of their deployment or a timetable for operability. Some estimates suggest that 2,000 soldiers – likely marines and special operations forces – will eventually be stationed at the base.

By the end of the year, the facility will hold weapons and ammunition and will include wharves for stationing Chinese navy ships. It will cost the Chinese $20 million annually to rent the base, which covers 36 hectares near a commercial port owned by Chinese companies.

There are plans to build an airfield, although they exist only on paper. There is one helicopter pad that should be completed by the end of the year. Notably, military expert Zhou Chenming told the South China Morning Post that the facility "is not a military base in the full sense" but that its capacity could be expanded later to repair ships and accommodate planes. From this, we suspect that the base has no aircraft and cannot service vessels. This doesn't say much about the facility's capabilities, and since so little is known about the nuts and bolts of the base, it would be difficult for anyone to reasonably conclude that it can help China project power abroad.

But more important is the fact that China's navy lacks blue-water capabilities – the ability to operate in the deep waters of the world's oceans. The navy has ambitious plans to develop these capabilities, but doing so takes a long time – at least one or two generations, assuming no major disruptions or pauses in the process. The navy does not currently have any operational aircraft carrier battle groups. Its sole operational aircraft carrier, the Liaoning, is a refurbished ship that initially launched in 1988. The Liaoning can carry about half the number of planes a U.S. aircraft carrier can. Its first live-fire exercises were held in December 2016, and its accompanying fighter pilots are only now graduating from initial training. The crew has little experience and requires years more training before the ship can be operationally effective. The Chinese navy, moreover, has yet to overcome basic logistical problems, including refueling. Most of the country's naval vessels are not nuclear powered and must therefore stop at ports to refuel, limiting their capabilities and reach.

China can't project power globally. It has to be selective in setting its priorities, and Africa isn't at the top of this list. China's real concerns are much closer to home. Any imports coming through the Indian Ocean destined for China must pass through the Strait of Malacca, a major chokepoint bordered by Malaysia, Indonesia and Thailand. Passage through the strait is secured by the U.S. Navy, but the Chinese don't want to rely on the U.S. for access to such an important route. Chokepoints are also an issue in the South China Sea, where China and several other East Asian states are competing for territory. What capabilities and resources Beijing does have will be focused on this region rather than the Horn of Africa.

AFGHANISTAN & CENTRAL ASIA

India after independence due to loss of territory in Pakistan Occupied Kashmir found itself cutoff from Afghanistan & Central Asia. Post 1962 after the war with China any possibility of a trade route through Tibet & western China also evaporated. As in the great game Central Asia was a region where the influence of the erstwhile Soviet Union & now Russia looms large. China's economic prowess has allowed it to make forays on the economic front in Central Asia. Russia while facing a threat from US including crippling sanction requires co-operation from China both politically & also in the economic sphere where it needs to sell oil & gas to China to generate much needed revenue to keep its economy afloat. Russia for time being has not raised any objections to the Chinese investment in this region (which it considers its own "backyard"). Afghanistan since the withdrawal of Soviets has been an unstable failed state. Pakistani military wanting to exert influence in Afghanistan propped up the Taliban in the 1990's to maintain their hold over the country. The US invasion post 9/11 brought end to Taliban rule but through covert support to the Taliban through Haqqauni network, Pakistan has continued to meddle in the internal affairs of Afghanistan. Afghanistan has always enjoyed warm relations with India (except during the Taliban rule). The schizophrenic Pak military establishment cannot digest good relations between India & Afghanistan & try to scuttle this affability between its eastern & western neighbors. In Dec 2015 the new Afghan parliament building was built with Indian aid. Indian projects in Afghanistan have proved tricky as they invariable attract the attention of Taliban – Pakistani military nexus which tries to disrupt or scuttle them with threats & terrorist attacks. When India wanted to trade with Afghanistan through the land route post 2001 they were denied by Pakistan. India then smartly decided to go around Pakistan by using Chabahar port in Iran. India in 2016 offered to develop the Chabahar port in Iran from which they planned to construct a road to the border with Afghanistan. The port was inaugurated late last year & the first batch of wheat was shipped from India to Afghanistan via Chabahar bypassing the need to go through Pakistan. The success of this route (in bypassing Pakistan) can be partially gauged by the volume of hysteria it generated in Pakistani media lamenting "the waning of Pakistani influence" when the route opened up last year. A future goal is to have Chabahar port connect up with the INSTC (International North South Transit Corridor). Goal of this corridor is to connect India with the markets in Central Asia, Europe & Russia via shorter route compared to the standard sea route vs the Suez Canal. Once completed it would cut short the transit time by this land route (Suez Canal) by upto 20 days vastly reducing costs

PM Modi understanding the importance of Central Asia became the first PM to visit these countries in a very long time. He visited all 5 Central Asian Soviet republics of Uzbekistan, Kazakhstan, Turkmenistan, Kyrgyzstan & Tajikistan in a single trip. Goal of the trip was to improve the paltry $1.2 billion trade with the region, improve connectivity via INSTC (International North South Transit Corridor) TAPI (Turkmenistan Afghanistan Pakistan India) gas pipeline. He was able to get commitments of 5,000 & 2,000 tonnes of uranium respectively from Kazakhstan & Uzbekistan to cater to India's growing civilian nuclear energy needs. India a few months ago was invited to join the Ashgabat Agreement, which was instituted in April 2011 to establish an international multimodal transport and transit corridor between Central Asia and the Persian Gulf. Its objective is to enhance connectivity within the Eurasian region and synchronize it with other regional transport corridors, including the International North–South Transport Corridor (INSTC).

ASEAN/SOUTH EAST ASIA

Post economic liberalization in the early 90's former PM PV Narasimha Rao launched the "Look East" policy to increase economic & security cooperation to deepen ties with countries in South East Asia. When the current government came to power in 2014 they launched a revised "Act East" Policy. One of the plans is to extend the Trilateral Highway beyond Thailand upto Cambodia, Laos & Vietnam thus connecting India to all the land based nations of ASEAN. India has also offered $1 Billion in loans for infrastructure projects in the ASEAN region. India during the Republic Day usually hosts one foreign head of state (with some exceptions). This year saw India in a huge diplomatic coup inviting all the 10 heads of state of ASEAN during the Republic Day parade as chief guests. This was in backdrop of the India ASEAN summit in New Delhi where a whole host of issues on regional connectivity, trade & security were discussed.

The vast majority of nations in the Asian have territorial disputes with China in the South China Sea. South China Sea has several small islands which are in between two or more countries in the region. They have never been demarcated by the neighboring countries due to the disputing claims. Most of these have been uninhabited uptill few years ago when China began to aggressively to move on to these islands & building permanent infrastructure to colonize these islands. This militarization of these islands by China is part of a plan to then eventually convert the South China Sea into a Chinese controlled water body where they can deny both sea & air access to any friend or foe. They have claimed all the territory within an arbitrary "9 Dash Line" which is based on bogus historical claims. The Unite Nations Convention on Law of the Sea (UNCLOS) says that a country can claim an exclusive economic zone upto 200 miles from its shores. China has willfully ignored any such convention while trying to take over this territory in a brazen land grab. It has actually claimed territory which is much closer to its neighbors than itself which also defines a logical equidistant boundary principle. Phillipines took its case to the tribunal at Court of Arbitration at Hague which ruled in its favor saying China has no legal basis to claim the infamous "9 Dash Line" in the South China Sea. China called the ruling "null & void" without "binding force" & continued to stand by its claim. Malaysia, Brunei, Philippines & Vietnam due to their economic & military asymmetry haven't stood up to China's bullying. It has been left to United States to sail ships every so often through the South China Sea calling it a Freedom of Navigation Operations (FONOPS). Even though this region is far away from Indian shores but due to India's trade with the Far East including Japan depends on freedom of navigation through the South China Sea it is a significant issue for India.

Singapore has the closest defense relationship with India in the region. India already had Army & Air Force Bilateral agreements in place & signed in 2017 the naval pact which would now allow India warships to dock in Singapore which is crucial as it sits in the strategically important Malacca Straits.

Vietnam fought a war with China in 1979 & is one of the countries with one of the most anti-China sentiment in this region. Crucially India has enjoyed good relations with Vietnam. Vietnam is viewed by many in China as a counterweight against China similar to what China uses Pakistan against India.

Vietnam has openly encouraged India to jointly explore & invest the oilfields in South China Sea (in dispute with China). India had given a $500 million line of credit to purchase military equipment in 2016. With Vietnam also having a large no. of Russian weapons in its arsenal India has provided a good source of weapon procurement & training. Just a few days ago when the Vietnamese President visited India a deal was signed for civil nuclear energy cooperation & for India to develop a port in Vietnam. There were some talks a couple of years ago about selling the supersonic cruise missile Brahmos to Vietnam. Some analysts have proposed that India shed inhibitions about Chinese blowback on this matter as China regularly sells weapons to Pakistan without taking into account Indian sensitivities. Selling Brahmos missiles to Vietnam will send a strong message that if China is going to actively engage with India's neighbors in the IOR, India is not averse to doing the same in China's own backyard.

JAPAN, AUSTRALIA & THE "QUAD"

Japan is another of China's neighbor that it has had territorial disputes with. The dispute is over the Senkaku islands in the East China Sea. Japan fought & conquered parts of China in World War 2 & the relations are still strained due to the Japanese invasion & atrocities during the Japanese rule then. The mutual distrust & hatred for each other is present on both sides of the China Sea. The rise of China in the recent times has caused much consternation in Tokyo. Post World War 2 Japanese constitution included an amendment (Article 9) that prohibits Japan from keeping offensive armed forces for war (to prevent a repeat of the legacy of World War 2 when Japan invaded multiple countries in Asia) i.e. Japanese armed forces are strictly for "self-defense". The Chinese threat has led PM Shinzo Abe to propose changing the constitution to get rid of this Article 9 a thought unthinkable even just a few years ago. This has drawn protests from the Chinese who suffered during the Japanese occupation in World War 2. Modi after the travel visa ban by the US & Europe became a pariah in the

West. Modi looked east while he was CM of state of Gujarat for investments & found a willing partner in Shinzo Abe one of Modi's earliest overseas friends. The warm camaraderie shared by both is reflected in the very close Indo Japanese relationship today. Japan has decided to loan India $17 billion at an extremely low 0.1% interest rate which is to be paid back in 50 years for construction of a bullet train between Mumbai & Ahmedabad.

Many nations around the world suffered during one or more the major financial shocks of last 30 years: Asia financial crisis, Dot-com bubble, post 9/11 recession & global financial crisis of 2008. Australia has been a major global outlier which has survived all of these events (no recession since 1991). It enjoyed the increase in exports of commodities to China to power its growth without experiencing a recession. Today China is Australia's biggest export destination $93 billion (4.5x next closest one US at $20 billion). Since Australia is island all of its exports are via sea & the issue of FONOPS (Freedom of Navigation) is of paramount importance to it. Around a decade ago when The QUAD a strategic dialogue between India, US, Japan & Australia was proposed but Australia eventually bowed out as it wanted to stay neutral between US & China. Overt last few years there have been quite a few exposes about the Chinese infiltration of the political institutions of Australia. . Australian PM Malcom Turnbull was forced to bring in new laws on espionage & intelligence due to this belated realization of massive Chinese penetration in Australia. On a separate front Chinese foreign students in Australia have become more vocal in protests pressuring professors to drop or alter teaching material on subjects like Tibet, Taiwan, border dispute with India, etc. that they deem as offensive to China. Frederic Grare, a fellow at the Carnegie's South Asia Program in his book India Turns East rightly says that Australia will soon have choose between its economic partner China & it's security partner US (with which it shares a military alliance). Ten years later woken up by the Chinese threat Australia signaled its willingness to join the QUAD as counter balancing force to the

Chinese threat. The main theme of the QUAD is to have "free and open Indo-Pacific," (referring to Indian & Pacific Oceanic region encompassing the disputed South China Sea) Goals for the QUAD include a rules-based order in Asia, freedom of navigation and overflight in the maritime commons, respect for international law & enhancing connectivity & maritime security. The common perceived threat from China has brought together 4 democratic "like minded countries" from three different continents together to uphold rules based order. US the 4^{th}member in the QUAD has warily seen the rise of China from across the Pacific Ocean. During the Obama administration there was the famous "Pivot to Asia" but they avoided calling it a bid to contain the Chinese as to not raise Chinese hackles. Trump administration has made the right noises about standing up to China & FONOPS but they can't press China too hard as they need their cooperation on North Korean nuclear issue. Quad is movement by various countries who know that it is not possible for them to deal with the Chinese threat by themselves joining hands to keep China in check.

OTHER EMERGING POWERS: BRAZIL AND SOUTH AFRICA

Although China and India are the only countries likely to become global powers in the next decades, several other rising states are poised to exert markedly increased regional and multilateral influence. Russia, a member of the BRIC group of countries, is sometimes considered in that light. It is also, like China, both a nuclear power and one of the "permanent five" with veto power on the United Nations Security Council. Russia, however, is not yet a member of the World Trade Organization, which China joined in 2001. Moreover, Russia is a special case: it is less an emerging power than a re-emerging one – a successor state to a former superpower (the Soviet Union) attempting to regain a leading role in international affairs despite its reduced circumstances.

The two other non-Asian emerging powers that bear closest attention are both the leading diplomatic actors on the other continents of the developing world. Brazil, the most populous country in the Americas after the United States, has clearly become the dominant country in South America and a leading voice for developing-country interests internationally. In Africa, that leadership role seems to have been taken up by South Africa over a decade after emerging from the dark period of apartheid. While not the continent's most populous country (that distinction belongs to Nigeria), South Africa has its largest and most dynamic economy. South Africa has also achieved an enviable degree of democratic stability and it has become increasingly engaged in multilateral diplomacy both regionally and globally. Brazil and South Africa are the most likely candidates from their respective continents for membership in an enlarged UN Security Council. Both Brazil and South Africa have, along with India and China, become key members of the majority developing-country bloc within the WTO that has challenged traditional G7 leadership in the conduct of multilateral trade negotiations. Brazil and South Africa have joined the inner circle of countries (which does not include Canada) with real influence on whether the current WTO Doha development round can succeed.

Brazil and South Africa have also been in the forefront of promoting "South South cooperation." A significant development in that regard was the creation in 2003 of the Trilateral Commission of India-Brazil-South Africa (IBSA) Dialogue Forum with the explicit mission to develop a common agenda of multilateral action as leading democracies from three continents and to foster South-South partnerships. The Forum meets annually and set out a plan of action for trilateral cooperation at its inaugural meeting in New Delhi in March 2004. How Brazil performs could set the pace for Latin America as a whole. The National Intelligence Council projection foresees that:

Brazil's success or failure in balancing pro-growth economic measures with an ambitious social agenda that reduces poverty and income inequality will have a profound impact on region-wide economic performance and governance during the next 15 years. Luring foreign direct investment and advancing regional stability and equitable integration – including trade and economic infrastructure – probably will remain axioms of Brazilian foreign policy. Brazil is a natural partner both for the United States and Europe and for rising powers China and India and has the potential to enhance its leverage as a net exporter of oil.

At the same time, the Goldman Sachs study on the BRICs noted that, although Brazil had posted an average annual real GDP growth rate above 5% over the past 50 years, growth had faltered as a result of financial and currency woes in the 1990s. Compared to China and other large Asian economies, Brazil remains less open to trade, its levels of investment and savings are lower, and its public and external debt are much higher. Hence Brazil's advance into the front rank of world economies will be slower and less certain.

In the case of South Africa, there are additional public health and demographic risk factors in addition to the factors of poverty and crime.

Principally these are related to the HIV/AIDS epidemic, its impact on the labour force and the strains on public services. According to Goldman Sachs projections, South Africa could become a high-growth economy, though their long-range (50 years) forecast predicts a more moderate GDP growth rate per annum of about 3.5%. South Africa will still have an economy much smaller than any of the BRICs in a few decades' time. However, as a result of declining population growth rates, it could have a higher per capita income level.

As well, on the diplomatic front, South Africa is reaching beyond its leading role in southern African regional forums and the African Union. Its role in the WTO has already been noted. But it has also been actively pursuing regional and bilateral free-trade and investment partnerships with the European Union, the European Free Trade Association, the United States, and the MERCOSUR bloc (Brazil, Argentina, Uruguay, and Paraguay), as well as growing links with China and India.

Implications for Canada

Canada will be unlikely to exert much influence in South America or in Africa without strong ties with Brazil and South Africa. Canada must also take into account these countries' increasing role in multilateral forums, notably the WTO and the UN.

Brazil has traditionally been Canada's largest trading partner outside of NAFTA in the Americas. There has also been a long-standing, if rather narrowly based, investment relationship. Progress has been made in recent years, with Canadian FDI in Brazil reaching about $7 billion in 2003, and Brazilian investments in Canada exceeding that amount. This is considerably greater than Canada's investment relationship with China and India combined. At the same time, Canadian exports to Brazil are well down from their peak level of 1997, and two way trade flows account for only about 0.4% of Canada's global total (just 0.2% of exports and 0.7% of imports in 2004).

Moreover, bilateral relations remain in question overall. A November 2004 visit to Brazil by the Canadian prime minister and trade minister, which gave a push to the negotiation of a limited free-trade arrangement with MERCOSUR, was a positive sign coming after a series of frictions. These include a 2001 Canadian ban on Brazilian beef imports over BSE fears and the ongoing dispute over export subsidies for regional jets built by Bombardier and its Brazilian competitor Embraer.

More broadly, Canada and Brazil have not been in sync over the now stalled negotiations over a Free Trade Area of the Americas (FTAA), and that appears to have also bogged down the bilateral negotiation with MERCOSUR.

One analyst argues that, while Brazil is interested in a deal with Canada, it is intent on pursuing its own hemispheric strategy, not one driven by North American interests. Furthermore: "Canada does not control the agenda [of the FTAA] – the US and Brazil do. Canada will have an increasingly difficult time influencing the agenda, and creative thinking will be needed if there is to be a renewal of productive Canadian-

Brazilian relations." In regard to South Africa, Canada has provided considerable bilateral assistance in support of the country's post-apartheid democratic transition (some $150 million in the decade after the new constitution of 1994).

South Africa is also Canada's largest trading partner in sub Saharan Africa. That total is still very small, however, accounting for only about 0.1% of Canada's global two-way trade (0.1% of exports and less than 0.2% of imports in 2004). Investment is also small and has been concentrated in the mining and resource sectors.

Diplomatically, Canada has sought to engage South Africa through the Commonwealth and through pan-African initiatives such as the New Partnership for Africa's Development (NEPAD) that was a centrepiece of the agenda for the G8 summit hosted by Canada in Kananaskis, Alberta, in June 2002. Bilateral relations have been mostly positive. However, Canada does not as yet appear to figure significantly in South Africa's ambitious approach to forging strategic free-trade and investment links outside of Africa.

CONCLUSION

Forecasts of global power shifts and long-term economic projections must be treated with caution, given the number of variables in play. They can, however, point to key trends that need to be taken seriously by prudent policymakers. Better preparation for probable international scenarios may also result in more effective responses to such anticipated events.

In the next several decades, it seems virtually certain that at least two Asian "emerging-market" countries, China and India, will move into the front rank of the world's economies and will increasingly exercise influence as global powers.

A change of such magnitude in the global power balance is likely to challenge the positions of even the most powerful Western countries. At the very least, the current G7 countries will have to adjust their policies to accommodate the interests of these rising powers.

Outside of Asia, several other countries – notably Brazil and South Africa – are also likely to exert growing leadership within their regions, within the developing world as a whole, and within important multilateral forums including the United Nations and the World Trade Organization. In addition, these countries are forging links among themselves and with Asian powers. They are building networks and alliances that promote common agendas of "South-South" cooperation.

As a smaller player in a world of contending giants, Canada is likely to experience a continuing decline in its relative power on the world stage. As a trade-dependent nation, Canada will also remain highly exposed to international economic trends. And in an environment of intensified multi-polar competition, Canada may not be able to rely as much as it has on proximity to the United States, which will be preoccupied dealing with its own power shift challenges. Canada's choice of competitive options within and beyond North America, whether that includes deeper economic integration, or more diversified relationships with other regions, perhaps a combination of both, will be greatly affected by the changes that China, India and other leading emerging-market countries bring to the international system.

If Canada is to avoid being marginalized, it will have to be innovative both at home and abroad, equipping Canadians for this new era of globalized competition with an increasingly "Asian face," and developing stronger Canadian ties to the emerging powers of the international system. It is certainly not too soon to be devising strategies to meet that challenge.

6

Diplomacy Toward "Pivot Countries"

To carry out OBOR effectively, China needs to find some "pivot countries," by which I refer to those states having strong strategic ties with China and able to develop the model of OBOR. They are mainly from the SSGP category, secondarily SSCCs. Neighborhood diplomacy should propel this process. Pakistan, China's only all-weather partner and with a population of 200 million, is one of the best candidates for a pivot country. Even so, projects for cooperation must go through feasible evaluations. China should slow down a bit on investment in Pakistan, as many failed programs will no doubt harm both bilateral relations and OBOR. Thailand, Malaysia, New Zealand, and Papua New Guinea are other candidates for pivot countries; possibly Uzbekistan as well. It is Bangladesh, rather than Sri Lanka and Myanmar, that will grow to become a pivot country. Based on intensive bilateral military cooperation, solid political relations (perhaps only next to Sino-Pakistani relations in South Asia) and economic complementarity, China and Bangladesh may expect a rapid and huge increase of bilateral cooperation.

According to my analytical framework, Indonesia and Kazakhstan will not become pivot countries, though both are enthusiastic toward OBOR. Their internal dynamics have created ceilings for bilateral political and economic cooperation. However, it's possible they could provide pivotal fields for cooperation.

DIPLOMACY TOWARD RUSSIA

Russia, the most important country in China's neighborhood diplomacy, deserve special attention. Russia plays an irreplaceable role for China when it comes to national security, international strategic collaboration, bilateral military cooperation, bilateral energy cooperation, and the construction of China's envisioned economic corridor and land bridge. Thus, some Chinese scholars advocate rebuilding the Sino-Russia alliance. I disagree — Russia always fails to maintain stable relations with the United States and Europe; it keeps strategic prevention toward China in many ways; and its civilian technology, economic structure, and GDP are all far behind China's.

If China and Russia form an alliance, China's loss will obviously surpass China's gains. Russia will dominate bilateral military cooperation while becoming China's burden, economically and technically. The United States, together with its allies, will shift its China policy from engagement with prevention to total prevention. That will be a disaster for China's foreign trade, inward/outward investment, technology imports, international education exchanges, etc. Under those conditions, many Silk Road countries would hesitate to join international institutions led by China.

Russia always views itself as a part of the Western world and keeps its main economic and cultural links with the West. Putin has also expressed many times that it is impossible to form any formal military alliance with China.

Sino-Russian relations should benefit both OBOR and China's peaceful rise. Generally speaking, Sino-U.S. relations will prevail over Sino-Russia relations, though Russia is crucial for China's neighborhood diplomacy.

CHINA'S NEW POLICY OF 'PERIPHERAL DIPLOMACY'

A very important meeting which approved China's new policy for relations with its neighbours seems to have attracted little attention and comment, possibly because it was overshadowed by the anticipation surrounding the Chinese Communist Party (CCP) Central Committee (CC)'s Third Plenum which was held a couple of weeks later in November 2013. All seven members of the CCP CC Politburo Standing Committee (PBSC) attended the entire two days (October 24-25, 2013) of this meeting, along with representatives of the various departments of the Central Committee, State Councillors, the Central Leading Small Group for Foreign Affairs and China's Ambassadors to important countries. Convened for the first time in the history of the People's Republic of China (PRC), the meeting approved far-reaching major changes in China's diplomatic strategy and significantly, also for the first time ever, categorized China's neighbours as 'friends' and 'enemies'. It decided to forge regional, sub-regional and bilateral 'cooperative' security relationships and gave a definite role to the CCP.

Prior to this 2-day meeting in October in Beijing, the Politburo convened at least twice over the space of the past year to deliberate the issue. China's new strategic policy towards its neighbours, labelled by Chinese analysts as 'Peripheral Diplomacy' (*zhoubian*), heralds a significant shift in the manner in which Beijing will henceforth conduct relations with its neighbours. Elements of the policy focusing on South Asia were being put in place by Chinese leaders, including Xi Jinping and former PBSC member Zhou Yongkang, over the past three years.

It is now clear that Beijing's categorization of nations as 'friends' and 'enemies' will guide its conduct of bilateral relations. Key features of the new policy aimed at securing global leadership for China will include emphasis on the "China Dream", promotion of bilateral security relationships, and the forging of regional, sub-regional, or 'cooperative' security ties. The new policy strives to strike a balance between the defence of national sovereignty and the maintenance of regional stability. It simultaneously stresses that efforts will be made for better political and economic relations with neighbouring countries, closer security cooperation and people-to-people contact.

Official reporting of Xi Jinping's speech at the 2-day conference was predictably guarded. Still, they noted his emphasis that 'most of the neighbouring countries have a friendly and mutually beneficial relationship with China' and, importantly, that the strategic goal of China's diplomacy with neighbouring countries is to serve the cause of 'national rejuvenation'. This was clarified to mean consolidation of friendly relations with neighbours and making the best use of current strategic opportunities. Emphasising that 'peripheral diplomacy' is intended to make neighbouring countries 'feel safe', he said China's interests must be better integrated with theirs. Regional economic cooperation, establishment of a 'Silk Road economic belt', 'a maritime silk road for the 21st century' and an economic corridor through India, Myanmar, and Bangladesh (BCIM) were listed as among the key objectives. Other features include accelerating the opening up of border areas, deepening reciprocal cooperation between China's border areas and neighbouring countries, and promoting regional and sub-regional security cooperation.

Xi Jinping specifically highlighted a role for the CCP in safeguarding peace and stability in the region. This points to the CCP, and particularly the CCP CC's International Department and United Front Work Department (UFWD), playing a more pro-active role in bilateral relationships including establishing and enhancing party-to-party ties. An example is the UFWD's growing profile in Nepal and direct involvement in Buddha's birth-place of Lumbini. The main objective, Xi Jinping stressed, is to ensure favourable external conditions for China's reform, which includes development and stability, safeguarding national sovereignty, security and development, maintaining world peace and stability and promoting common development. He said 'common ground and converging interests' should be emphasized to achieve these objectives.

Salient elements of the new strategy of 'Peripheral Diplomacy' have filtered out through commentaries and clarifications offered by senior CCP cadres. China's strategic analysts and academics are unanimous that relations with the

US are crucial to China. Reputed Tsinghua University Professor Yan Xuetong, who is Dean of the Institute of Modern International Relations and Chief Editor of 'The Chinese Journal of International Politics', recently underscored this while explaining the 'new type of big power relations' proposed by China's President Xi Jinping to Obama while on a 'working' visit to the US. Yan Xuetong's proximity to Xi Jinping adds considerable importance to his observations and analyses. Yan Xuetong said that far from denoting an alliance, this new type of relations is intended to prevent Sino-US relations deteriorating from one of "competition" to "confrontation". He specifically acknowledged the "complete lack of trust", but suggested this is "not a prerequisite to a relatively peaceful accommodation". He candidly stated that "China and the U.S. have not trusted each other since 1989 and are not likely to in the future. But interests will form the cornerstone of this relationship....although China and the U.S. are strategic competitors". He said the most desired relationship would be termed "cooperative", like that between China and Russia. The other two categories of relations are "competitive" as with the US and "confrontational" as in the case of Sino-Japan relations.

China's Ambassador to the US, Cui Tiankai, conveyed the same idea more diplomatically in context of the new policy of 'Peripheral Diplomacy' to a US audience on February 20, 2014. He underlined the need to shift the orientation of Sino-US relations from one of "crisis management to opportunity management" adding that using coercive language is not constructive.

He also cautioned against "unilateral interpretations of some international legal instruments, and attempts to impose these interpretations on others". Cui Tiankai acknowledged that "the United States is a powerful and very strong country...the most powerful and strongest country in the world, and will remain so for many years to come" and that China's effort to build the 'new model of relationship', is based on full recognition of this fact. Chinese on Jan 28, 2014, Yan Xuetong said the conference on 'Peripheral Diplomacy' signalled China's strategic shift in its foreign policy outlook. He said that unlike the US or West, China will use alternative strategies "to achieve global leadership" and attributed this to the compulsions of nuclear weapons and globalization.

Of the two core principles that have guided Chinese foreign policy since the early 1990s, Deng Xiaoping's famous dictum of 'lie low bide your time' (*taoguang yanghui*) has been discarded while the other, of according first priority to relations with the US, has been modified. The new dictum allows that although China and the U.S. are "strategic competitors", they "have common interests, complementary interests and conflicting interests". This provides both countries room for active cooperation when interests converge and a degree of preventive cooperation where interests conflict.

A major change is that while for the past two decades China opted for a neutral stance avoiding confrontation at all costs and never opposing the US, the new policy advocates engaging with neighbouring countries so as to "align their interests with China's rise". Xi Jinping's stress on "friendship and loyalty between China and its neighbours", he said, "is more significant than it sounds".

Yan Xuetong clarified that henceforth China's foreign policy will reflect the different treatment for China's "friends" and "enemies". China will find ways to ensure that greater benefits and gains flow from China's development to those willing to play a constructive role in China's rise. In this manner it hopes to give its neighbours an incentive in China's development. With some select 'key' neighbours China will even try to create "communities of shared common destinies". In addition to economic interests the latter will "include a wider range of strategic elements" and a strong political dimension. This could extend to building security relationships, including providing security guarantees as in the case of China's agreement with Ukraine in December 2013.

Referring to the three specific strategic areas of focus identified by China's leadership, namely, the "new silk road" with Central Asia, a maritime silk road with South East Asia, and the economic corridor through India, Myanmar, and Bangladesh, Yan Xuetong said these regions can expect considerably increased willingness by China to underwrite substantive economic, security, and other benefits in exchange for political support for China's regional objectives.

At the same time, Yan Xuetong emphasized that China's new policy of 'peripheral diplomacy' means that those who are hostile to China, or oppose it, will be confronted with sustained periods of tough sanctions and isolation. He assessed that China's new foreign policy outlook in the region will provide an expanded set of strategic options and ample chances to avoid using "military conquests" to achieve regional dominance.

China's official news agency 'Xinhua' on February 7, 2014 separately clarified the kind of political support for regional objectives that China seeks as part of "peripheral diplomacy". Describing Russia as a "good example of China's regional diplomacy, the core of which is to treat neighbours as friends and partners and help them to develop", it regretted that "some countries in the region chose to ignore history and international law inciting territorial disputes with China and disturbing peace and development of the Asia-Pacific region". Referring to Japanese Prime Minister Shinzo Abe's visit to the Yasukuni Shrine, the Xinhua despatch accused Japan of continuously "irritating its neighbours and even US allies by attempting to downplay its fascist history and revise a pacifist constitution to make overseas deployment of soldiers possible." It said Russia and China should both, therefore, commemorate the 70th anniversary of victories in the World Anti-Fascist War and Anti-Japanese War in 2015.

Some features of the new strategy have been clarified by Chen Xulong, Director of the Department for International and Strategic Studies at the China Institute of International Studies (CIIS), a think-tank directly subordinate to China's Ministry of Foreign Affairs (MFA). Observing that China's leadership is aware that many of China's neighbours have reservations about the country's rise and that in some cases it has even generated friction, he said handling and readjusting relationships with international institutions and neighbouring countries is one of China's biggest challenges. China's leaders, he said, are conscious that the US pivot had "disturbed" China's strategy in Asia and that Japan and the Philippines had "misinterpreted" its message thereby creating a number of immediate and potential challenges in China's periphery. China can no longer keep a low profile but has to take the initiative and create a favourable periphery. He said the strategy on 'peripheral diplomacy' "strikes a balance between the defence of national sovereignty and the maintenance of regional stability". Efforts will be made for better political and economic relations with neighbouring countries, for closer security cooperation and people-to-people contact.

Qin (closeness), *cheng* (earnestness), *hui* (benefit) and *rong* (inclusiveness) were identified as the four basic principles of 'peripheral diplomacy'. Chen Xulong said with them China will be able to realize "virtuous interaction" with the United States, India and other major countries.

He clarified that 'closeness' refers to developing close relations through frequent visits; 'earnestness' means to show enough sincerity in solving neighbourhood problems; 'benefit' refers to the principle of mutual benefit, on which cooperation with neighbouring countries will be strengthened to weave a network of common prosperity thus bringing them benefits from China's development; and 'inclusiveness' means that the Asia and Pacific regions are big enough to include all parties for common development.

Problematic in China's efforts to implement the strategy of 'peripheral diplomacy' will, however, be its insistence on achieving its sovereignty and territorial claims and desire to project power.

Reiterating the explicit assertions made on two separate occasions in 2011 by the official 'Xinhua' news agency, the CCP's 'People's Daily' (*Renmin Ribao*) on Nov 4, 2013 declared that 'China pursues an open strategy of a win-win situation through beneficial cooperation, but will absolutely not trade the nation's core interests away, and definitely will not brook other countries' wilful hurting of China's legitimate rights and interests'. Severe complicating factors that could be introduced by the beginning of the next decade will be the survival and livelihood issues of acute water and food scarcities.

A change is discernible in Beijing's posture from the time in 2010, when during Hu Jintao's visit to the US it opted to drop its description of the South China Sea as an 'issue of core national interest', to the present when it has clarified that it will not back off from its maritime territorial claims. Beijing's unrelenting insistence on its maritime territorial claims in the South China Sea and East Sea, together with its assertive posture, underscores its ambition for dominance over the entire region.

This ambition is evident in China's occupation of the Mischief Reef and Scarborough Shoal and latest bid to gain control over the Second Thomas Shoal, all claimed by the Philippines; repeated encounters with Vietnamese and Philippines vessels; renewed claims over St James' Shoal claimed by Malaysia and the Ieodo Rock of South Korea; unilateral declaration by Beijing that non-Chinese citizens and vessels must obtain prior permission to enter or fish in a maritime territorial zone that covers virtually half the South China Sea and which directive is being enforced by China's maritime agencies and Hainan Island authorities who, according to the Hainan Party Secretary, push back fishing vessels each week; refusal to clarify the U-shaped line on maps on which basis Beijing claims sovereignty over territories in these waters; and Djakarta on March 12, 2014, designating as a 'dispute' the doubts raised by the U-shaped line on Chinese maps over Indonesia's Exclusive Economic Zone.

Beijing's handling of its disputes with rival claimants has varied, but the end objective of securing control over the territories preferably without conflict, is unchanged. Chinese officials have, for example, warned the Philippines to be prepared for a tough four years for taking the contested claim over the Scarborough Reef to international arbitration while its patrol vessels continue to muscle Philippines Navy ships out of waters claimed by China. With Vietnam, the communist parties of both countries have been active in trying to keep ties friendly. The situation is more complex with Japan, which has been singled out as a major potential threat. In the dispute over the Senkakus, called Diaoyu in Chinese, China is trying to isolate Japan and has adopted a tough military stance with its aircraft, ships and submarines going up to the Senkaku Islands and beyond Okinawa. It has ceased all official contacts, but at the same time allowed tourism and economic ties to remain unimpeded.

The current tensions in the Asia-Pacific and their effect on Sino-US relations were present in the remarks Cui Tiankai made on US soil on February 20, 2014 when, referring to the interests of both countries in the Asia Pacific, he clarified that Beijing is not about to resile from its maritime territorial claims. He said the "United States' presence, interests, and influential role in the Asia Pacific is fully and widely recognized" and that China welcomes a "constructive role by the United States in the region". Equally important was his observation that "China is also a Pacific country, and China is also an Asian country. Geographically, China is just situated in the centre of the Asian continent. And we have been here for centuries, perhaps a little bit longer than the whole history of the United States. So I think it may be fair to say that neither Chinese nor Americans are aliens from Mars in the Asia Pacific, but we are somehow more indigenous than you are". Warning that "any attempt to manage or manipulate the regional affairs at the expense of China's legitimate interests in the region, cannot be justified, and would indeed be detrimental to the stability and prosperity of the entire region, and eventually will serve nobody's interests", he implied that the new model of big power relations was intended to address such issues.

Shanghai-based Chinese venture capitalist and commentator, Eric X Li, more bluntly echoed similar thinking at a conference in Seoul around the same time. He argued that there had been no missteps by China in the territorial disputes in the South China Sea and East China Sea and that history will "probably prove" that China had dealt with these situations with unmatched agility. China's strategic objective in the region, he said, is to change the status quo — the establishment of which it did not have enough power to participate in or influence — to its advantage while avoiding military conflict. He described China's most important achievement in the past thirty years as its mastering of the international economic system, established by the US, without being absorbed by it. He concluded by saying that China has, and always will, act in its own best national interests. He emphasized that consistent with the cultural roots of the Middle Kingdom, China's "world view is to keep out barbarians and not invade them".

Soon after the policy of 'Peripheral Diplomacy' was approved, the China Institute of Contemporary International Relations (CICIR), subordinate to China's Ministry of State Security (MoSS), convened a round-table the same month. Entitled "Current situation in China's surrounding areas and its Strategy", its proceedings were published in CICIR's *Xiandai Guoji Guanxi (Contemporary International Relations)*. The summary of this round-table prepared by the European Council on Foreign Relations observed that its focus was on China's relations with the US, India, Mongolia and Central Asia. It said while participants differed in their views, they were unanimous about the role of the US.

Lin Hongyu of Peking University made the interesting disclosure that the Boeing XB-37, the new US space orbiter, overflew Beijing at the beginning of the crisis over the Air Defence Identification Zone (ADIZ) set up by China in the East China Sea in November 2013. Discussants at the CICIR meeting allanticipated there would be an escalation of global competition among the major powers: China, Russia, India, and the US. Almost all speakers took serious note of the TPP, even though they thought its goals very ambitious, and with the discovery of new energy resources such as shale oil and gas and Japan's invention of a process that can tap methane from underwater ice blocks, viewed it as signalling a "third Industrial Revolution". The Regional Comprehensive Economic Partnership (RCEP) was viewed as China's counter-strategy and some suggested that China and RCEP should join with the TPP. Lin Limin, Editor-in-Chief of the CICIR journal '*Xiandai Guoji Guanxi*' (Contemporary International Relations) acknowledged these differences and warned that China's "aspirations" should not exceed its "capabilities", because this has in the past spelt disaster for powers such as Russia, Germany, and Japan.

Discussions on India at the CICIR round-table were interesting with general agreement that there has been a "gradual maturing process" (*zou xiang chengshu de guocheng*) in China-India relations since 1988 as evidenced by the lack of open conflict over the border dispute. Li Li, Associate Professor at CICIR who has studied at a university in India, took a generally benign view of the relationship though she blamed lack of trust and mutual understanding for the failure to arrive at any agreement.

She said this had been exacerbated by the 'malicious' assertions made by Western researchers and part of the Indian media who were creating a "confrontational point of view" (*duikang shijiao*) and presenting relations between China and India as antagonistic. To deal with this, political leaders of the two countries have increased the number of high-level meetings and set up a formal exchange mechanism.

Indo-US relations figured prominently in discussions, with a consensus that these would harm China's security and national interests and had already generated challenges in the maritime arena. It was apprehended that India will obtain technologically advanced long-range weapons from the US to extend its reach deep into China and acquire leverage over China in negotiations. On land, India-US security cooperation was said to be already causing friction on China's western borders. The need for China to take precautions was stressed.

India-China relations are a key component of China's new strategy of 'Peripheral Diplomacy', which has obvious implications for India and Japan. The new policy signals that Beijing will intensify efforts for economic engagement with India, including making investments, and accompany this with high-level visits. The visit proposed by Chinese President Xi Jinping for October-November 2014 is a good example as he is likely to be accompanied by more than 150 Chinese Chief Executives (CEOs). Beijing will try to focus on the development of economic ties while setting aside resolution of the contentious border dispute till what it deems a more opportune time. Repeated assertions that China will not barter away its "core national interests" substantiate this.

During the premeditated intrusions in the Depsang Plains in Ladakh too, China's media and officials in India and Beijing were insistent that the PLA personnel were well inside Chinese territory. The influential '*Zhongguo Qingnian Bao*' (China Youth Daily) on May 14, 2013 accused India of triggering tensions by adopting a "forward policy" and stressed that "Ladakh was unified with China's Yuan Dynasty as part of Tibet in the 13th century" and was "under the jurisdiction of the central government of China's Qing Dynasty until 1830s". Stating that it was important for access to Central Asia, it added that "although it is under Kashmir, Ladakh shares similarities with Tibet in terms of culture, religion, customs, and language, and it has long been dubbed "Little Tibet." The objective will be to maintain India-China relations at a 'competitive' level while trying to prevent emergence of uncomfortable warmth in Indo-US relations.

India will have to contend with the policy's likely fall-out on its neighbours. Beijing's initiatives in Myanmar and Nepal reflect its new approach. Qiu Guoheng, China's former Ambassador to Nepal and presently Director General of External Security in China's Ministry of Foreign Affairs (MFA) visited Kathmandu in early December 2013. While there he conveyed that as part of 'peripheral diplomacy', Beijing had decided to revise upward the quantum of foreign assistance to developing countries in its neighbourhood and that Nepal and Pakistan will particularly be beneficiaries. He said development of the 'new Silk Road economic belt' would benefit Nepal. Talks are separately underway for extending the 1200-kilometers Qinghai-Lhasa-Shigatse railway to Kathmandu, agreed to by Chinese

Premier Wen Jiabao during his unannounced visit to Nepal in 2012 and which, once completed, will alter the geostrategic balance in the region. The CCP CC's International Department and UFWD have both stepped up activities in Nepal, where suppressing pro-Dalai Lama Tibetan activists is not China's sole interest.

China initiated steps to safeguard its interests in Myanmar in early 2013. It replaced its Ambassador in Yangon and, quite unusually, appointed 74-year old Wang Yingfan, a retired diplomat related to former PBSC member Qiao Shi, as Special Envoy for Asian Affairs. Beijing also, for the first time since the Mao era, interfered in the internal affairs of a country – albeit at its request – and brokered at least three rounds of meetings between the rebel groups in north Myanmar and Myanmar's army.

Reliable reports from Beijing state that Xi Jinping has taken personal charge of the 'Silk Road economic belt' project. This project envisages an outward westward push from Yunnan towards Bhutan, Nepal, Pakistan and Central Asian countries up to and possibly beyond Turkey. India's north east is part of this as well as the Bangladesh-China-India-Myanmar (BCIM) corridor. The economies of India's north eastern states are very fragile and connectivity is extremely poor. Acquiescing to both these proposals, which will certainly be accompanied by enormous pressure, by India would be premature. It would mean allowing the free influx of Chinese goods and nationals with the attendant danger of the latter settling down in these areas.

'Peripheral Diplomacy' envisages sub-regional, regional and "cooperative" security relationships. China already has an all-encompassing military relationship with Pakistan. The People's Liberation Army (PLA) has been steadily upgrading ties with the Nepal Army and Beijing recently secured a maritime cooperation agreement with Sri Lanka.

A serious precedent is that set by the security agreement signed between China and Ukraine on December 4, 2013. It states that "China promises...to provide security guarantees to

Ukraine if Ukraine is attacked by nuclear weapons or threatened by such aggression". China and Bangladesh signed a civil nuclear cooperation agreement, which has remained inactivated. Enticed by economic largesse these countries could in future be drawn into a sub-regional, regional or "cooperative" security relationship with China. The end objective of China's 'peripheral diplomacy' is to use alternative strategies "to achieve global leadership".

CHINA'S UNPLEASANT IN SOUTHEAST ASIA

Most mornings, activity in Phnom Penh all but stops when the morning heat begins to rise. But on that day, the city resembled a festive papal visit to a devoutly Catholic nation. Nearly a hundred thousand Cambodian children lined the streets, many in threadbare school uniforms and waving tiny Cambodian and Chinese flags or small photographs of Jiang's face. The children cheered and screamed for Jiang as his open car toured through the city, chanting as if he were David Beckham or Bono, rather than an elderly politician with thick glasses and an oily, swept-back hairdo. Jiang's route did not take him past one of the city's most important attractions. Only a few blocks from his motorcade, foreign tourists wandered through Tuol Sleng, an old high school that Cambodia's Maoist Khmer Rouge regime had converted into a killing factory in the 1970s. Tens of thousands of Cambodians were brought to Tuol Sleng between 1975 and 1979. Fewer than 10 made it out alive.

During the Khmer Rouge's murderous four-year reign, during which they killed as many as 2 million Cambodians, China served as the regime's most important foreign patron. Beijing sent the Khmer Rouge over 15,000 military advisers and provided the bulk of its external aid. Beijing knew what was going on in Cambodia. Before Jiang's visit, Chinese leaders had actively worked to forestall a special international tribunal for the Khmer Rouge officials still alive.

But standing alongside Jiang that day, Cambodian Prime Minister Hun Sen did not mention the Khmer Rouge era or the tribunal. Instead, he praised Jiang's "historic" visit to Phnom

Penh and called China's relatives with Cambodia "a precious gift." A beaming Jiang replied that he was "overwhelmed by friendship and joy" and promised that the relationship would become much closer.

Jiang was right. Within five years, China had become probably the most important foreign influence in Cambodia, and Hun Sen shuttled to and from Beijing constantly. Beijing became Cambodia's most important provider of foreign aid, giving Cambodia one of the largest Chinese aid packages of any nation in the world while also forgiving Cambodia's entire debt to China. Chinese language programs quickly dominated downtown Phnom Penh: one Chinese-language school alone drew over 10,000 students. As a result, although older Cambodians who remember the Khmer Rouge remain suspicious of China, their sons and daughters, who once would have headed to Australia, France, or the United States for higher education, now look to universities in Shanghai and Beijing. Chinese newspapers, films, television, and radio have become increasingly popular. Thousands of Chinese businesspeople have moved into Phnom Penh and northern Cambodia, creating entire villages of recent migrants. Chinese tourists descend en masse on the capital. Today, even when the prime minister has concerns about China's influence, he keeps quiet.

Cambodia is hardly unique. Since the late 1990s, perceptions of China in Southeast Asia have shifted significantly, so much so that elites and publics in a most importantity of the 10 members of the Association of Southeast Asian Nations (ASEAN) now see China as a constructive actor—and, potentially the preeminent regional power.

China's image transformation has resulted from a range of factors. China has benefited from missteps by the United States and Japan, ranging from the response to the 1997 Asian financial crisis to Washington's post–9-11 focus on counterterrorism in Southeast Asia. But the transformation also stems from a rise in China's "soft power" in Southeast Asia—that is, China's ability to influence Southeast Asian countries by persuasion, rather than coercion. This growing attractiveness is conveyed through various means, including culture, diplomacy, participation in multinational organizations, businesses' actions abroad, and the gravitational pull of China's economic strength.

When Joseph Nye coined the term soft power, he originally used a more limited definition that excluded investment and aid and formal diplomacy—more traditional, harder forms of influence. But in the context of Asia today, both China and its neighbors enunciate a broader idea of soft power, implying all elements outside of the security realm, including investment and aid. Soft power stems from both governments and nongovernment actors—from businesspeople and pop stars and language teachers. Nongovernment actors do not necessarily operate in concert with the state, and no state can be said to have a completely coherent foreign policy. Still, it is possible to identify broad strategies Beijing has enunciated and policy tools it has used that allow nongovernment actors to more effectively wield soft power. Just as us policies between World War II and the end of the cold war made Washington popular in the region and smoothed the way for American soft power, it is these frameworks that today make it easier for Chinese soft-power actors, from language schools to businesspeople, to have a growing impact on the ground.

The Unpleasant Begins

Nineteen ninety-seven provides a convenient date to mark China's soft-power emergence in Southeast Asia. Whether or not Beijing explicitly recognized that the United States and Japan were fumbling their responses to the Asian financial meltdown that began with the Thai baht's collapse and soon spread across the region, China's own reaction proved savvy. Beijing refused to devalue its currency, which would have exacerbated devaluations in Thailand and Indonesia, and portrayed its decision as standing up for other Asian nations. After the crisis, ASEAN Secretary General Rodolfo Severino announced, "China is really emerging from this smelling good."

Since then, Beijing has begun to employ several strategies to boost its soft power in Southeast Asia. In statements and speeches, Chinese leaders enunciate a doctrine of "win-win" relations, highlighting that Southeast Asians can benefit from their relationship with China even as China benefits from its relationship with them.

China will not interfere or meddle: foreign nations benefit because China will not make demands on other nations' sovereignty, economic models, governance, or political culture. "We don't believe that human rights should stand above sovereignty," the head of Beijing's premier state think tank says. China implicitly contrasts its "win-win" philosophy with that of the United States, a non-Asian actor that Beijing portrays as disrespectful of sovereignty, imposing a web of sanctions on Southeast Asia and demanding economic and political concessions.

The Chinese have backstopped this "win-win" rhetoric with real initiatives. Over the past five years, China has ended nearly all of its old border disputes and has signed Southeast Asia's Treaty of Amity and Cooperation, a document that commits the signers to mutual respect for a country's sovereignty and equality. Beijing has committed to creating a code of conduct on the South China Sea. It has enthusiastically signed bilateral cooperative agreements with several Asian states. Beijing seems willing to sign these agreements en masse, leaving details to be hammered out later. (In the lawyerly—and democratic—US political system, this type of sign first, talk later diplomacy would be virtually impossible.)

Beijing also has reversed its previous disdain for multilateral organizations, which older Chinese leaders had seen as constraints on China's power. It has not hurt that, as the United States became less interested in multilateralism between the late 1990s and today, China's participation in multilateral groups has made it look better by comparison. Again, Beijing has backed up its changing strategy with real initiatives. As a dialogue partner with ASEAN, China works closely with the organization, trying to strengthen it and, according to Asian diplomats, initiating far more joint projects than other partners, such as Japan or the United States.

China's strategy also includes focusing on developing nations whose bilateral relationships with the United States or Japan are faltering. After President Gloria Macapagal-Arroyo pulled Filipino troops out of Iraq in 2004 as part of a deal to win the freedom of a Philippine hostage, the United States cut assistance to Manila. Shortly after, China invited Macapagal-Arroyo for a state visit, and then aggressively wooed Philippine policy makers, offering greater cooperation and aid.

Another most important component of China's appeal to developing nations involves Beijing's portrayal of China as a potential ideal, as a model. China emphasizes top-down control of development and poverty reduction and the sidelining of political improvement for economic improvement. China's model particularly appeals to rulers in authoritarian or semi-authoritarian nations. With the Chinese model, the regime has time to think of ways to co-opt businesspeople and other elites that it needs to keep on its side to remain in power.

Flaking Old Insecurities

Until the past decade, China exerted minimal soft power in Southeast Asia. Following Chinese leader Deng Xiaoping's advice, an insecure Beijing still pursued a defensive foreign policy and focused on rebuilding China's domestic economy from the ravages of the Cultural Revolution. The Chinese public still lacked confidence that Beijing could become a global actor, let alone a regional power. A poll taken by the research organization Horizon Group in 1995 asked Chinese citizens their views of the "most prominent countries in the world": one-third ranked the United States most prominent, with only 13 percent choosing China. The Chinese imperial court's treatment of mainland Southeast Asia as vassal states, and the modern history of Maoist China supporting communists in Thailand, Malaysia, and, most disastrously, Cambodia, left a residue of mistrust in the region. China's limited engagement with Southeast Asia foundered on Beijing's continuing claims to the South China Sea, China's suspicion of ASEAN's multilateral forums, and concern among ASEAN nations that China's continuing economic growth would siphon foreign investment from Southeast Asia. Meanwhile, China's policy tools remained weak. It was not a most important aid donor, its diplomatic corps remained dominated by older envoys, and its public diplomacy was blunt.

In the late 1990s all this began to change. China's breakneck economic growth fostered greater confidence within the Chinese public. By the end of the 1990s, many Chinese urbanites were too young to remember the Cultural Revolution. They no longer shared an inherent distrust of the state's wielding of power and ideology. In 2003, the Horizon Group again polled Chinese citizens. This time, nearly 40 percent picked China as "the most prominent country in the world." America came in a distant second. China's leadership was also becoming more confident. Until the mid-1990s, the generation that had grown up around Mao still dominated China's inner circle. But this generation passed away in the 1980s, or was forcibly retired to make way for younger officials. After the crackdown at Tiananmen Square, the leadership recognized that China could not rely on the United States, but had to develop better relations with its neighbors and become a greater international player.

China recognized, too, that its hard power was still limited. In the mid-1990s, Beijing tried to signal its rising military strength to the world by aggressive moves like sending ships to unoccupied, disputed reefs in the South China Sea. This approach backfired. Provocative military exercises, including missile tests in the Taiwan Strait, frightened neighbouring states and evoked old memories of Chinese military adventurism.

Even as they saw that China's aggressive moves triggered Southeast Asian balancing against Beijing, Chinese leaders could not help but notice another trend. Wang Jisi, director of American studies at the Chinese Academy of Social Sciences in Beijing, one of China's elite think tanks, noted in Chinese publications that America's weakness might be its soft influence, not its unrivaled hard power.

Wang was right. After the finish of the cold war, America had retreated from the world, consumed with its own economic boom, its culture wars, and its political scandals. Significant pluralities of Americans opposed US interventions abroad and called for Washington to slash foreign aid, and the White House listened. Washington cut public diplomacy abroad and merged the United States Information Agency, the main public diplomacy outfit, into the State Department. The Clinton administration sidelined many of the multilateral institutions that America had built after World War II, creating perceptions of the United States as a unilateral actor— a perception that would only increase as the Bush administration eviscerated multilateralism.

Support and Trade Tools

China's economic tools also have become more sophisticated. China's aid has undergone a serious transformation. According to a study by Henry Yep of the National Defence University in Washington, in 2003, China's aid to the Philippines was roughly four times greater than America's, China's aid to Laos was three times greater, its aid to Indonesia was nearly double, and its aid to Cambodia nearly matched US levels. Beijing has revamped its aid programs to better tie assistance to discrete policy goals, including promoting Chinese companies abroad, cultivating important political actors, and bolstering China's benign regional image. In Thailand, for instance, Chinese aid has been used for the kind of lobbying familiar in Washington: to bring important elected Thai politicians to study trips and conferences in China. Beijing has also used funds to purchase surplus Thai agriculture, mollifying Thai farmers worried about the impact of China's free trade agreement with Southeast Asia.

China's embrace of free trade in the region and its promotion of the idea that it will become a most important source of foreign direct investment also bolster its image. In addition to the ASEAN-China Free Trade Agreement, Beijing is negotiating closer bilateral trade ties and economic partnerships with individual Southeast Asian states. By the end of 2006, Southeast Asia's total trade with China probably will eclipse Southeast

Asian trade with the United States or Japan. (China-ASEAN total trade in 2005 was roughly $130 billion; US-ASEAN total trade in 2005 was about $150 billion.) By comparison, the United States struggled to complete a bilateral free trade agreement with Thailand.

On visits to the region Chinese leaders set targets for future Chinese investment into Southeast Asia. These targets, usually for five or even ten years in the future, tend to be enormous, and obscure the fact that, at present, Chinese direct investment still lags far behind investment from the United States and other wealthy countries like Japan.

Finally, over the past decade the Chinese government has not only lifted restrictions on migration within China but has also made it vastly easier for Chinese to leave the country for business and tourism. Partly as a result, Chinese migration, often on overstayed short-term visas, is transforming the demographic makeup of northern mainland Southeast Asia, from northern Burma to northern Vietnam. Because of outmigration from Yunnan and other border provinces, ethnic Chinese now dominate entire towns in places like Luang Namtha, in northern Laos. The recent migrants are much more attuned to trends in China than older generations of ethnic Chinese, and they also have created a kind of renminbi zone in northern mainland Southeast Asia, where the Chinese currency serves as a de facto second currency.

Beijing's Fresh Toolbox

As China's engagement with the world has become more sophisticated, its tools of soft power have become more sophisticated as well. In the past decade, China has upgraded its public diplomacy, which has focused on selling the idea that China will not be a threat to other nations. China's public diplomacy efforts reinforce the idea of peaceful development. They include museum exhibits in Malaysia and Singapore to celebrate the 600th anniversary of the voyages of Zheng He, a Chinese admiral who sailed across Asia, encountering but never conquering other nations. Part of this new public diplomacy has been increasing cultural exchanges with Southeast Asia. China has begun hosting overseas scholars, the kind of programming the US State Department has long done. Beijing also has created a Chinese version of the Peace Corps, run by the China Association of Youth Volunteers, to send idealistic young Chinese on long-term volunteer service projects to developing nations like Laos and Burma. China has expanded the international reach of its media as well. It has upgraded the Chinese newswire Xinhua and expanded Xinhua's output in languages other than English and Chinese, and it has expanded and professionalized the international broadcasting of CCTV, Chinese state television.

The new Chinese public diplomacy includes setting up networks of informal business and cultural summits in China designed to bring together Asian opinion leaders. These meetings allow China to subtly emphasize its role as a potential partner for investment and trade and its position as a regional leader. The most prominent include the Boao Forum for Asia, which brings together Asian businesspeople for a Davos-style World Economic Forum-like event; and the ASEAN-China Eminent Persons Group, which unites former statesmen.

As China has upgraded its public diplomacy, it also has invested in improving its diplomatic corps. Over the past 15 years, the Chinese Ministry of Foreign Affairs has begun to retire older, more ideological diplomats, replacing them with a young generation of envoys who speak better English and local languages: one 2005 study suggested that one-half of the country's 4,000 diplomats are under 35. China can keep these diplomats in the region because unlike the United States, which gives its Foreign Service officers leeway to choose where they want to be posted, the Chinese foreign affairs ministry can mandate postings. Top Chinese diplomats in nations like Cambodia or Thailand now often have done three or even four rotations in those countries before rising to the rank of ambassador, building their language skills and developing extensive contacts in the local business and political communities.

Beijing supports its diplomacy through constant visits by senior Chinese officials to Southeast Asia, a short hop from Beijing in contrast with the 20-hour flight from Washington. According to a recent study of visits by top Chinese and US officials to Thailand and Cambodia in 2004 and 2005, senior Chinese officials made at least twice as many visits to Bangkok and Phnom Penh.

Promotion of Chinese culture and Chinese verbal communication studies are most important components of this public diplomacy. Beijing now funds at least the first year of what it calls Confucius Institutes, Chinese language and culture schools created at leading local universities. Beijing has tried to push instruction in Mandarin and in Chinese culture in overseas primary schools, partly by signing agreements with countries like Thailand to help integrate Chinese into public school curricula, and partly by helping students in poor nations like Cambodia attend private local Chinese-language primary schools.

While promoting Chinese studies in other nations, Beijing has tried to lure more foreign students to China. The ministry of education advertises Chinese universities abroad and has boosted financial aid and loosened visa policies for foreign students. After 9-11, in contrast, the United States tightened its student visa policies, making it far harder for students from Southeast Asia to attend school in America. Even students already in the United States have had a harder time. In 2003, Washington announced that all Indonesian men residing in America would have to register with immigration authorities. Many of them simply left. Between 1999 and 2003, the number of Indonesians studying in the United States fell by over 20 percent.

THE OPPORTUNITY OF CHINA'S SOFT POWER

What will China's charm offensive mean in the long run, for Southeast Asia and for the United States? There are signs that China's rising power, and its engagement with the world, will prompt Beijing to wield its soft influence responsibly. China has begun to mediate other nations' disputes—a task of responsible great powers. After anti-Thai riots in Phnom Penh in Cambodia led to a serious break in relations between Cambodia and Thailand in 2003, Chinese Deputy Foreign Minister Wang Yi called in the Thai and Cambodian representatives in Beijing and helped them lay out their grievances. In private the Chinese minister then warned the neighbors to normalize relations as soon as possible. Chastened, the two sides began to patch up their relationship. China also has proved influential on nontraditional security subjects, working with the Southeast Asian states to address drug trafficking and human trafficking. One regional expert on human trafficking lauds Beijing for taking progressive stances on human trafficking education—stances that have put pressure on governments in Cambodia and Laos to do the same.

Some of China's soft power hardly comes at America's expense. The United States continues to receive strong cooperation on many subjects from most important nations like the Philippines, Singapore, Malaysia, and Thailand. The United States and Japan remain the most important investors in Southeast Asia. America is still the region's premier hard power. It also stands as the biggest source of foreign films, television, popular music, and books in the region. As Catharin Dalpino of Georgetown University found, even during waves of virulent anti-Americanism in Indonesia, the country remained the world's biggest market for MTV.

Most important, the United States still offers a political and social model that appeals to average people in the region, even if Washington itself does not always live up to American values. China's values—noninterference, respect for other nations' internal affairs, economic gradualism—enjoy appeal as well. But they appeal only to specific groups: elites in authoritarian nations like Vietnam; average people in countries like Indonesia that equate the American model with the financial crisis; publics in some states willing to trade some degree of political freedom if they could obtain Chinese-style growth rates. In surveys of Asian publics taken by the East Asia

Barometer and published by the Journal of Democracy, most importantities in every country say they desire democracy rather than any other type of political system.

Meanwhile, as China's soft power grows, it could begin to encounter blowback—particularly in Southeast Asian countries like Vietnam that historically have had the most troubled relations with China. As China becomes more powerful, other nations will begin to see beyond its benign face to a more complicated reality. They will realize that despite China's promises of noninterference, when it comes to core interests, China, like any great power, will put its priorities ahead of others.

China ultimately could employ its soft influence to push nations to make a more explicit choice between it and the United States. This could threaten US alliances and other close bilateral relationships, undermine America's forces, and hurt its standing in international organizations. Across Southeast Asia, as China has become more popular, it has been able to create a web of multilateral groups that put China at the centre of the region. These organizations could exclude the United States, like the recent East Asia summit in Malaysia, which eventually could turn into a forum for important security subjects.

Indeed, in some respects China is already trying to draw on its charm to push back against American power. When Dennis Blair, commander of US forces in the Pacific, proposed "security communities" in which the United States would increase its defence cooperation with several Asian nations, many countries rejected the idea, in part because China quietly applied pressure on them to reject it. In early 2004, Blair's successor, Thomas Fargo, suggested that American marines or Special Forces could be stationed in Southeast Asia to patrol the Straits of Malacca, the narrow waterway between Malaysia and Indonesia that serves as a vital shipping channel. China gingerly leaned on other countries in Asia to block the idea. Indonesian and Malaysian leaders spoke out against it, and the idea of posting US Special Forces to the straits collapsed.

In the future, China could prod countries like the Philippines or Thailand to downgrade their close relations with the United States, or push countries like Singapore to stop providing basing rights for America. It could also pressure them not to intervene if the United States and China went to war over Taiwan.

The Authoritarian's Helper

But the most dangerous part of China's rising soft influence—the most dangerous to average people in Southeast Asia and, potentially, to American influence—is China's support for authoritarian regimes in opposition to US support for democratization. Despite its smooth highways and flashy shopping malls and reams of Starbucks, China remains an authoritarian country, with a Leninist regime if no longer a Marxist one.

China's influence can be felt most in Burma, the region's most backward, politically isolated nation. At the most important moments in recent Burmese history, when pressure might be applied on Rangoon, China has protected the leaders of the Burmese junta. In May 2003, thugs dressed as monks attacked the convoy of Burmese opposition leader Aung San Suu Kyi on a rural road, leaving 70 or more people dead. A close associate of Burmese junta leader Than Shwe was suspected of masterminding the massacre. Western governments quickly decried the attack. The State Department's chief spokesman, Richard Boucher, called it a "premeditated ambush," and Washington extended a visa ban on Burmese leaders and tightened economic sanctions.

The Measure of Achievement

To gauge the success or failure of China's charm offensive in Southeast Asia, it is important to understand China's goals in the region. One goal is simply to maintain peace on China's periphery. Peace allows China's economy to continue growing, for border provinces like Yunnan to build economic links to Southeast Asia, and for China to gain access to resources. Beijing also wants to reduce Taiwan's influence in Southeast

Asia, a strategy first enunciated in 1994. In addition, Beijing wants to change regional perceptions of China, so that it is seen as a positive, benign actor in the region. Finally, and most important, China may want to shift influence away from the United States to create its own sphere of influence, a kind of Chinese Monroe Doctrine for Southeast Asia. In this sphere, countries would subordinate their interests to China's, and would think twice about supporting the United States should there be any conflict in the region.

Beijing clearly has had success maintaining peace and boosting its image as nonthreatening. As one Southeast Asian diplomat notes, it is almost impossible now to hear any Southeast Asian leaders question China's rise, a sharp contrast from only five years ago. In the past five years, China's trade with the region has grown by 20 to 30 percent annually, and Chinese officials have predicted that trade will reach $200 billion annually by the end of the decade. Yet Southeast Asian leaders take pains to downplay the possible negative effects of this growth in China-dominated trade.

Chinese businesspeople and policy makers are increasingly given the type of welcome and access in Southeast Asia that once were reserved for American and Japanese elites. Sometimes, they receive grander welcomes. Chinese Prime Minister Wen Jiabao was toasted with frequent ovations during a 2003 visit to Indonesia; when President George W. Bush visited Indonesia the same year, many of the country's cultural and political leaders would not even meet with him for fear they would be tainted in the public's mind by association with the president.

Southeast Asian publics seem to agree with their leaders' views of China. Polling in the region suggests many Southeast Asians now regard China as a benign presence to be emulated—a sharp contrast with current regional views of the United States. Likewise, whereas a decade ago leading newspapers in Southeast Asia frequently criticized China's economic and security policies, today such coverage is rare and muted. The public sentiment is reflected in Chinese language and cultural studies, which have skyrocketed in popularity in the region. Between 2002 and 2004, the number of Cambodian students in China grew by nearly 20 percent, while the number of Indonesians rose by nearly 50 percent, and the number of Vietnamese by 90 percent. In Indonesia, the demand for Chinese has become so great that the country faces a shortage of some 100,000 Chinese language instructors.

Another way to measure China's growing soft power is by looking at the position of ethnic Chinese in Southeast Asia. Again, as perceptions of China change, the position of ethnic Chinese in the region has been radically transformed. In Thailand, leading politicians now tout their Chinese heritage, advertising their ability to boost ties with Beijing. In Indonesia, where only a decade ago riots targeting ethnic Chinese laid waste to Jakarta, a much wider spectrum of ethnic Chinese now provides close input into government policy making. Indeed, being ethnic Chinese in Southeast Asia is increasingly viewed as an asset, not a detriment.

Meanwhile, governments in Southeast Asia are wounding even their informal links to Taiwan. In the 1990s, leaders from nations in the region that officially recognized Beijing would travel to Taipei for informal visits, as Malaysian Prime Minister Mahathir Mohamad did in 1997. They also allowed Taiwan to open informal embassies in their countries, typically known as Taipei Economic and Cultural Offices. In 1998, Cambodian Prime Minister Hun Sen announced that he did not want a Taiwanese informal embassy in Phnom Penh. Other Asian nations have halted informal diplomatic visits.

Countries have proved willing to isolate other perceived enemies of China. At the request of the Chinese government, Cambodia in 2002 barred the Dalai Lama from attending a Buddhism conference. In 2001, the Thai government prodded Falun Gong to cancel an international meeting in Bangkok. Explaining Thailand's actions, Thailand's police minister bluntly told reporters, "We want to keep good relations with China." In following years the Bangkok government deported or arrested Falun Gong members for protesting in front of the Chinese embassy, Indonesia prohibited marches by Falun Gong supporters and sentenced Falun Gong activists to jail, and Malaysia filed charges against nine Malaysian Falun Gong adherents.

Ultimately, soft power can be used to persuade other nations to take actions they otherwise might not. Measured this way, China's influence in the region clearly has grown. China has persuaded other countries to take China's interests into account almost reflexively. Southeast Asian diplomats say that in the past three years, consensus at ASEAN meetings is often delayed as member nations analyse how Beijing will react to any decision. Although Chinese dams on the upper portion of the Mekong River may be contributing to decreased water flow on the river, China's growing influence, including its aid to nations like Cambodia and Laos, has kept a lid on Mekong region leaders' complaints about China's policies.

CHINESE DIPLOMACY IN THE SOUTHEAST ASIA REGION

The relatives that exist among these states however, emanates from the spirit of communism, led by communist parties and conducted by communist government and finally acted by communist actors or leaders. As a background however, we need to provide a prelude of the relations that exist between china, North Korea, Vietnam and Laos, which can be termed to be 3+1 diplomatic relations. China is North Korea's most important ally, biggest trading partnerand main source of food, armsand fuel. In the hope of avoiding regime collapse and an uncontrolled influx of refugees across its 800 mile border with North Korea (Bajoria, 2008). China has helped sustain Kim Jong-Il regime and opposed harsh international economic sanctions. After Pyongyang tested a nuclear weapon in October 2006. Experts say that China has reconsidered the nature of its alliance to include both pressure and inducements. But Beijing, arguably, continues to have more leverage over Pyongyang than any other nation and has played a central role in the ongoing Talks, which is clearly a multilateral framework aimed at denuclearizing North Korea (Bajoria, 2008). The chemistry of Chinese political relations with countries in the South East Asia region is rather paternalistic in an outlook, maternal in characteristics and peaceful in conduct. This is primarily because these countries regard china as a mother and a father to them, relying holistically to her economic and political advantages from the angles of political support and relations; economic and commercial exchanges and even cultural exchanges. This study will focus on such paternal type of diplomatic relations between main-land China and her communist ideologically oriented countries within the region, by instrumentalising the communist party influence and party relations.

While on the other hand, however, Vietnam's size and resources make it a politically and militarily predominant country in the Indo-China peninsula; Vietnam's geographical configuration with a coast-line of over 3.300 km (Subhash, 2005) in length gives it a strategic footing in the naval waters extending from China's doorstep in the Gulf of Tonkin, a long littoral on the South China Sea and ending with another dimension in the Gulf of Thailand.

While, the above was earlier significant only to the United States and Japan in terms of lifeline sea lanes running parallel to the Vietnamese littoral, it is also increasingly becoming important to China. With China soon becoming a net importer of oil, the security of sea lanes becomes equally critical for China. In any future China containment policy of the United States, Vietnam is a prospective component on China's Southern periphery.

For China, now in a Cold War mode with the United States, Vietnam revives the view of the 1950 and 1960s of an entirely monolithic Communist dominated Western Pacific littoral. China is more prominent in this game and has made concerted efforts to build meaningful political relations with Vietnam, in parallel to emerging as its largest trade partner. Chinese President Hu Jintao's visit to Vietnam from October 31 to November 2, 2005 needs to be analyzed in the above light (Subhash, 2005).

While, Laotian relation with China has traditionally consisted of trade and aid largely in road construction in the Northern provinces of Laos, without directly challenging the interests of Thailand or Vietnam in the central and southern regions. However, Vietnam's invasion of Cambodia in December 1978 to unseat then prime minister Pol Pot, provoked China into a limited invasion of Vietnam approximately 19 km deep to teach Vietnam a lesson. Laos was caught in a dangerous bind, not wanting to further provoke China, but not able to oppose its special partner, Vietnam (Arthur, 2001). The Laotian leadership survived the dilemma by making slightly delayed pronouncements in support of Vietnam after some intraparty debate and by sharply reducing diplomatic relations with China to the chargé d'affaires level without a full break. The low point in Sino-Laotian relations came in 1979, with reports of Chinese assistance and training of Hmong resistance forces under General Vang Pao in China's Yunnan Province (Arthur, 2001).

Materials and Methods

This research is a manufactured goods of literature materials, which envelope the use of library data such as text books, journals, periodicals, magazines, government reports and others. Since, the research deals with comparative diplomatic phenomenology, the methodology used in the research is the comparative methodology as used in international relations and politics. According to Macridis (2000), comparative methodology deals with: abstraction and concrete situations; it determines criteria of relevance of the particular components of social and political situations to the problem under study. The methodology emerged as a critique to the traditional methodology due to its dissatisfaction especially after the Second World War.

Results and Conversation

The development of communist parties in South-East Asia: The Chinese Communist Party (CCP) was established in Shanghai by Chen Duxiu and Li Dazhao in June 1921 as a result of the political and revolutionary inspiration of the

Russian federation. The original members of the party included: Mao Zedong, Zhou Enlai, Zhu De and Lin Biao. Mao Zedong soon became the most important member of the CCP. He adapted the ideas of Lenin who had successfully achieved a revolution in Russia in 1917. He argued that in Asia it was important to concentrate on the countryside rather than the towns, in order to create revolutionary elite (Lubell, 2002).

Accordingly, the Kuomintang gradually increased its power in China. Its leader, Sun Yat-sen died on 12 March, 1925. Chiang Kai-Shek eventually emerged as the most important figure in the organization (Lubell, 2002). He now carried out a purge that eliminated the communists from the organization. Those communists who survived managed to establish the Jiangxi Soviet. The nationalists now imposed a blockade and Mao Zedong decided to evacuate the area and establish a new stronghold in the North-west of China. In October 1934 Mao, Zhou Enlai, Lin Biao, Zhu Deand some 100,000 men and their dependents headed west through mountainous areas. The marchers experienced terrible hardships. The most notable passages included the crossing of the suspension bridge over a deep gorge at Luting (May, 1935), travelling over the Tahsueh Shan mountains (August, 1935) and the swampland of Sikang (September, 1935). The marchers covered about fifty miles a day and reached Shensi on 20th October, 1935. It is estimated that only around 30,000 survived the 8,000 mile Long March (Lubell, 2002).

It was during the hegemonic and invasive era of expansionism that Japanese Army invaded the heartland of China in 1937. Chiang Kai-Shek was forced to move his capital from Nanking to Chungking. He lost control of the coastal regions and most of the most important cities to Japan. In an effort to beat the Japanese he agreed to collaborate with Mao Zedong and his communist army. During the Second World War the communist guerrilla forces were well led by Zhu De and Lin Biao (Lubell, 2002). As soon as the Japanese surrendered, Communist forces began a war against the Kuomintang. The communists gradually gained control of the country and on 1st October, 1949, Mao Zedong announced the establishment of People's Republic of China. In 1958 Mao Zedong announced the Great Leap Forward, an attempt to increase agricultural and industrial production. This improvement programme included the establishment of large agricultural communes containing as many as 75,000 people. The communes ran their own collective farms and factories. Each family received a share of the profits and also had a small private plot of land. However, 3 years of floods and bad harvests severely damaged levels of production. The scheme was also hurt by the decision of the Soviet Union to withdraw its large number of technical experts working in the country. In 1962 Mao's improvement programme came to an end and the country resorted to a more traditional form of economic production (Lubell, 2002).

As a result of the breakdown on the Great Leap Forward, Mao retired from the post of chairman of the People's Republic of China. His place as head of state was taken by Liu Shaoqi. Mao remained important in determining overall policy. In the early 1960s Mao became highly critical of the foreign policy of the Soviet Union. He was appalled by the way Nikita Khrushchev backed down over the Cuban Missile Crisis. Mao Zedong became openly involved in politics in 1966 when with Lin Biao he initiated the Cultural Revolution. On 3rd September, 1966, Lin Biao made a speech where, he urged pupils in schools and colleges to criticize those party officials, who had been influenced by the ideas of Nikita Khrushchev (Lubell, 2002).

Mao was concerned by those party leaders such as Liu Shaoqi, who favoured the introduction of piecework, greater wage differentials and measures that sought to undermine collective farms and factories. In an attempt to dislodge those in power who favoured the Soviet model of communism, Mao galvanized students and young workers as his Red Guards to attack revisionists in the party. Mao told them the revolution was in danger and that they must do all they could to stop the emergence of a privileged class in China. He argued, this is what had happened in the Soviet Union under Joseph Stalin and Nikita Khrushchev. Zhou Enlai at first gave his support to the campaign but became concerned when fighting broke out between the Red Guards and the revisionists. In order to achieve peace at the end of 1966, he called for an end to these attacks on party officials (Lubell, 2002). Mao Zedong remained in control of the Cultural Revolution and with the support of the army was able to oust the revisionists. The Cultural Revolution came to an end when, Liu Shaoqi resigned from all his posts on 13th October 1968. Lin Biao now became Mao's designated successor. Mao now gave his support to the Gang of Four: Jiang Qing (Mao's third wife), Wang Hongwen, Yao Wenyuan and Zhange Chungqiao. These four radicals occupied powerful positions in the Politburo after the Tenth Party Congress of 1973. Mao Zedong died in Beijing on 9th September, 1976. After the death of Mao the power of the Gang of Four declined dramatically. In 1980, they were found guilty of plotting against the state. Jiang Qing and Zhange Chungqiao, who were considered to be the leaders, were sentenced to death (later commuted to life imprisonment). Wang Hongwen and Yao Wenyuan received lengthy prison sentences (Lubell, 2002).

The communist party of North-Korea: The Communist Party of Korea was founded in 1925, by Kim Yong-bom and Pak Hon-yong during a secret meeting in Seoul. The secret meeting was a result of Japanese occupation regime, which vividly banned communist parties under the Peace Preservation Law. The party became the Korean section of the Communist International at the 6th congress of the international in Aug-Sep, 1928. But after only a few months as the Korean Comintern section, the perpetual feuds between rival factions that had plagued the party from its foundation led the Comintern to disband the Communist Party of Korea in December the same year. However, the party continued to exist through various party cells. Some communists, like Kim Il-sung went into exile in China, where they joined the Communist Party of China. In the early 1930s, Chinese and Korean communists began guerrilla activity against the Japanese forces (Lankov, 2001).

After the second World War and the liberation from Japanese rule, the situation for the Korean communists changed considerably. The country was divided into US and Soviet occupation zones and the working conditions for the party were very different in the two zones. In the US occupied South, the party leader Pak Hon-yong, who had been a prisoner of the Japaneseand became active in Seoul upon his release in 1945. He reorganized a Central Committee, of which he became the Secretary. Being based in Seoul, he had limited contact with the Soviet occupation forces in the North. The Soviet Red Army liberated Northern Korea from the Japanese occupation in August, 1945 (Lankov, 2001).

Most members of the Communist Party of Korea were in Southern Korea, which was occupied by the United States and there were very few Communist cadres in the Soviet occupied zone. The practice of the Soviets in most countries, it occupied after World War II was to rely on the domestic Communist Party to transform the occupied state into first a pro-soviet and then a Soviet style socialist state but this was initially difficult in what became North Korea because of the lack of a strong domestic Communist presence. The Soviets began to rely largely on exiled Communists who returned to Korea at the end of World War II as well as ethnic Koreans who were part of the large Korean community in the USSR and therefore, Soviet citizens (Lankov, 2001). Kim Il-sung became a prominent figure of the party in the Northern areas. After his years as a guerilla leader, Kim Il-sung had moved to the Soviet Union (where, historians believe his son Kim Jong-Il was born in 1941) and had become a Captain in the Red Army. His battalion arrived in Pyongyang just as the Soviets were looking for a suitable person who could assume a leading role in North Korea. On October 13, 1945 the North Korea Bureau of the Communist Party of Korea was established (Lankov, 2001).

Though, technically under the control of the Seoul based party leadership, the North Korean Bureau was had little contact with Seoul and worked closely with the Soviet forces (termed the Soviet Civilian Authority). The first chairman of the Bureau was Kim Yong-bom who had been sent to Korea by the Comintern in the 1930s to conduct underground activity.

Kim Il-sung was a member of the Bureau at its founding and replaced Kim Yong bom as chairman in December, 1945. Official North Korean historians later disputed this, claiming that Kim Il-sung had become its chairman from the onset of the Bureau. Moreover, official North Korean sources claim that the meeting was held on October 10 and it is regarded as the Party Foundation Day in North Korea, on which Kim Il sung formed the first genuine Marxist-Leninist party in the country (Lankov, 2001).

The communist party of vietnam: The Chinese communist party was 9 years older than the Vietnamese communist party (Viet Nam cong san Đang), which was established in 1930. The Party was founded by Ho Chí Minh and other political exiles living in China, which was first rooted at a conference in Hong Kong. At the Hong Kong conference two competing communist factions, Indochinese Communist Party (Đông Duong cong san Dang) and the Communist Party of Annam (An Nam cong san Đang), merged. Although, the third Vietnamese communist group, the Indochinese Communist League (Đông Duong cong san lien Doan), had not been invited to the Hong Kong conference its members were allowed to become members of the new united party (Smith, 1998).

It was however, at its first plenum the party's name was altered to Indochinese Communist Party (Đang cong san Đông Duong), The First National Party Congress was secretly conducted in Macau in 1935. Similarly, a Comintern congress in Moscow adopted a policy towards a popular front against fascism and directed Communist movements around the world to collaborate with anti-fascist forces regardless of their orientation towards socialism. This required the ICP to regard all nationalist parties in Indochina as potential allies. The party was dissolved in 1945 and refounded as the Vietnam Workers' Party (Đang Lao dong Viet Nam) at the Second National Party Congress in Tuyen Quang in 1951. The Workers' Party of North Vietnam was merged with the People's Revolutionary Party of South Vietnam to form the Communist Party of Vietnam At the 4th National Party Congress held in

1976 (Smith, 1998). The nature of chinese diplomatic relations with the three countries: It is in the argument of David (2005) that the traditional underpinnings of international relations in Asia are undergoing profound changeand the rise of China is a principal cause. China's new regional posture rests on the following four pillars:

- Participation in regional organizations
- Establishment of strategic partnerships and deepening of bilateral relations
- Expansion of regional economic ties
- Reduction of distrust and anxiety in the security sphere.

On the other hand, however, the Chinese diplomatic principles as adopted by the CPC, one was derived from the principle of peaceful coexistence constructed by Leninand the other four principles were formulated by Chairman Mao. Lenin upheld that the first socialist country should and could coexist peacefully with the surrounding capitalist world and strive for its existence and development. Chairman Mao formulated the other principles on April 30, 1949, almost half a year before the founding of the People's Republic as the guiding principles for new china's foreign policy (Huang, 1995). The principles of Chinese foreign policy, however are:

- Mutual respect for territorial integrity and sovereignty
- Non-aggression
- Non-interference in states' internal affairs
- Equality and mutual benefitand
- Peaceful co-existence.

China has raised its profile in meetings with regional leaders. This new embrace of regional multilateralism was highlighted by China's hosting of the 2001 APEC meeting in Shanghai and the attention given by President Hu Jintao at the 2003 APEC meeting in Bangkok. Another example of China's efforts to raise its profile was Beijing's hosting of the 3rd International Conference of Asian Political Parties on Sep. 3-5, 2004. The meeting, organized by the International Department of the Chinese Communist Party, brought together

350 delegates from 81 political parties in 35 Asian countries, including eight heads of state. On the last day of the conference, the convocation agreed on a 12-point Beijing declaration on principles of cooperation (David, 2005).

The communist party of Laos: It has its origin in the Indochinese Communist Party founded by Ho Chi Minh in 1930. The ICP was completely Vietnamese at its inception but grew throughout French Indochina and was able to found a small Lao section in 1936. In the mid-1940s, a campaign to recruit Laotian members was instigated and in 1946 or 1947, Kaysone Phomvihan, a law student at the University of Hanoi, was recruited, along with Nouhak Phoumsavan (Arthur, 2001).

In 1973, a peace agreement was signed that brought the Pathet Lao into the government and was supposed to result in the Vietnamese leaving the country. The Vietnamese army did not leave. In early 1975, the Pathet Lao and North Vietnamese began attacking government outposts again. Without the support of the US, the non-communists elements in the government had little choice other than to gradually allow the Pathet Lao to take power. In the spring of 1975, Pathet Lao forces consolidated their power throughout the country. The royal government fell in May 1975 and the LPRP took power. The LPRP on taking power showed itself to be closely connected to Vietnam. The LPRP signed a treaty of friendship, which allowed Vietnamese army units to base themselves in Laos and also brought political advisors from Vietnam into the country (Arthur, 2001). The LPRP economically isolated Laos by cutting off trade with all neighbouring countries except for Vietnam. The LPRP has shown itself to be remarkably resilient. Transitions of power have tended to be smooth, the new generation of leaders has proven more open to improvementand the Politburo now has some ethnic diversity. Organised opposition to the LPRP is weak (Arthur, 2001).

Sino-Korean relations: China was stimulated to act in early 2003 by a drastic fear that North Korea might be the next target of us invasion after Iraq, China on his effort to see the continuity of North Korea, it deployed a diplomatic strategy to bring Washington and Pyongyang to the same table in Beijing thrice in the space of 10 months: three party talks in April, 2003, six party talks in August 2003 and February 2004. The recommendations made from the Chinese diplomatic submissions were:

- Don't expect too much from Beijing
- Don't underestimate China's commitment to protect its own national interest
- Don't force China to choose sides
- Don't expect much movement from Pyongyang
- North Korean distrust of outsiders may be almost insurmountable
- Don't count on china to dissuade North Korea from going nuclear (Andrew, 2004).

China has assisted North Korea in fighting the Korean war. It was estimated that china lost about 360,000 lives including 130,000 wounded and noncombatant losses were >380,000 (Bonnie, 2009). China remained in what can be described as brother-in-arms relationship with North Korea even after the war. Due to an unprecedented relations of the two countries, the Chinese forces remained on the Korean peninsula for an additional 5 years (until 1958), assisting in national reconstruction projects. This however, culminates into signing a military cooperation and assistance pact between the two countries in 1961. It was a kind of a de facto alliance formalized when the two signed a treaty of friendship, cooperation and mutual assistance, which was committed to one country coming to the aid of the other if attacked (Andrews, 2004).

Despite, the changing phases of international politics and economy; the Chinese ties with Seoul, especially in the 1980's and early 1990's. China sent a large delegation of athletes to South Korea for the 1986 Asian games and the subsequent attendance of the Seoul Olympics, coupled with the increasing trade and investment relations and formal establishment of full diplomatic relations with Seoul in 1992, it angered North

Korea, but did not change the diplomatic historiography of the two or crumble their diplomatic ties (Andrew, 2004).

Investment from China: China has a direct interest in economic improvement and recovery in the DPRK. Chinese business interests with support from Beijing are beginning to invest widely in the North Korean economy. Unlike, South Korean investors, Chinese are allowed to invest in enterprises fully integrated into the DPRK economy. They also have provided machinery and equipment to existing North Korean factories. Chinese investment in mineral extraction in the DPRK seems to represent an easing the DPRK constitutional ban against cultural infiltration. This has been interpreted to include international economic integration and globalization. However, Pyongyang seems to be treating investment from China as being not contaminated relative to those from South Korea or other nations (Dick, 2008). South Korean investments are carefully walled off from the average North Korean citizen.

Whereas, China has been able to invest in production facilities in various locations. According to Chinese sources, from January-October 2006, the Chinese side approved 19 new investments in the DPRK, with negotiated investment of $66.67 milliond (Dick, 2008). Cumulative investment up to the end of October 2006 included Chinese government approval of 49 investments in the DPRK with negotiated investment of $135 million. The projects of the investment covered such fields as food products, medicine, light industry, electronics, chemical industry and minerals. Most important Chinese investments involving mining and minerals in the DPRK according to Dick (2008) include the following:

China Tonghua Iron and Steel Group has invested 7 billion yuan (Approximately, $875 million) in developing the DPRK's Musan Iron Mine. Two billion yuan (approximately, $250 million) is to be used for the preliminary construction of communication facilities and cables from Tonghua, China, to the DPRK's Musan area; 5 billion Yuan (approximately, $625 million) is to be used mainly on technology and equipment in developing the mine as well as in Musan's overall planning). This mine is the largest open cut iron mine in Asia with verified iron rich ore reserves reaching seven billion tons (Bonnie, 2009).

On October 20, 2007; China's Tangshan Iron and Steel Company (China's third largest steel company) and the DPRK's Department of Foreign Economic Cooperation and Taep'ung International Investment Group signed a letter of cooperation intent. The two sides are to cooperate on the DPRK Kimch'aek Metallurgy Park Projectand the DPRK So'ngjin Iron, Steel, Coaland Electricity Project. Tangshan is to build a steel smelting plant in the DPRK with an annual steel output of 1.5 million tons. It is to be jointly funded by the DPRK side and is to involve joint development and utilization of nearby iron ore.

The China Iron and Steel Group reportedly is ready to develop a Molybdenum mine in the DPRK with a goal of producing >10,000 tons of molybdenum concentrates per year. China and the DPRK have signed a PRC-DPRK Inter Governmental Agreement on Joint Development of Offshore Oil to pursue joint energy projects.

China's Jilin Province also has cooperated with the Hyesan Youth Copper Mine (containing the largest copper deposit in Asia), Manp'o Zinc and Lead Mineand the Hoeryo'ng Gold Mine in the DPRK. One project is to transmit electricity from Jilin's Changbai County to the DPRK in exchange for the gold, copper and other ores. The joint project is to install power transmission facilities with an estimated total investment of 220 million yuan ($27.5 million).

China's Heshi Industry and Trade Company along with the International Mining Company have set up a joint venture with the DPRK's So'gyo'ng 4 Trade Company called the DPRK-China International Mining Company.

In October 2005 China Minmetals also signed with the DPRK side an Agreement on Establishing a Joint Venture in Coal Industry in the DPRK, which called for establishing a joint venture with the DPRK at the Ryongdu'ng Coal Mine.

On August 23, 2004 China's Zhaoyuan Shandong Guoda Gold Stockholding Company and the DPRK Committee for the

Promotion of External Economic Cooperation agreed to establish a joint venture mining company to mine the gold in the DPRK's Mt. Sangnong and to ship all the mined gold concentrates to Zhaoyuan for smelting. The DPRK's Sangnong Gold Mine is estimated to have at least 150 tons of mineable gold.

However, due to a shortage of capital and backward technology, it has been in a state of semi-stoppage of production. Guoda is to provide equipment and technology and is to ship the mineral ores by sea to Zhaoyuan for smelting (Dick, 2008). Still on china-Korean relations, Esther (2006) has summarized the nature of the benefit derived by North Korea in her diplomatic relations with the mainland when she wrote:

Pyongyang is economically dependent on China, which provides most of its food and energy supplies. North Korea gets about 70% of its food and 70-80% of its fuel from China. Beijing is Pyongyang's largest trading partner and an estimated 300,000 North Koreans live in China, many of them migrant workers who send much needed remittances back home.

Politically, china has been the driving force of putting a stoppage against any form of international sanction on North Korea, at the same time, trying to concede North Korea to compromise with the world in subjects pertaining her nuclear development. It is however, in this respect that Adam (2006) pointed out:

China has repeatedly blocked UN Security Council resolutions against North Korea, including some threatening sanctions. China has also hosted the Six-Party Talks, a series of meetings in which North Korea, South Korea, Japan, China, Russia and the United States have tried to resolve the security concerns associated with North Korea's nuclear weapons program. There and in other international forums.

The emergence of a soaring relationship between the two countries was manifest in the aftermath of Korean test of a nuclear technology. The test took China by surprise and was strongly opposed by Beijing. China viewed it as not only an act of defiance to the international community and a threat to regional stability, but specifically as an act of defiance toward China. In the aftermath of the test, China supported a UN Security Council resolution that condemned North Korea's action and imposed limited sanctions. Chinese officials privately admitted that their toolbox for managing the North Korea nuclear weapons challenge has relied too much on carrots in the past and now needs to include a combination of pressure and inducement (Bonnie, 2009).

On trade relation: China plays an important role especially in his investment projects in Vietnam. Economic and trade relation between Vietnam and China has seen significant development with the two way trade volume standing at 1.345 billion US dollars in the first 7 months of 2000 (Phan, 2000). On the Sino-Vietnam economic relations, the following areas have been of great importance as written by Brown and Joseph (1986).

Vietnam-China trade, which reached a record US $7.2 billion last year, is likely to reach $10 billion by 2007, 3 years ahead of the schedule set by Vietnamese Prime Minister Phan Van Khai and Chinese Premier Wen Jiabao at a meeting in Beijing last year. Trade, which has grown at an amazing annual rate of 40% in recent years, has emerged as a bright spot in bilateral relations, thanks to many advantages, including the shared 1,643 km land borderand mutual access to the Gulf of Tonkin.

Since, the resumption of Vietnam-China economic relations in 1991, the two countries have seen stable and rapid growth in trade, from $32 million in 1991 to nearly $2.5 billion in 2000 and $7.2 billion in 2004. Vietnam exports in great volumes crude oil, coal, coffee, sea products, fruits and vegetablesand footwear to China, while China has registered large increases in the export of pharmaceutical products, machinery and equipment, petroleum, fertilizers, motorbike parts and cars to Vietnam.

At present, China is the second biggest trading partner of Vietnam after the European Union (EU). It is the fourth largest buyer of Vietnam's goods and the biggest seller to Vietnam. Yet the value of two-way trade accounts for just 12% of Vietnam's total trade turnoverand represents only 0.6% of China's. The Vietnam Chamber of Commerce and Industry (VCCI) suggested that to further boost bilateral trade, both countries businesses should look to long-term contracts on supplying products not only to their countries but also to a third country.

A glorious example of the fruits of Sino-Vietnamese cooperation is the Thai Nguyen Steel Complex in Vietnam, which last year produced 430,000 tons of rolling steel, 300,000 tons of steel ingot and 210,000 tons of pig-iron, grossing a turnover of VND2, 500 billion (US $157 million). Its products have gone to almost all key projects in the country, occupying a firm foothold in the market. The steel complex, located about 80 km North of Hanoi, was built with Chinese assistance in 1959. At the end of 2001, the first phase of an extension project of the Thai Nguyen Steel Complex was completed with a total investment of nearly $46.7 million, with China contributing $22 million. The second phase of the extension (2005-2007), with a total investment of $200 million, aims to raise the complex's capacity to 750,000-1,000,000 million tons a year.

The Ha Bac Nitrogenous Fertilizer Factory, another gift from China to the Vietnamese people in the 1960s, has markedly contributed to Vietnam's development. Producing nearly 2 million tons of fertilizer for Vietnam so far, the factory over the past 4 years has had an average annual growth rate of 18%. The growth rate was achieved thanks to a $32 million investment from the Chinese partner to raise the factory's capacity to 150,000 tons a year.

Other most important projects jointly carried out by Vietnam and China includes the Sin Quyen copper project, the Cao Ngan thermal power project and the Dac Nong bauxite project. In addition, the Chinese government has decided to provide 150 million yuan (US $18 million) as non-refundable aid to help build a Vietnam-China Friendship Palace. In the 1992-2004 periods, China pledged $312 million of official development assistance for Vietnam, including $50 million as non-refundable aid for the upgrade of a number of Chinese-funded industrial projects in Vietnam. According to Roger (2006), similarly, China may be the second largest source of foreign aid to Vietnam (including grants and loans). In 2005, the PRC reportedly offered nearly $200 million in grants and loans, 28 in 2006. Beijing provided loans to Vietnam for railways, hydro-power developmentand ship building facilities. Japan and France are the largest donors of ODA to Vietnam, providing an annual average of $670 and $116 million, respectively (2004-2005).

Sino-Vietnamese relations: For >2000 years, Vietnam's development as a nation has been marked by one fixed and immutable factor the proximity of China. The relationship between the two countries is in many ways a family affair, with all the closeness of shared values andbitterness of close rivalries.

No country in Southeast Asia is culturally closer to China than Vietnamand no other country in the region has spent so long fending off Chinese domination, often at a terrible cost in lives, economic development and political compromise.

China has been Vietnam's blessing and Vietnam's curse. It remains an intrusive cultural godfather, the giant to the North that is always there. Almost, a thousand years of Chinese occupation, between the Han conquest of Nam Viet in the 2nd century BC and the reassertion of Vietnamese independence as Dai Viet in AD 967, marked the Vietnamese so deeply that they became, in effect, an outpost of Chinese civilization in Southeast Asia (Andrew, 2007).

While, the other countries of Indochina are Theravada Buddhist, sharing cultural links with South Asia, Vietnam derived its predominant religion a mix of Mahayana Buddhism, Taoism and Confucianism popularly known as tam giao or Three Religions from China. Until the introduction of romanized quoc ngu script in the 17th century, Vietnamese scholars wrote in Chinese characters or in chu nho, a Vietnamese derivative of Chinese characters. Over the centuries, Vietnam developed as a smaller version of the Middle Kingdom, a centralized, hierarchical state ruled by an all-powerful emperor living in a Forbidden City based on its namesake in Beijing and administered by a highly educated Confucian bureaucracy.

Both countries are deeply conscious of the cultural ties that bind them togetherand each is still deeply suspicious of the other. During the long centuries of Chinese occupation, the Vietnamese enthusiastically embraced many features of Chinese civilization, while at the same time fighting with an extraordinary vigor to maintain their cultural identity and regain their national independence Asia (Andrew, 2007).

Traditional friendship between China and Vietnam as well as the people of the two countries has enjoyed a long history. On January 18, 1950, the two countries established diplomatic relations. The Chinese Government and people rendered full support to the long-term revolutionary struggle of Vietnam against France and the US and provided Vietnam with huge military and economic aid. Vietnam regards China as its strong backingand the two countries have developed extensive cooperation in the political, military and economic fields. In late 1970s however, Sino-Vietnamese relations deteriorated. In November 1991, at the invitation of General Secretary Jiang Zemin and Premier Li Peng, General Secretary of the Central Committee of the Vietnamese Communist Party Do Muoi and Chairman of the Council of Minister Vo Van Kiet visited Chinaand both sides declared in end to the past and the start into the future. So that the party and state relations between the two countries were normalized (Sina, 2005).

Since then, the party and state relations between China and Vietnam have seen an overall restoration and in-depth development. There were frequent contacts and exchanges of visits between the leaders of the two countries and friendly exchanges and mutually beneficial cooperation in various fields between the two sides were continuously strengthened.

It was on October 8, 2004; the governments of the People's Republic of China and the Socialist Republic of Viet Nam subjectd a joint communiqué. The full text of the communiqué as revealed by Phan (2000), is as follows:

At the invitation of Prime Minister Phan Van Khai of the Socialist Republic of Viet Nam, Premier Wen Jiabao of the

State Council of the People's Republic of China paid an official visit to Vietnam from October 6-7, 2004. During the visit, Premier Wen Jiabao held a talk with Prime Minister Phan Van Khai and met with Secretary General Nong Duc Manh of the Central Committee of the Communist Party of Vietnam, Vietnamese President Tran Duc Luong and Chairman Nguyen Van An of the National Assembly. Leaders of the two countries exchanged views on strengthening bilateral relations and on international and regional affairs of common concern in a sincere, friendly and practical atmosphere and reached consensus in a variety of fields. The visit achieved full success.

Both sides are glad to see that guided by the principle of long-term stability, orientation to the future, good neighborliness and friendship and all-round cooperation defined by the leaders of the two countries Sino Vietnamese relations are developing rapidly, deeply and comprehensively. The leaders of both sides have exchanged visits frequently, mutual political trust is being strengthened, significant achievements have been made in the fields of economic and trade cooperation, most important progresses have been realized in the settlement of such historical problems as boundary and territoryand exchange and cooperation in other fields are also being expanded. The two sides support and coordinate with each other in both international and regional affairs.

Both sides believe that China and Vietnam have common strategic interest on many most important subjects. To maintain the stable, sound and smooth development of bilateral ties at a time of fundamental changes in the international situation is in the interest of the two countries and their people and conducive to regional and world peace and development as well. The governments of both countries, taking into account the overall situation and starting from a strategic perspective, are determined to follow the above principle, carry on the traditional friendship, expand mutually beneficial cooperation, appropriately handle sensitive subjects in a timely manner and constantly push the relationship between China and Vietnam to new levels.

Both sides agree to maintain frequent exchanges between leaders of the two countries, strengthen the friendly exchanges between their government agencies, local governments and civil organizations, strictly implement the cooperation documents signed by the ministries of foreign affairs, national defence and public security of both countries and effectively strengthen mutual understanding and trust. Both parties express willingness to deepen all-round cooperation, encourage and support their practical cooperation in the fields of economy and trade, technology, education and cultureand try their best to seek and expand common interest. They also agree to enhance exchange of experiences in running the party and state and the theories and practices of socialism, promote the development of the Friendship Meeting of Chinese and Vietnamese Youth, accelerate exchanges of the youth of both countries and enhance publicity of the friendship between China and Vietnam.

Both sides are satisfied with the progress in their economic and trade relations and express commitment to continuing to deepen mutually beneficial coordination. They reach consensus on expanding transactions of bulk commodities, maintaining the rapid and sustained growth of bilateral trade so that the trade volume between the two countries can reach $10 billion by 2010 and gradually narrow down imbalance in bilateral trade relations. Both sides note that they will accelerate the implementation of the already established cooperative projects, encourage and support businesses of both sides to conduct long term cooperation in most important infrastructure and industrial programsand improve the quality of bilateral economic and trade cooperation. They also agree to establish an expert panel, under the framework of China Vietnam economic and trade cooperation commission, to discuss the feasibility of building the Kunming Laojie Hanoi Hai Phong Quang Ninh and Nanning Liangshan Hanoi Hai Phong Quang Ninh economic corridors and the Beibu Bay economic rim.

Both sides agree to jointly promote the development of China-ASEAN Free Trade Area. Vietnam acknowledges China's complete market economy status and promises not to use Articles

15 and 16 of the protocol on Accession of China to the WTO and the 242 paragraph of the Working Party Report on China's Accession to the WTO. China recognizes the market economy status of Vietnam supports Vietnam's efforts to join the World Trade Organization at the earliest date possible and is willing to make joint efforts with Vietnam in this regard. Both parties, in the spirit of being practical and flexible, will complete the negotiations on bilateral market access as soon as possible.

Both parties hold that the special meeting between the chief negotiators on the boundary subject of the two governments held in August 2004, the agreement on implementing the most important consensus reached by the leaders of the two countries and the minute of that meeting are conducive to furthering mutual trust, effectively preventing the emergence of boundary and territorial problems and tackling such problems in a timely manner, whenever they occur. Both parties agree to take effective measures to implement the minute as soon as possible.

Both sides agree to accelerate the process of boundary survey and the erection of boundary markers along the land border between China and Vietnam. Related government departments and local governments of the two countries will be required to work hard to strengthen mutual trust and cooperate sincerely so as to accomplish the survey and erection of boundary markers as scheduled and build the land border into a boundary of peace, friendship and cooperation between both countries. During the process of boundary survey and the erection of boundary markers, both sides will faithfully maintain the status quo of border and manage the boundary strictly following the Interim Agreement on Handling Border Subjects between the People's Republic of China and the Socialist Republic of Viet Nam reached in 1991.

Both sides highly compliment the Beibu Bay Demarcation Agreement and the Agreement on Fishery Cooperation going into effect on June 30, 2004 simultaneously, which they believe is a significant event in the Sino-Vietnamese relations, conducive to the permanent peace and stability of Beibu Bay region and of great importance to the long-term stable development of bilateral ties. The two countries are satisfied with the implementation of the above two agreements and stress that they will continue to coordinate closely in implementing the two agreements strictly. They express the commitment to jointly maintaining peace and stability in the Beibu Bay, promoting long-term cooperation and bringing benefit to the two peoples in the spirit of mutual understanding and concessions and without resort to radical action or force Phan (2000).

Both parties agree to strictly follow the consensus reached by the high-level leaders of both governments and the purpose and principles of the Declaration on the conduct of parties in the South China Sea (DOC) signed between China and the member states of ASEAN. Thetwo parties will remain restrained, neither adopting unilateral action, which might add to the complexity or expand existing disputes nor resorting to force or threats by force, including not resorting to force against fishing boats. Both sides will take tangible actions to maintain the stability of the South China Sea Phan (2000).

Both sides emphasize that they will retain the negotiation mechanism on marine subjects and increase rounds of negotiations. They insist to seek fundamental and permanent solutions, which are acceptable to both parties through peaceful negotiations. Prior to the final settlement of those subjects, both sides will follow the spirit of addressing easy problems first and then difficult ones, continue to strengthen cooperation in fields with lower sensitivity, which are of common concern to both parties and gradually explore how to expand cooperation in other identified fields.

The Vietnamese government reiterates that it will continue to firmly uphold the one China policy, support China's lofty cause of national reunification and oppose the separatist activities of Taiwan independence in whatever form. Vietnam only maintains non-official economic and trade contact with Taiwan and resolutely refrains from establishing official relations with Taiwan.

Both sides agree to continue to strengthen cooperation and coordination of the two countries in the United Nations, ASEAN,

ASEAN Regional Forum, APEC, ASEM, Greater Mekong Sub-region and other multilateral organizations. They also express commitment to building a fair and rational new international political and economic order and contributing to the regional and international peace, stability and development.

Sino-Laotian relations: The two countries' relations have virtually consisted trade and aid, which primarily, become manifest in road construction in the Northern provinces of Laos, without directly challenging the interests of Thailand or Vietnam in the central and Southern regions. However, Vietnam's invasion of Cambodia in December 1978 to unseat then prime minister Pol Pot, provoked China into a limited invasion of Vietnam approximately 19 km deep to teach Vietnam a lesson. Laos was caught in a dangerous bind, not wanting to further provoke China, but not able to oppose its special partner, Vietnam. The Laotian leadership survived the dilemma by making slightly delayed pronouncements in support of Vietnam after some intraparty debate and by sharply reducing diplomatic relations with China to the chargé d'affaires level without a full break. The low point in Sino-Laotian relations came in 1979, with reports of Chinese assistance and training of Hmong resistance forces under General Vang Pao in China's Yunnan Province (Brown and Joseph, 1986).

This hostile relationship gradually softened however and in 1989 Prime Minister Kaysone paid a state visit to Beijing. In 1991 Kaysone chose to spend his vacation in China rather than make his customary visit to the Soviet Union. Diplomatic and party-to-party relations were normalized in 1989. Trade expanded from the local sale of consumer goods to the granting of eleven investment licenses in 1991 including an automotive assembly plant. Following the establishment of the Laotian Chinese Joint Border Committee in 1991, meetings held during 1992 resulted in an agreement delineating their common border. China's commercial investments and trade with Laos have expanded quietly, but not dramatically, in 1993 and 1994. Unlike its other neighbors, China has not historically dominated the Laotians. In the final analysis, China represents the most powerful remaining communist state to which Laos might turn for support against Thai or Vietnamese hegemony (Brown and Joseph, 1986). According to Bouasone (2008), Sino-Laotian relation is identifiable from the following angles:

Political relations: China and Laos are friendly neighbors linked with mountains and waters and the people of the two countries have co-existed in peace and harmony since the ancient times. On April 25, 1961, China and Laos established diplomatic relations and have maintained neighborly and friendly relations ever since. Between the late 1970s and mid 1980s, their relations suffered twists and turns. In 1989, however, Sino-Laotian relations returned to the normal.

Over the last 10 years and more, Sino-Laotian relations have seen comprehensive restoration and development and exchanges of visits between leaders of the two countries become frequent. President Jiang Zemin, Premier Li Peng and Chairman of the Standing Committee of the NPC Qiao Shi visited Laos respectively while, President of Laos Kayson Phonvihane and Nouhak Phoumsavanh, Premier Khamtay Siphandoneand Boungnang Vornchith, President of the National Assembly Samane Vignaket and Central Chairman of the Nation-Building Front Sisavath Keobounphan visited China many times. The two countries have witnessed growing friendly contacts and cooperation in the political, economic, military, cultural and health fieldsand maintained close coordination and cooperation in international and regional affairs. The Laotian Government abides by one-China position and supports the Chinese people in the peaceful unification cause of their motherland.

In November 2000, President Jiang Zemin paid a state visit to Laos. As it is the first visit to Laos by the president of China, it stands out as a milestone in the history of bilateral relations. During this visit, the Joint Statement on the bilateral cooperation was signed and subjectd, confirming the development of comprehensive cooperation between the two countries based on long term stability, neighborliness and friendship and mutual trust. connections and cooperation in other areas: There has been good cooperation between the foreign ministries of the two countries, the Chinese and Laotian foreign ministers, respectively visited the other country. Laos opened its consulate-general in Kunming. In 1999, the two countries reached an agreement on Laos opening another consulate-general in Hong Kong (Bouasone, 2008).

Military relations between China and Laos have developed very well. China's military leaders Chi Haotian, Zhang Wannian and Yu Yongbo visited Laos one after another, while Laotian Vice-Premier cum Defence Minister Choummaly and other military leaders visited China many times. Since 1989, China and Laos have signed agreements on cultural and press cooperation as well as memorandums of understanding on cooperation in education, health, broadcasting, film and TV. There were frequent exchanges of visits between performing artists, writers and journalists of the two countries. The two countries started to exchanged students and vocational trainees since 1990.

Economic and trade relations: Over the recent years, China and Laos have seen sound development of their economic and trade relations. Documents on cooperation in trade, investment protection, tourism and automobile transport were signed respectively and the committee on bilateral economic, trade and technological cooperation was set up between the both sides. In 2000, Sino-Laotian trade volume reached US $40.84 million, up 28.8% from the previous yearand in 2001, it rose to US $ 61.87 million, up 51.4% from 2000 (Bouasone, 2008).

Since 1900, Chinese companies started building plants in Laos with their investment. By the end of 2001, the contractual investment had totaled US $75 million, covering such areas as building materials, cultivation and aquicultureand pharma ceutical production. On the other hand, they actively participated in labour and project contracting in Laos, with the contractual total exceeding US$ 0.5 billion. The following however, are the aid projects built by China in Laos: ground station for receiving satellite TV programmes, hydropower station by Namgao River power transmission project and cultural palace of Laos. The project under construction now is the 2nd phase of Vangvieng

Cement Plant and Langprabang Hospital and other projects will come later (Bouasone, 2008).

Border subject: China and Laos share a joint boundary of 500 km long. In October 1991, the two countries signed the Sino-Laotian Boundary, Treaty on the Sino-Laotian Boundary System and Supplementary Protocol to the Treaty on the Sino-Laotian Boundary System. Having found a successful solution to their boundary dispute in a relatively short time through friendly consultations, the governments of the two countries have set an example for states to resolve boundary questions through peaceful talks. The Sino-Laotian boundary has become a peaceful, friendly and stable border (Bouasone, 2008).

7

China's South Asian Diplomacy

The fact that Indo-Sino ties have been noticeable by suspicion and distrust also because of Beijing's strategic ties with Pakistan in the military and nuclear fields makes for a complex brew. On top of it, the tension between Islamabad and New Delhi that resurged after the 2008 Mumbai attacks has made it trickier to walk the tightrope. What China did right was not to take sides nor make pathetic attempts to please either of the two by making unwarranted comments. For instance, Premier Jiabo pointedly refrained from castigating Pakistan in New Delhi unlike Nicholas Sarkozy and David Cameron who gave the Indian media a field day by doing exactly that.

China's increasingly practical diplomacy now includes a renewal of ties with adversaries. Cognisant of India's economic growth and potential, China has astutely set the tone for the next few decades. By earmarking a staggering \$100 billion target in trade by 2015, China and India can only move forward together. The good thing is that such an economic waltz will make it challenging to indulge in arm-twisting on other fronts. It also sets a good precedent for neighbouring Pakistan and India to move beyond the downtrodden path and not allow instigating elements to sabotage the laboriously achieved peace. While Pakistani officials may deny harbouring apprehensions about the Chinese premier's visit to New Delhi, it is only natural that every detail was followed anxiously. Much to their relief, China maintained the status quo in its relations with Pakistan. Even more important than the $25-35 billion worth of trade deals and MoU's signed in Islamabad was China's defence of Pakistan's counter-terrorism policy, likely to prove a bigger boost.

It is not that Beijing is not concerned about the go up of militancy and the threat it poses region-wide, but the Chinese being master players in astuteness, know when to strike the right note. The presence of separatists from China's restive southern Muslim province of Xinjiang in Pakistan's tribal areas is a major concern.

While both states are said to be sharing intelligence on this front, Beijing expects Islamabad to do more to ensure the non-collusion of Chinese anti-state elements with terror groups in the area. Realistically speaking, this is a tall order since it is difficult to monitor the coming and goings from across the border in Afghanistan or even from the northern areas. Despite difficulties, intelligence cooperation was increased manifold as witnessed at the time of the 2008 Beijing Olympics and the recent Shanghai Expo to ward off possible threats.

Pakistan has rightfully reminded Washington that the government in keeping with environmental dynamics will decide the timing of future military operations in North Waziristan. The preposterous increase in US drone strikes besides the consequent build up of pressure on Pakistan with the planned withdrawal of US troops from Afghanistan next year has revealed deeper fissures in the US-Pakistan relationship. Furthermore, the latest allegations pertaining the leak of identity of the CIA station chief by the ISI—(allegedly) in retaliation for the naming of ISI Chief, General Ahmed Shuja Pasha in a criminal case in New York by Mumbai terror victims' families—thereby necessitating his removal from duty is likely to create bigger ripples.

Already the US Afghan Review has shift the focus on Pakistan blaming it for ineptitude and an ambivalent and half-hearted attitude in dealing with home grown and foreign insurgents. China for one was quick to contradict this. Wen Jibao while addressing the Parliament in Islamabad praised Pakistan's role in halting the proliferation of terror and for the sacrifices it has made so far. Instead of lashing out at Pakistan for not doing enough, the Chinese leader urged the (international community to do more to help Pakistan cope with the situation. It maybe that China may have relayed its concerns on the situation to Pakistan's leadership in private differently but it did well not to embarrass its long time ally and friend. Maybe the Americans and its NATO allies could learn a lesson or two from China in diplomacy and dealing with critical allies.

It maybe also be occasion for Pakistan to realise that some of its behaviour patterns are beginning to resemble that of a servile and shackled state, negating the whole purpose of its existence. The US is a friend and ally, not a master. Sadly, over the decades, Pakistan's leadership may have given a contrary impression but that does not translate for the state or the people. It is imperative that the state puts its own house in order and takes a firm stand as far as external diktat is concerned. No sincere leader will find it a problem to unify the masses to jointly take arms against any threat to the state—external and internal. The problem lies in who will don the mantle.

INDIA FALLING BEHIND CHINA IN SOUTH ASIAN DIPLOMACY

India has always been a local superpower, being by far the largest country within South Asia, and is, in fact, the only one in the group that borders every other South Asian country except Afghanistan, which shares a border with Pakistan. But India's economic performance was stunted by years of state control of the kind now prevalent in Iran.

Over the past 15 years, however, economic growth has been strong, enabling the country to have a much greater diplomatic reach than at any time since the 1950s when India briefly emerged as the leader of those countries that were being de-colonized by the European powers. Given this situation, it ought to have been the case that New Delhi would be preeminent in its own backyard. Instead, over the past two decades, India has lost the status of being the lead player in any South Asian country barring Bhutan, a country with which it still has a treaty relationship. In almost the entire region, China has overtaken India in that intangible quality - influence - especially in Nepal and Sri Lanka, while Beijing's existing alliances with Pakistan and Bangladesh are growing stronger.

This is not due to a lack of quality within India's diplomatic service. Instead, the Indian Foreign Service (IFS) has produced a modern corps of skilled diplomats, many experts in different regions of the world, and eager to do more to advance their country's interests. The wall they face is the ambivalence that has become second nature to the country's top policy makers, both within the political crust as well as the administrative backup. Phrases such as "going all the way" and "going for the kill" are inelegant. Yet they represent a reality that is that sometimes a country has to formulate and then determinedly implement a clear policy to be carried out till success is achieved.

In South Asia, such a quality was recently displayed by President Percy Mahinda Rajapaksa of Sri Lanka. He succeeded in wiping out the terrorist group known as the Liberation Tigers of Tamil Eelam (LTTE) where, over the past three decades, all his predecessors had failed. Unlike them, President Rajapaksa did not heed (well-meaning but disastrous) advice to slow down his offensive or agree to a cease-fire, the latter being a device that the LTTE used since 1987 to gain time to recover after having lost the initiative in the field. Once the LTTE recovered its strength, the ceasefire would be abandoned. This point was repeatedly made by Rajapaksa to the peacemakers who clustered around him, especially in the final months of the brief, brutal war against the LTTE that began with his coming to office in 2005.

Once India, because of political considerations such as the need to avoid alienating the country's sizable Tamil population, refused to give the Sri Lankan army equipment, Rajapaksa turned to Pakistan and China. Both countries opened their warehouses to him, and so built up immense capital both within Sri Lanka's Sinhala most importantity as well as the country's policy establishment. Rajapaksa showed none of the half-heartedness that has characterized so much of Indian policy and, as a result, emerged a winner. In the case of India, the desire to win brownie points with key international players (by heeding their sometimes incorrect advice) as well as an aversion to risk ensured that much of Indian diplomacy was too watered down to be effective. This is especially the case in its immediate neighbourhood.

This on-again, off-again excellence can be seen in Indian diplomatic policy towards Pakistan especially in regard to the long-term pattern of instituting confidence building measures (CBM) being followed - usually after a mass terror attack - with strong rhetoric and a withdrawal of contact.

The reality is that in the case of Pakistan, conventional war may have ceased to be an option. This is because the Pakistan army has itself lost control of many of the jihadis that it has trained, equipped and funded for so long.

Instead of reducing the risk of a terror attack, going after the Pakistan military would inflame a large segment of the Pakistani population thus making them susceptible to recruitment in the ongoing jihad against India.

Given that situation, it may have been preferable for Indian policymakers to publicly resort to a conventional war except in the case of a conflict started by Pakistan, an unlikely possibility. The military option would work only if (a) the Pakistan army controls the jihadi networks and (b) is comprehensively defeated in battle. Neither condition exists.

A "No War" declaration by India would remove the Pakistani military establishment's most frequently used excuse to station more than 60 percent of its army along the India border, even as the force is engaged in a life-and-death struggle with the Pakistan Taliban.

Instead, even though New Delhi has no intention of going to war, the prospect of one is deliberately kept open especially after terror strikes such as Mumbai 11/26-28. Thus, the benefits of India's "No War" declaration are denied, while the other side is aware that the mock-aggressive posture is a bluff and hence will not change its behaviour as a result of the threat.

A glaring example of how promoting the idea that India would go to war over Pakistani provocations has hurt New Delhi can be seen in the 2002 standoff with Pakistan in the mountains separating the two. Ostensibly to scare the international community into putting pressure on Pakistan to call off its Kashmir jihad, the then-Vajpayee government mobilized two Indian army strike corps on the border, keeping them and their support units on a hair-trigger alert for the greater part of the year. Aware that the Indians were bluffing, the Pakistan government refused to budge from its policy of helping jihadists active in Kashmir. The long Indian army mobilization created a perception of regional instability that affected India's status as a safe investment destination even as it exhausted the elite army units on the front line. Given the information that India would not attack, the 2002 mobilization came at a horrendous cost and no benefit.

In a system where posturing comes easily to the higher levels of the Indian policy establishment, Prime Minister Manmohan Singh has thus far resisted jingoism and has made it evident that India would not be stampeded into military action. In the case of Sri Lanka, the policy was to intensify conflict until victory. What is needed is a clear policy that is carried out effectively, not a zig-zag routine that confuses the international community and results in a loss of credibility for India.

Military sales can become an effective instrument of diplomacy, were they deployed by India. Within the region, including in Sri Lanka and Nepal, the military is a significant component of the policy process, often the crucial player. Because of New Delhi's longstanding policy of not permitting foreign military sales save for exceptional situations, China has been provided an opportunity to fill the gap. Had Bangladesh, Nepal and Sri Lanka been more reliant on Indian equipment and training for their armed forces, New Delhi would have been in a much stronger position to influence policy in those places than it is today. Instead, the "weapons gap" isincreasingly being filled by China.

The mantra of "non-alignment" has in most instances become a cover for lack of action. Even during the period of the Cold War, when India suffered many of the consequences of being seen as a Soviet ally, not a single Soviet soldier was ever stationed in India or trained here, nor did any Indian soldier undertake any sort of mission in the USSR. In contrast, there are regular exchanges of U.S. and Indian soldiers and joint training exercises have become routine. The warming of ties is because there is a natural fit between the two sides. India has a significant pool of trained (and trainable) manpower, while the United States has abundant stocks of equipment that could be transferred to New Delhi rather than mothballed or left under-utilized. This is especially the case with naval vessels, where India is now being made to pay $3 billion for a secondhand Russian aircraft carrier that it is finding it difficult to float and move at the same time.

Progress in U.S.-India military to military relatives has been slow and is still far below its potential in substantial part because of the wariness of the Indian establishment over China's reaction. Compare this with Pakistan which has built up close military ties with both China and the United States, its friendship with one not affecting the other. In the military field, the choice is between going with the United States or going alone, because a military alliance with China is not an option. Beijing sees New Delhi as a potential competitor and has repeatedly shown through its actions its commitment to a strategic policy that inhibits the growth of Indian power. Unfortunately, in this case, Indian ambivalence is now being matched by the United States under the Obama administration, which has downgraded ties with India to a level much below that set under President George W. Bush. It seems inevitable, however, that both countries will, hopefully within the present presidential term, awaken to the need for a partnership that can ensure that Asia does not fall under the sway of any single power.

The persistent Indian ambivalence in policy was visible in Sri Lanka, where India simultaneously called for a cease-fire while backing the unity of the island nation. As a consequence of simultaneously conveying two contradictory messages, neither the Tamil nor the Sinhala zealots have anything other than distaste for India, while the abundant provision of military supplies has led the Sri Lankan military towards becoming as close to Beijing as are their counterparts in Pakistan.

In Nepal, after first helping to get King Gyanendra to abdicate, New Delhi threw its support behind the Maoists, who promptly reacted by threatening to scrap the India-Nepal agreement and replace it with a similar deal with China. After its embrace of the Maoists, which ended only after their tilt to Beijing became manifest (by the end of 2008), no other Nepali party is willing to trust New Delhi and see it as a reliable partner, even the once-friendly Nepali Congress. Meanwhile, in a show of deft footwork, Chinese diplomats have been active in Kathmandu renewing ties with the non-Maoist parties that today run the government (after the departure of the Maoists), so as to accelerate the growth of PRC influence in Nepal.

Today, there are almost as many radical training camps located within Bangladesh as there in Pakistan, camps whose specific purpose is to replenish the stream of jihadis into India. Yet, unlike in the case of Pakistan, the Indian government is not posturing as if was is likely. A hostile Pakistan, an unfriendly Bangladesh, and Nepal and Sri Lanka heading towards the PRC.

These are the wages of a diplomacy that refuses to go for the jugular in the pursuit of objectives, but almost invariably crafts a compromise that gives much less geopolitical benefit. India presents an example of how a most important power that avoids a clear policy line or a better deployment of its assets gives way to the other who is ruthless and willing to complete the marathon rather than slow down and stop before the finish line. Such a policy is the delight of politicians and anathema to statesmen, who understand the need for not just vision, but for will and perseverance.

INDIA IN CHINA'S "NEW AGE DIPLOMACY"

India needs to carefully monitor China's "New age diplomacy", a new slogan, being energetically pushed by the sixth generation leadership of President Xi Jinping and Premier Li Leqiang. The 'blue book' published by China's top think tank, the Chinese Academy of Social Sciences (CASS), looks squarely at the Indian Ocean Region, its littoral states, and India's 'Look East' policy. Although the blue book is not yet available in India in an English translated version, media reports from Beijing suggests it is concerned that China was falling behind India and the US in the strategic domination of the Indian Ocean. It warns that if India, the US and China did not engage each other in this region then the Indian Ocean will become an Ocean of conflict.

The book also exhibits some concerns about India's Look East Policy. The Chinese official media has been showing some discomfort with this. In fact, this issue became prominent when Prime Minister Manmohan Singh visited Japan recently for upgrading of India-Japan relations to a new level. Liu Zhangyi, a research fellow at the Shanghai Institute of International Studies (SIS), an important think tank, wrote this in the official Global Times (May 31): "As an embodiment of the Look East Policy, India has strengthened economic, strategic and security co-operation with countries like Japan, South Korea and Vietnam. It has interfered in the South China Sea disputes in a high profile manner against the backdrop of the US pivot to Asia. Some Indian scholars acknowledge that some parts of the Look East Policy target China".

To make things clear, the 'blue book' produced by the CASS is not an official publication. But the CASS is finally under the Communist Party and the government, and the President of CASS holds a position equivalent to a member of the politburo of the Party Central Committee. Such books and papers are produced as per the parameters laid down by the establishment not only for the consideration of the policy makers, but also to elicit reactions from abroad.

The media is fully in control of the Party and the government, though views of powerful factions on internal issues are also carried by them. A Party propaganda department directive announced earlier this year that the media is not independent and serves the Party and the government.

Before Premier Li Keqiang embarked on his historic (historic, because it was the first time that a top Chinese leaders made India the first stop on his maiden foreign trip) to India, the authentic Party mouthpiece, the People's Daily (May 14) said China's diplomatic stance "especially in the matter of core interests" had become "strong and bold". The article gave several reasons for this boldness including its comprehensive national power with its military strength increasing by the day, and a clear understanding of "enemies and friends" in its diplomatic strategy. Very interestingly, the article added maritime security had become China's focus, and its diplomacy had become "particularly ruthless" in protecting its maritime interests. The reference was obviously to Japan over the Senkaku/Diaoyu Islands' sovereignty issue and South China Sea disputes.

The Li Keqiang visit did not yield any spectacular result, nor was it expected to. The visit was proposed by Xi Jinping to Manmohan Singh at the BRICS Summit in the last week of March, and he arrived in India on May 20.

The visit was initially clouded by the establishing of a camp by a Chinese People's Liberation Army (PLA) battalion on April 15 at Daulat Beg Oldi (DBO) in the Western Sector of the India-China border, in India's perceived side of the Line of Actual Control (LAC). The incident made news in the Indian media though not a word was mentioned in the Chinese media. From the military point of view it did not appear the PLA detachment had come to engage the Indian border troops. They had no back up. It can, therefore, be concluded that they came in to make a point – that the Indians should not think the border issue was going to be smooth.

In this connection it may be recalled that on the last day of Prime Minister Vajpayee's visit to China in 2003, a PLA detachment surrounded an Indian non-army patrol in the Eastern Sector, disarmed them, and sent them back with a lecture. Only one Indian newspaper reported the incident which was, otherwise, brushed under the carpet by the Indian government.

The Chinese should have been very happy by Prime Minister Vajpayee's visit to China in 2003. He had signed off India's Tibet position by signing on the dotted lines presented by the Chinese. But the incident in the Eastern Sector conveyed the message that it was not enough.

Premier Li's visit and the joint statement with Prime Minister Singh would suggest the resolution of the border issue has been put on the fast track. It is, however, difficult to accept this assumption. Certainly, Prime Minister Singh told Premier Li that the Chinese camping in DBO was not acceptable and should not recur. He also asked that China work to correct the huge imbalance in bilateral trade, and open up China's markets to Indian exports. Premier Li agreed to work on both. Given China's track record with other countries, India will be frustrated on both accounts.

Li Keqiang came with a business delegation of exporters and investors interested especially in the Indian infrastructure area which has huge potential. The Indian side, however, appears to have shied away from critical issues. These include Chinese obstruction to India's membership of the Nuclear Suppliers Group (NSG), Chinese constructions in POK which is a disputed territory, Chinese opposition to India's membership of an expanded permanent UN Security Council, among many others. This includes the strategic river flows from China to India, a lower riparian. Equally important is the issue of China's nuclear empowerment of Pakistan in the weaponization sector with Beijing having set up four plutonium processing plants in Pakistan according to international observers.

Li Keqiang went to Pakistan from India reassuring Islamabad that his visit to India in no way reduces their "all weather" friendship. The visit detailed that China was poised to establish a much stronger position in Pakistan, considered an IOR littoral state and gateway to the Gulf and West Asia.

China has been concerned for quite some time now, especially after the India-US nuclear deal, up-gradation of India-US defence co-operation including joint military/naval exercises, and a possible India-US-Japan coalition to encircle China.

The CASS 'blue book' is not correct in saying that China lags behind in the Indian Ocean region while India has made significant progress from South East Asia to East Asia and North East Asia.

The truth is the other way round. For decades China has tried and succeeded in keeping India enclosed in South Asia, using India's neighbours and keeping Pakistan as the anchor. China and Sri Lanka entered into a strategic co-operation partnership when Prime Minister Manmohan Singh was in Tokyo. The co-operation includes co-operation in security and defence. China's push into Nepal to reduce India's influence is well known. In the mid-1990s, China had devised a policy to gain in Indian Ocean Rim countries through cheap or free military transfers to encircle India. This policy is not dead, but a more sophisticated policy with more than one military dimension is in the offing.

Li Keqiang wanted India to support its claims in the South China Sea. This was a preposterous suggestion. India cannot afford to support the Chinese demand which will close one of the busiest international commercial maritime routes. If China objects to Indian oil companies exploring in Vietnamese waters for oil and gas, it will be against all international laws.

There is an apprehension in Beijing that India will be a partner to Japanese Prime Minister Shinzo Abe's "democratic security diamond" comprising Japan, the US, India and Australia. China should have understood that such a security concept no longer exists, and India's independent foreign policy will persist. On the other hand, India has never objected to

China's relations with India's neighbours even when they were pointedly inimical to India.

India has historical relationship with most of the South East Asian countries which were based on culture and trade, and not war. India has never tried to teach any country a "lesson" which China has done on record.

India and Japan, and also the other countries need each other for natural development. The problem is that China wants to dominate Asia. No one wants to contain China, and a collapsed China will be a much bigger threat than a strong China. But if this strength translates into dominance, there will be trouble. India and China are the two biggest countries in Asia. Both have to work together. If China tries to restrict India it will only be inviting a serious problem. China must stop strategizing in cold war terms. The "I, me, and mine" syndrome has to be dropped.

INDIA-US NUCLEAR DEAL – THE DIPLOMACY-CULTURAL CONTEXT

A cross-cultural analysis of current issues in the India-United States nuclear deal will demonstrate that there are two key issues that have cropped up in recent days that merit a better understanding of the calculus of the negotiations that are going on to consummate the civil nuclear cooperation between the US and India. Both the issues must be examined with the lens of cross-cultural communications to explain such baffling developments.

Two Key Issues

The first is the question of why the Americans are adding conditions after conditions to the deal, which supposedly has been agreed to between the two governments at the highest levels?

The second is why several lawmakers in the US are seemingly supportive of the deal, yet there is no action on the ground ? A large part of the answer to both these questions lies in cross-cultural communications. Let us first deal with the seeming propensity of American interlocutors to add conditions to the deal even while India keeps fending off such amendments or additions.

The latest spanner in the works is the insistence by American interlocutors that India should return any material or equipment acquired under the deal if either side terminates the deal or is perceived to be in violation of the letter or spirit of the agreement for cooperation in civil nuclear energy.

The diplomacy in public, and public diplomacy, over the next few days on this issue can be well forecast — bowing to its domestic constituencies, India will need to publicly reject such a proposal, and the US State Department will probably have to go back to the drawing board. Such a tango on several propositions between the US and India has already played out often in the public sphere and one can safely hazard a guess that this latest proposal too will meet a similar fate.

Remember the brouhaha about the 123 agreement a few weeks ago? (Taking away India's rights for nuke tests.) Once it became known that the American interlocutors were keen on including that as one of the conditions of the deal, India's response was an immediate and reflexive public denial and rejection. So, why are such conditions being added to the deal on an ongoing basis?

The Culture Context

The US is traditionally a "low context" culture, whereas India is typically a "high context" culture. A low context culture assumes no context to any relationship and safeguards itself by spelling out each and every term of the relationship on paper.

High context cultures, on the other hand, assume that there is a significant context and trust to the relationship, and therefore do not reduce the complete understanding to pen and paper.

When the US President, Mr George Bush, and the Prime Minister, Dr Manmohan Singh, signed the nuclear framework, it was signed in an atmosphere of high context — where the overall context and trust of the relationship was deemed primary and the contractual details were deemed secondary. This approach suited the Indians well.

On the other hand, the Americans, once back home just to be sure, started drafting the detailed contractual terms. Of course, pressure from lawmakers and opponents of the deal in the US added to the clauses in the fine-print and therefore the American approach clashed with the Indian approach.

So, given the propensity of a culture to crossing the *t's* and dotting the *i's* of an agreement, propelled by the opponents of the deal, it is but obvious that such conditions will keep on creeping into the agreement.

'Yes' but 'no'

The second trend, which is lately coming into public view, pertains to the fact that several lawmakers are seemingly supportive of the deal and yet when rubber hits the road, they are not in favour of voting to approve the deal, as it is being presented by the US administration. Statements or sound bytes such as, "I support closer US-India relations and also support civil nuclear cooperation", that are often reported and understood by many in India as being supportive of the deal, are in fact misleading for those who do not understand American culture.

Sure, they are supportive of nuclear cooperation with India and sure they support Mr Bush's pioneering efforts to transform US India relations, but do they support the exact deal, which has been presented by the US administration?

The answer in many cases is a resounding no. They support nuclear cooperation, but they have concerns or they wish to add certain clauses, or they wish to wait and see the final draft submitted to the Congress.

The enthusiasm of many proponents of the deal and the fast paced sound-byte-driven media cycles miss out on the cultural context in which the statements are being made by the US lawmakers. The fine-tuned and nuanced communication style of the US lawmakers is well understood within American culture; however, it can be misleading for the Indians. The relations between the US and India are truly on an inflexion point — a good deal between the two nations will offer a plethora of dividends for both, though there may be some interests being compromised by both. However, a non-deal will lead to an altogether different orbit for India in international affairs. Not to say that that orbit will be good or bad for US-India relations, but it certainly will be a different path.

Anyone who has participated in strategic dialogues between the two countries will tell you that the primary aspect that concerns Indian leadership the most about America is the issue of trust. Trust is the cornerstone of the whole issue. Crossing the *t's* and dotting the *i's* are the premise of low context cultures. A fusion of the two is now needed.

THE LIMITS OF CHINESE POWER IN SOUTHEAST ASIA

That China is one of the most powerful states in the world is no longer a contested claim, but cataloguing China's increasing material resources does not in itself demonstrate that China is powerful. Southeast Asia presents an apparently 'easy' case for investigating China's rising power. Given the significant asymmetry of power, if China's power has grown we would expect to see altered preferences and behaviour among these weaker neighbours in response to coercion, persuasion or inducement. Results so far are mixed. While China has been able to harness much of the region's economic energy in a favourable direction, it does not always get its way in territorial and resource conflicts.

In mainland Southeast Asia, China's participation makes feasible region-wide economic development plans for the Greater Mekong Subregion initiative of the Asian Development Bank, drawing international investment for infrastructural projects. These connect the poorer states — Cambodia, Laos and Vietnam — to the markets of China and Thailand while improving China's access to raw material supplies and ports in the Indian Ocean and East China Sea. These schemes also spur Japanese and American interest and investment in Mekong regionalism. More prominently, China's initiative for an FTA with ASEAN overcame the nagging problem of galvanising an economic integration project. When it came into effect in 2010, the China-ASEAN FTA formed the world's largest free trade area, comprising 1.9 billion consumers and US$4.3 trillion in trade.

Situations in which the pre-existing preferences of other states are unclear or undecided — such as the 1990s debate about whether rising China was a threat — present opportunities for China to influence its neighbours by persuading them that its own narrative is more accurate and certainly more profitable. This campaign, from the mid-1990s, involved an alternative narrative about China's cooperative New Security Idea, and its 'peaceful rise' or 'peaceful development' as it strives for a 'harmonious world.' The message was intended to reassure neighbours that China's resurgence would not threaten their economic or security interests because of its peaceful intentions, limited national capabilities, mutually beneficial development trajectory and pluralist international mindset.

Rhetoric was accompanied by policy action. In Southeast Asia, China negotiated land (though not maritime) border disputes with Vietnam; fully participated in ASEAN institutions; and undertook highly publicised restraint and aid during the 1997 and 2009 financial crises. China's persuasive power encompassed economic inducement. Its China-ASEAN FTA Early Harvest Programmes with some ASEAN countries — the partial lifting of trade barriers on selected goods — is portrayed by Chinese analysts as China 'giving more and taking less', working towards harmony and enrichment of its neighbours.

Yet there are limits to how much policymakers in Southeast Asian states are reassured regarding the China threat. China's power to persuade is rooted in its ability to sustain benign policy action. Apart from efforts to offset some of the adverse effects of Chinese economic competition, China's neighbours are also watching its behaviour in more serious conflicts of interest. The best way to gauge the change of power into influence is in cases where the powerful actor causes another actor to change policy on a significant subject of disagreement. In the case of China and Southeast Asia, such subjects include policies on Taiwan, defence relations with the US and policies on territorial disputes. On these potential hard cases, it is difficult to find significant changes in Southeast Asian states' policies in response to Chinese actions to date.

Of these, China has expended most effort in the disputes over atolls in the South China Sea. China and ASEAN agreed to a Declaration of Conduct in 2002, committing to peaceful negotiations. Yet the Chinese navy continued manoeuvres to assert its claims, leading to skirmishes with Vietnam and the Philippines. Two months into a Vietnamese concession to develop gas fields off the Vietnamese coast in 2007, BP suspended operations, reportedly as a result of Chinese threats to exclude it from future energy deals in China. In March this year, Chinese naval vessels tried to interrupt oil exploration by the Philippines in waters that Manila considers its own.

At a regional defence ministers' meeting in June 2010, statements suggesting that China now regards the South China Sea as part of its 'core national sovereignty interests' led US Secretary of Defence Robert Gates to warn that the US 'oppose[s] the use of force and action that hinder freedom of navigation.' One month later, Secretary of State Hillary Clinton reiterated US 'national interest' in the peaceful resolution of these multilateral disputes. In September 2010, after the Japanese Coast Guard detained a Chinese fishing trawler for allegedly intruding into Japanese waters, a Sino–Japanese standoff ensued. One direct result was the further strengthening of US interest in China's behaviour in maritime disputes. The Obama administration publicly affirmed that the US-Japan treaty umbrella extends to the Senkaku/Diaoyu Islands and reiterated the importance of peaceful dispute resolution, freedom of navigation and respect for international maritime laws in the South China Sea.

China's behaviour in these disputes constitutes a critical test of its intentions, and its hard line backfired seriously in that it led to a closing of ranks across Southeast Asia, Japan and the US. Beijing's actions lend weight to regional pessimists who are not persuaded of its peaceful rise, and sustained coercive action may prompt its neighbours towards the very containment policies that it wishes to avoid.

So far, there are few good cases of China making Southeast Asian states do what they otherwise did not want to do. Alongside Beijing's successful record of persuasion and inducement, it has shown caution in exerting pressure on its neighbours with the most challenging subjects. The recent backlash in the South China Sea is likely to make Beijing more cautious. China's still limited military capacity provides an important explanation since, particularly in the maritime access and security arena, the presence of the US still serves as a significant deterrent.

GLOBAL DIPLOMACY AND EMERGENCE OF PLURALISM

The emergence of pluralism as an idea is not as early as the emergence of those influential religions, like Christian or Islam, although it has close relations with them. In oriental world, the religious diversity was a case, accordingly, those different religions in some time could not exist peacefully. In 3 century B.C., the India's king Asoka issued one order, which seems the first code of tolerance that set the base of religious pluralism in that region, through which Buddhism and Brahmanism could be preserved and boomed in their own ways in one society. If examining another important oriental country—China, it's interested to find that there is almost no religious persecution in history and the religious pluralism is almost accepted by both governors and publics in any dynasties.

But in the West, pluralism was discarded by Christians in the Middle Age. The diversity of religion in ancient Greece or Rome was not a myth, yet with the rising of Christian, tolerance and religious pluralism was not accepted. Typically after the Christian was legitimized in late Rome Empire and after the consolidation of Vatican's authority, religious pluralism was absolutely more unlikely in Europe. Even the movement of religious reforms led by Luther and Calvin in 16 century was not aimed at diffusing values of tolerance and religious pluralism, but at building protest's authority and expanding secular power. However, renaissance (14-16 centuries), religious reforms (16 century), and especially the enlightenment movement (18 century) lead by those famous Western thinkers with modern ideas, finally paved a road to the religious pluralism. From then, religious pluralism have become a very important modern value adhered not by religious but by secular world. When religious pluralism was consolidated in modern society, the diversity of religion is permitted or even encouraged, and no single religious code has the superiority to others' to explain the truth or to predict the future of humankind beings.

Around the 20th century, pluralism was also used to examine the political issues. British political scientist Harold J. Laski is famous to challenge the traditional political research based on state theory, with using the conception of pluralism. In accordance with his argument, state is not the single actor to practice sovereignty, and other societal actors like labour union and political parties are as important as the state—government is its representative—to control and manage the whole affairs of the state. His idea on political pluralism was also advocated by another famous scholar, the French lord Tocqueville who in his work on US argued that interests groups were also influential on policy-making and decision in US. To some extent, corporatism has shared some ideas with political pluralism, since both highlights the importance of societal groups for public affairs.

According to the meaning of pluralism, international pluralism should indicate the equality of different ideologies or values and international actors. Based on this idea, the intended expansion or penetration of social ethics, political systems, and social customs that are popular within one state to another country is not legitimate. Meanwhile, all states in the world are equal in sense of sovereignty, meanwhile, all international actors are equal to participate in global governance. Notwithstanding, the question maybe will be come here is that how those conflicted values or ideologies co-exist peacefully in international society, and how those non-governmental organizations share power with states in global governance? As for the first question, clearly the conflicted values and ideologies are very hard to compromise to each other, for example, the conflict between socialist camp and the capitalist camp that was happened in the Cold War era and the conflict between Christian world and Islamic world in the post-Cold War era, yet in light of international pluralism, international society should admit the equality of different values and ideologies in the world at first before solving the conflicts. Only based on equality, there would be a chance for each value or ideology to evolve in its own way and compete with one another in international community. Non-tolerance toward diverse values and ideologies and non-respect for equality of them give rise to many potential international conflicts and violence.

However, another more important question be supposed to be taken into consideration: does international pluralism imply there are no any shared international values and ideologies? If examining the concept of pluralism, we're unfortunate to find that pluralism always leads to human's misunderstanding on many issues, because this idea often makes people slide into relativist and even nihilist, when it's used to examine the diversity of values and ideologies. Anyway, this is a hard question that has been presented for several centuries and has not been answered implicitly yet. However, international pluralism which adheres to the equality of and the tolerance toward diverse values and ideologies is much better than inequality of and non-tolerance toward them. Actually, there are shared values and ideologies in international society. Thus although the international pluralism cannot explain or predict this reality, it can give a way for peaceful competition of these diverse values and ideologies in international society.

As for the second question, contemporary global governance with the participation of NGOs is one practice of the international pluralism. These non-state international actors are playing more and more important roles in this trans-national governance, especially in those so-called "low political" fields. As someone argues that one " important trend in international law is the expanding access to international legal fora by non-state actors". The multilateral structure of this governance is challenging nation-state's ability and legitimacy, pressing it to adjust and reform itself to apply to this new structure in globalized age.

Of course, equality of power is as well stressed by international pluralism in which sovereignty is one basic principle that international society should strictly adhere in order to keep national interests and respect for diverse cultures, values and ideologies. As one tactic of weak social group, pluralism was always used to fight against vested interests groups for more rights and power. In history, those strongest religions or political parties never actively agreed to give rights or power to their heretics or enemies if without strong exterior pressures. So in international society, only relatively weak states are willing to utilize pluralism as the approach to gain national interests and prevent their sovereign independence and equality from being attacked and harmed. Further speaking, pluralism in international society used by weak countries is aimed at fighting against international injustice such as the inequality of states, hegemonic intervention in domestic affairs, imperialist cultural penetration, and so forth.

RISE OF A MULTI-POLAR ASIA: A VIEW FROM INDIA

Continuing tensions over Ukraine notwithstanding, including a US-led boycott of the Victory Day Parade commemorating the 70th anniversary of Germany's surrender in World War II, Russia under President Vladimir Putin has retrieved much of its eminence as a great power and even managed a handsome recovery of its sanction-hit rouble. By tweaking its West-centric gaze towards Siberia and the Arctic (which Putin likely visited during a mysterious absence some weeks ago); towards Asia, the Middle East, South America and Africa, Moscow straddles a multipolar world and a multipolar

Asia. Given that the bulk of its vast territories embrace the Asian landmass, it would be a mistake not to think of Russia as an Asian power.

The reality that it is already a multipolar Asia would not have escaped Beijing, which in recent years is expanding its global footprint while seeking a commanding presence in its Asian neighbourhood. Given its deep economic and strategic ties with Moscow, Beijing obviously recognises that Russia will pursue its interests in Central Asia, Europe, Iran and the Islamic world, with India, and elsewhere.

The People's Republic will have to accept that there is no escape from sharing eminence with rising powers like India and Iran, which, like Russia and China, share strategic and economic interests in the same regions. Nor will it be possible to exclude countries like Japan, Vietnam, Australia, Indonesia and Malaysia, to name a few, from pursuing their interests in the Asia-Pacific. The Chinese leadership will therefore have to come to terms with the fact that Beijing is unlikely to enjoy the 'sole superpower' status that the United States briefly enjoyed after the collapse of the Soviet Union in 1991.

Currently, Beijing resents India's assertiveness in Asia and even more in the Indian Ocean where India has a commanding presence by virtue of its geographical location. More importantly, many countries feel less threatened by the rise of India and favour New Delhi assuming greater responsibilities in protecting the sea-lanes from the African coast to the Indonesian islands. India is accordingly prioritising modernisation of its navy and air force. By scaling down the strength of the new mountain strike force from a proposed 90,000 to around 30,000 troops, the Modi government has defanged the hardliners who were upping the ante on the border dispute with China, both before and during his visit to that country.

The Indo-China border dispute, a legacy of the British Raj, has been made intractable by China's annexation of Tibet and acquisition of Indian territory (Aksai Chin, to consolidate its hold on Tibet) from Pakistan, which the latter has illegally occupied in contravention of UN Resolutions. This unresolved dispute has been aggravated by Beijing nibbling at Indian territory in Ladakh (Jammu & Kashmir) in recent years.

In April 2015, Beijing announced an ambitious China-Pakistan Economic Corridor from its Xinjiang province to the Gwadar port in Baluchistan (Pakistan), via Gilgit-Baltistan which legally belongs to India, being part of the erstwhile princely State of Jammu & Kashmir. The plan is to link its New Silk Road and Maritime Silk Road ('One Belt, One Road') initiatives with Central Asia and later the Middle East, Europe, and Africa. While professional Cassandras loudly declaimed that China was challenging India in her maritime backyard (Arabian Sea), they omitted to mention that New Delhi is investing $100 million to develop the Chabahar Port in Iran, which will grant it access to Afghanistan and Central Asia, bypassing Pakistan. China's proposed corridor has, however, sparked deep resentment in Gilgit-Baltistan and may not be easy to implement. New Delhi summoned the Chinese envoy to protest against this project. However, the earthquake that that struck Nepal on April 26, with strong aftershocks hitting the region even after three weeks, could affect the viability of projects in this mountainous region.

There is also real danger from jihadist outfits that Pakistan has nurtured in pursuit of its strategic objectives in Afghanistan and India. Central Asia is the new frontier of radical Islam; Chechnya, Fergana, and Xinjiang are the new recruiting ground for the Islamic State in Iraq and Syria (ISIS), which recently established a base in the Afghanistan badlands. Hence, Russia, China, Iran, and India will have to cooperate in fighting the jihadi menace.

Chinese claims on the Indian State of Arunachal Pradesh – first articulated in 2006 when it was called South Tibet – are a baseless tactic to pressurise India. The claims were rebutted by the 14th Dalai Lama, who asserted that Arunachal Pradesh was historically never a part of Tibet. The claim seems to be a ruse to avert a situation in which Tibetans claim that the next incarnation of the aged Dalai Lama is born in territory outside Chinese control (the sixth Dalai Lama, Tsangyang Gyatso, was born near the Tawang monastery in Arunachal Pradesh). As an aside, one may mention that India's Kushan empire included Kashgar (Kashi), Khotan and Yarkant in the Tarim Basin, and Kushan control over the road from China to Gandhara (Afghanistan) facilitated trade and travel across the Khunjerab Pass and enabled the spread of Mahayana Buddhism to China.

While Beijing's hostility to Prime Minister Narendra Modi's visit to Arunachal Pradesh in February this year was unwarranted, it suggested that there would be no forward movement on the border issue, notwithstanding the high optics accompanying Modi's visit (May 14-16), which began with a trip to President Xi Jinping's hometown of Xi'an, from where Xuanzang set off for a pilgrimage of important Buddhist sites in India in the seventh century, and even arrived at a monastery in Modi's hometown, Vadnagar, Gujarat. But Xi'an is also the new axis of power in China, with three of the seven top leaders of the politburo standing committee, eight of 25 politburo members and four out of 11 members of the central military commission belonging to the 'Shaanxi group'.

Shrewd and pragmatic, Modi refused to allow establishment hawks to dictate the terms of engagement and accorded priority to civilisational, commercial, and civilian ties. At the Tsinghua University on the last day of his tour, he articulated the Indian position on all issues firmly while moving to improve bilateral trade and investment opportunities. India, he said, currently enjoys a growth rate of 7.5 per cent and is working to create next generation infrastructure – roads, ports, railways, airports, telecom, digital networks and clean energy. Yet, he said, it is imperative to bridge the doubts and distrust in the relationship, to settle the boundary quickly, and to first settle the ambiguity regarding the Line of Actual Control.

Modi specifically mentioned the tensions over trans-border rivers (from the Himalayas) and unilaterally extended electronic tourist visas to Chinese citizens, even as critics bemoaned the stapled visas for Indians from Jammu & Kashmir and Arunachal Pradesh. He refused to let Pakistan's growing strategic relationship with Beijing derail his engagement with China and remained focused on his larger perspectives: he inked fresh deals worth $22 billion (in addition to previously pledged investments of $20 billion), and sought China's support for India's permanent membership of a reformed UN Security Council and the Nuclear Suppliers Group.

A signature theme of India's security establishment for over a decade has been China's 'string of pearls' strategy to encircle India, a reference to China's growing ties with Sri Lanka, Myanmar, Bangladesh and Pakistan.

The decibels rose sharply when China began building the Hambantota port in Sri Lanka (a project declined by India) and again when, in 2014, then President Rajapaksa twice permitted a Chinese nuclear submarine to dock at the island nation. Modi intervened, quietly but decisively, and after Maithripala Sirisena came to power, the Colombo port project with China was deferred and the Mattala Rajapaksa International Airport, opened in 2013 with a Chinese investment of $200 million, rendered defunct.

Actually, an undue pessimism pervades India's security establishment because it continues to harbour a Nehruvian worldview, and has not been able to overcome the trauma of defeat in 1962. Yet, when the then Prime Minister Atal Bihari Vajpayee visited China in June 2003, he secured Chinese recognition of Indian sovereignty over Sikkim (which it once disputed), and for the first time since 1960, both sides appointed special representatives (SR) to negotiate the boundary dispute. In 2013 and 2014, China agreed to pull back its soldiers from eastern Ladakh.

In recent times, India's engagement with Russia has appeared rather muted. But the day before the Prime Minister left for China, President Putin telephoned him and Modi confirmed his participation in the forthcoming BRICS summit and Shanghai Cooperation Organisation summit, both in Ufa, in July. New Delhi's quest for full membership of the SCO may be approved at this meeting. The two leaders also discussed a range of issues concerning expansion of the Russia-India privileged strategic partnership.

Indeed, Russia, China and India and even Iran have converging interests in stabilising Afghanistan and curbing its multi-billion dollar drug trade, as well as containing terrorism in Central Asia and the neighbourhood. India does not endorse the Western line on Iran, Syria or Ukraine; at Fortaleza, Brazil (August 2014), Modi reportedly assured Putin that he would not support the US/EU (not UN) sanctions against Russia.

Fortaleza was Modi's first global engagement after coming to power, and it was here that the members decided to launch the New Development Bank with a $100 billion fund and currency reserve pool of $100 billion, to help third world countries access loans without 'unfair' conditions imposed by West-dominated multilateral financial institutions such as the World Bank, International Monetary Fund and Asian Development Bank. India has appointed KV Kamath as the first chief of the Shanghai-based bank. China's ambitious Asian Infrastructure Investment Bank (AIIB), mooted in 2013 to support infrastructural projects in the region, has acquired over 40 members, including America's western allies who are keen for Chinese investments and trade.

Modi was quick to understand that the coming era belongs to the non-West and is keen to receive the fruits of the Russia-India-China (RIC) grouping. Russia is reportedly keen on an India-China rapprochement, so that the RIC can emerge as an economic and strategic axis that can challenge the dominant West, especially the United States. To be stable and viable, such an alliance needs Iran (RICI), which is a force to be reckoned with in the Gulf region. The interests of all four nations converge in many areas.

In fact, China's One Belt One Road, India's Cotton Route and Project Mausam, and the Russian-led Eurasian Economic Union (EEU), are all complementary projects based on the old land and sea-based trade routes of the ancient world. Even in the centuries BC, the land and sea commerce between India, Persia, Egypt, up to the African coast, was protected by different dynasties; China joined this trade only under the Han dynasty, but expanded it exponentially.

Currently, the Sino-Russian alliance is the fastest growing. Trade between the two countries stands at $100 billion annually, and some long-term energy deals – driven by Moscow's need to counter a Western attempt to throttle its pipelines – have cemented the relationship. In May 2014, the two signed a 30-year $400 billion gas deal and another $325 billion gas deal in November 2014, sharply reducing Russian reliance on Europe. In fact, cash-strapped Russia has agreed to sell its most advanced air defence system, the S-400 missile, and 100 Sukhoi Superjet airplanes, to China. Beijing will invest $5.8 billion to extend the Moscow-Kazan high speed railway into China. In all, the two nations have signed 32 infrastructure related agreements during President Xi's visit to Moscow in May. Russia is also moving ahead with Turkish Stream, a trans-Black Sea pipeline that will deliver natural gas to Turkey by December 2016; Putin has offered Greece to fund an extension of the pipeline to the heart of Europe. So far, Serbia, Macedonia, Hungary and Greece have expressed a desire to be part of the project. The Turkish Stream is a Russian counter-offensive to the West's attempt to checkmate its South Stream pipeline at Bulgaria.

President Xi was the principal guest of honour at Moscow's Victory Day celebrations (an estimated 25 million Russians sacrificed their lives during the War), but leaders of around 30 nations attended despite Washington's boycott call. Nations who participated in the parade at Red Square included India, China, Mongolia, Serbia, Azerbaijan, Armenia, Belarus, Kazakhstan, Kyrgyzstan and Tajikistan. Beijing is now planning its own end-of-World War II military parade in September to highlight its contribution to the War (in which an estimated 15 lakh Chinese soldiers died) and challenge the West-centric narrative that has hitherto dominated the history books. This is yet another symbol of the rise of Asia.

ASSUMPTION AND PERFORM OF PLURALISM IN CHINESE INTERNATIONAL RELATIONS

In the post-Cold War era, Chinese diplomatic policy is aimed at realizing some basic and general goals such as respect for sovereign independence and non-intervention in domestic affairs, multilateralism, international democratization and multi-polarity in international society, and so on. The realization of these goals is the practice of pluralism in Chinese diplomacy. At first glance, it seems these goals are very different from each other. Yet in practice they're linked one another and each one is related to or can be explained by pluralism. In general, the core basic meaning of pluralism is tolerance based on which some other accessory values such as equality, peace, kindness, deliberation, coordination and others can be understood. As for Chinese diplomatic strategic goals, all of them are in line with the core meaning of pluralism and those accessory values.

Theoretical Psychoanalysis

Sovereign independence and non-interference as one basic goal or principle of Chinese diplomacy are grounded in a hypothesis which argues that each state regardless of its population, polity, territory or power is equal to any other in the world. That is, although one country has very different features in many dimensions from other countries, this country's sovereignty should be respected.

Difference and distinction of state's features are not the legitimate excuse for any country to intervene in other countries' internal affairs, if the influence of those affairs is only limited within its national borders. Isaiah Berlin argues that there is no universal ranking of moral rights and duties. He said "this idea [pluralism] has been unpacked to reveal two parts: the claim that values are plural because they are incompatible and the claim that they are plural because they are incommensurable". In terms of this idea, ay country should be equal in international dignity.

However, if one country's affairs can negatively influence other countries, other countries should take some action to solve their shared issues through multilateral approaches if pluralism as a basic international idea functions in international society. Multilateralism is a more constructive and peaceful means, if compared to unilateralism, to deal with most part of international issues. Commonly, unilateralists are inclined to use hegemonic and violent approaches to solve contradiction and conflict, which isn't in coincide with tolerance. Although the peaceful approach that multilateralism should adhere can meet the condition of pluralism, yet one big problem is that to a degree pluralism is very different to be put into practice in a multilateral institution or arrangement for solving problems, because pluralism means each idea or value should be tolerated and respected.

But under this condition, no agreement can be reached by virtue of the absence of shared values and ideas. This problem is stemmed from the dilemma of pluralism itself which argues that each value is equal in a given society but ironically, according to which one should not oppose others who have different ideas, because others should be respected at any time according to pluralism.

Allowing for this, based on pluralism, it's hard to reach a consensus on international issues in multilateral institutions since each international actor's different interests and ideas are in equal status and should be respected. Because it's hard to reach consensuses only through pluralism approach, correspondingly, the pluralism should not be defined as a useful approach to resolve substantive problems but defined as one spirit that directs participants in multilateral organization. In a word, multilateralism is somehow a result of pluralism since international multilateral talks or actions are dependent on sovereign equality and peaceful approach. Yet generally, pluralism cannot resolve all detailed problems under multilateral structure but is only helpful to build the base of the structure.

China also advocates that the international democracy and multi-polar system should become international common targets. International democracy implies not only the equal status of each country in international organization but also the open, true and heartfelt dialogues among all countries through peaceful approaches. Multi-polarity is an alternative of uni-polarity or hegemonic order in international society. Clearly, the idea of polarity is also the reflection of realpolitik which considers the world is always dominated by one or several big powers, however multi-polar system is closer to the meaning of pluralism than uni-polarity or hegemonic order. At least, Multi-polarity means relative equality of several big powers yet uni- or bi-polarity or hegemonic structure does not.

UNDERSTANDING CHINA'S SOFT AUTHORITY DIPLOMACY IN SOUTHEAST ASIA

ASEAN has sought to restrain Chinese power by enmeshing it in regional institutions. Whereas ASEAN is attractive China to tame the aggressive realpolitik that has characterised Chinese foreign relations, Beijing views the same institutions as a way to extend its regional influence and has sought to exclude the US. In planning for the first EAC summit, which was held in Malaysia, China tried to exclude India, Australia and New Zealand, but was overruled by Japan and ASEAN members. As China's regional influence grows, most ASEAN members are working to push against or balance Chinese power. While deepening trade and diplomatic co-operation with Beijing, many members, US allies such as Thailand and the Philippines, key 'swing states' such as Singapore, and emerging regional powers such as Indonesia, have also increased security ties with Washington (Twining 2005).

The question is why the US has changed its policy in the region from a benign power to one almost squarely focusing on hard power balance issues including terrorism as the overall obsession. For Southeast Asia, long under the United States' political and economic influence, times are rapidly moving in a new direction. A decade ago about three-quarters of US investment in East Asia went to Southeast Asia. That figure has now fallen to 10 percent. Approximately 80 percent of US investment in East Asia now goes to China (Thayer 2004: 178).

The United States remnants the region's single biggest destination for exports, and will be for some years to come. This is probably why the White House is on the defensive in terms of coming to grasp with the regional and multilateral setting in East and Southeast Asia. As one observer remarks: "Relations between Southeast Asia and the United States are perhaps best described as 'a policy without a strategy" (Banloi 2003). Asian leaders are organizing and building new regional institutions precisely to avoid the sort of power politics that America is practicing. Progress has been tenuous but real, and most regional leaders are cautiously optimistic about Asia's future. As long as this remains true, American emphasis on balance-of-power politics will continue to meet with only limited success. Indeed, this approach is likely to be under-mined by regional players, who are more interested in participating in economic integration and building regional communities than in divisive balancing behaviour. Most troubling for the United States, it will also cede its leadership role in Asia and limit Washington's ability to influence the future shape of regional institutions in the region.

China's ultimate strategic purpose remains a subject of debate and speculation among analysts. Southeast Asia, in this respect, is the sole region adjacent to China in which Chinese influence can most easily expand. A benign interpretation would see China as simply cultivating the sort of stable, peaceful, and prosperous regional environment that is required for its own successful modernization. A more sceptical view sees China playing a long-term game designed to curtail American influence and weave a close-knit economic and security community with China at the centre.

Beijing is in fact using nationalism and the 'glories of the Chinese civilisation' to instil a sense of unity among Chinese nationals domestically and among the Chinese Diaspora in Southeast Asia. Although Beijing may acknowledge that rampant nationalism could pose a danger to its own internal stability, it has astutely harnessed it to build a new Asian pride and identity, which it hopes might help establish a new Asian system of politics, economics, security and culture within the 'ASEAN+3' framework. The PRC ardently hopes this could be transformed ultimately into an East Asian Community under its leadership (Teo 2005). To realize its peaceful rise, China is using a sophisticated blend of trade, confidence building measures, and development assistance to establish itself as an important regional-cum-global leader.

Of course the appeal of Confucianism offers Beijing a definite comparative advantage in its soft supremacy approach. Moreover, the relationship China enjoys with the Chinese Diaspora in the region, who dominate the economic and, in some countries like Thailand, increasingly the political scene, is another advantage. The immediate implications of such an approach are that it would be naive to believe that China is not interested in exerting a dominant influence over its regional hinterland; commercial and financial muscle will eventually be the levers of choice, perhaps spearheaded by a strong regional currency. As much as the Chinese may be more ethnically exclusive than Americans and some Europeans, they are every bit as eager to see Chinese culture and traditions adopted by others - as a mark of civilization. As more and more Chinese tourists visit the region and even begin to dominate the tourist trade, the service sector response will be to tailor to Chinese taste and custom. This will inevitably result in a revival of Chinese culture and language in local communities once believed to have assimilated. Already one of the fastest growing Chinese language media groups is based in Malaysia, where Chinese language education has an unbroken history of more than a century. Up to the present, businesses have catered to a culture that projects modernity and sophistication in a Western guise - this could change and have an impact on U.S. and European influence (Vatikiotis 2003: 75).

The use of culture as a tool of diplomacy highlights the sense of theatre that China skilfully deploys to exaggerate kin, ethnicity and national bonds between the Motherland and the Diaspora. It also

reflects an increased appreciation by the Chinese government of the importance of norms and soft power in diplomacy. Chinese print media, television, music, food, and popular culture are spreading around the region as never before. So, too, are Chinese tourists fanning out across the region, often filling the void left by American tourists staying home after 9/11, the Bali bombing, and tsunami; 800,000 Chinese toured both Thailand and Singapore in 2004 (Shambaugh 2005).

In this way it is safe to say that ethnic Chinese business communities scattered in Southeast Asia have facilitated 'the rearticulation of mainland China into the global economy' not least through their reciprocal involvement in more than 100,000 joint ventures in China (Yeung 2000: 267; 271). It is also arguable that the Chinese Diaspora has been used not 'just as a financial resource in China to fund revolutions in the past and economic reforms in the present; they have been an important symbolic resource in the construction of Chinese nationalism' (Callahan 2003: 483). The combination of geo-political and geo-economic strategies and cultural expansion begs an answer to the question: 'what are the implications of China's policy of soft power for US influence in the region'?

Elizabeth Economy notes the important point that, China's rise to date appears to be less about the 'inevitable conflict of rising power' theory, popular in some circles, than about creeping power transition. Chinese thinkers, themselves, have recognized that the international community is concerned by the potential implications of China's rise and have taken pains to ensure that it will be perceived as non-threatening. This is well illustrated by Li Junru, Vice-President of the Central Party School at the Chinese Communist Party (CCP), who explicitly outlined the benefits to China's neighbours, stating, 'China's rise will not damage the interests of other Asian countries. That is because as China rises, it provides a huge market for its neighbours. At the same time, the achievements of China's development will allow it to support the progress of others in the region' (2005: 3-4).

In order to understand the motives and objectives of Chinese pragmatism, it is important to put both bilateral and multilateral diplomatic initiatives and foreign policy into the overall trade and security context and understand the internal and external constraints for a Chinese expansive strategy in Southeast Asia. The region as a whole maintains a trade surplus with China of US$8 billion annually, largely from its enormous exports of raw materials and precision machinery. China also agreed to an 'Early Harvest Package' that is perceived by ASEAN as 'largely a concession' to provide benefits through tariff reductions on 573 products including agricultural and manufactured goods. Individual Chinese entrepreneurs are also now expanding China's economic reach throughout Laos and Myanmar.

In some areas, locals now use only the Yuan and speak Chinese (Economy: 2005: 4). The forays of Chinese companies fit in with a broader strategic push by Beijing to establish closer economic cooperation with and among Asian countries. Unofficial reports by ASEAN officials claim that the foreign policy aim is part of a broader thrust by China to deploy multilateralism against what it sees as US unilateralist hegemony in the region and the world. 'This is a long-term game that China is playing,' says a senior ASEAN official. 'They want a situation in Southeast Asia that automatically takes into account China's interests. The whole objective of the policy is to avoid strategic encirclement by the U.S.' (Vatikiotis and Hiebert 2003).

Critical voices note that ASEAN's trade with Japan of $136 billion and that of the United States of more than $136 billion in 2004 exceeds trade with China. At the same time, in both Indonesia and Malaysia, people complain that jobs are being lost to China. Not least because Chinese textile exports since January 2005 have increased, thus implying down-ward competition for Cambodia and Vietnam. A growing mainland Chinese economic presence could also fuel latent resentment against the sizable ethnic Chinese economic elites in the region (Economy 2005: 5). In fact, almost no research has so far been done to investigate the impact of China's FDI on labour markets, environment and social issues and the question is whether China is exporting its own poor labour practices (Frost 2004).

Factors inhibiting Chinese private investment and tourism are sensitive to the treatment of Chinese minorities in Southeast Asia and in particular in the Philippines and Indonesia. The Indonesian racial riots in the aftermath of the financial crisis in 1998 which targeted ethnic Chinese created long-term damage to the 'bamboo network' (Low 2003: 73). There are also cultural impediments when it comes to expansion as noted by a senior ASEAN official: 'Unlike Americans, Chinese don't embrace foreigners - you cannot 'become Chinese" (Vatikiotis 2003: 75).

China's approach has been subtle, using soft power and economic diplomacy to build a benign multilateral framework in the shape of a free-trade agreement with ASEAN. 'China has shown a great deal of sensitivity,' says Singapore Prime Minister Goh Chok Tong. 'China realizes that it is a huge elephant, and even if it treads softly, it can still shake the ground.' One observer notes that 'China is seen by some to be slowly filling the vacuum left behind by the United States in the political, economic and security spheres in the region. This implies that 'U.S. Influence in Asia under Bush is Waning' (Agence France Presse, August 29, 2004.) and being replaced by China.

Beijing has also enthused the dynamics of regional cooperation in many other ways. One example is China's enthusiasm for developing the ASEAN-China dialogue into a vibrant web of multilevel and multi-sector cooperation. As noted above, the 1997 financial crisis was the main catalyst for the creation of a full-fledged diplomatic mechanism spanning summit, ministerial, and senior official levels. As Cheng-Chwee notes, the mechanism has stretched into various semi-state and civil society organizations that include research departments, media outlets, youth organizations, and the business sector. Also cooperation in agriculture, transport infraarrangement, as well as energy has been included. Over time, these ties have interwoven into a web of interdependence between China and ASEAN. The PRC has also taken the initiative in pushing for the creation of the Network of East Asia Think-Tanks (NEAT) (2005: 115). These moves are not merely tactical but part of PRCs overall goal to utilize the ASEAN-plus-three as the main vehicle of East Asian cooperation and the creation of the hybrid East Asian Community. Although there are other factors at play, China has played a decisive role in pushing in that direction. 'China's enthusiasm for East Asian cooperation is clearly driven by its aspiration to shape the direction of the existing regional institutions' (2005: 115-116).

Diplomatically, China's goals and vision in Southeast Asia are clear as it rivals the US and Japan world-wide and regionally. Moreover it may be again considering ASEAN as its own Monroe sphere, as it was during the 400 years of the Chinese tributary system under the Ming-Qing Emperors. Southeast Asian countries appear to be accepting sub-ordination as they seek to profit from the rising China.

8

Russian-Chinese Relations: A Study in Contemporary Geopolitics

The disappointment which a number of Russian politicians feel over the way their country's relations with the West evolved in the decade following the end of the Cold War, has led many of them to discuss various „eastern options". Since 1994, one hears the talk of new axes, alliances and partnerships with countries ranging from India to Iran to Iraq, but above all, with China. This harkens back to a traditional adage of Russian diplomacy: when checked in the west, look for opportunities in the east.

This largely self-contained elite discussion received much wider attention in December 1998 when then Prime Minister Evgenii Primakov casually mentioned the need for creating a „strategic triangle" consisting of Russia, China and India. The offer found no immediate takers and was subsequently downplayed by Primakov himself, but it left a trace. Never before had a senior Russian leader been so explicit about the idea of counterbalancing the global domination of the West, led by the United States, by means of a Eurasian alliance. A few months later, during the Kosovo crisis, Russia and China moved even more closer together in their opposition to U.S. „hegemonism". Symbolically, as the Russian military forces were holding their first major exercise dubbed „West-99" which for the first time in a decade again designated NATO as the enemy, a visiting high-level Chinese military delegation was given unprecedented access to Russian nuclear bases. Moscow and Beijing are beginning to live up to the notion of a strategic partnership through taking a common position on the issue of theatre missile defenses in Asia, which they oppose. There are signs that Moscow is relaxing its self-imposed restrictions regarding the quality level of the arms and technologies it sells to China.

Only recently, the Sino-Russian relationship was carefully analysed and found to be of rather limited nature. Is this changing now? Is a new geopolitical realignment in the works? Will the current Moscow-Beijing entente eventually lead to an alliance? Or, conversely, are the inherent constraints in the bilateral relationship strong enough to keep China and Russia from forming an anti-Western bloc? Or, to completely reverse the discussion, can it be that the present improvement in the Moscow-Beijing ties is only a short-term phenomenon, and in the medium and long term the two countries will collide again, as China becomes more powerful and assertive? What, in short, are the prospects and limitations of the geopolitical relationship which is likely to be among the most important and complex anywhere in Eurasia?

Geopolitics, of course, is only one aspect of the broader Russo-Chinese interaction. Economic relations, cross-border migration, contacts at regional and local levels, and not least among ordinary people, the impact of information technology and the exponential growth of communication, leading to cross-cultural influence, i.e. everything which is usually associated with the world of the future, is not covered by geopolitics. A narrowly geopolitically-focused perspective is not just deemed to be old-fashioned and plainly obsolete, it can be distorting and misleading. Still, it is highly useful for a number of important reasons. First, much of the government-to-government bilateral relationship between Beijing and Moscow today is about geopolitics. There is little else, at least for the moment, to back the claim of a „strategic partnership". Second, the bulk of Chinese and Russian elites are keen students or at least admirers of geopolitics, which informs many of their actions. Third, for much of the outside world it is the prospect of a geopolitical realignment of China and Russia – and not, say, the chances for their economic cooperation-which evokes the most intense interest.

This article starts with an assessment of the new status quo between Russia and China, the vaunted correlation of forces between them, which has undergone dramatic changes in the last ten years. It then proceeds to take stock of the geopolitical gains resulting from the improvement in the bilateral relations. Lastly, it examines the potential for geopolitical cooperation and conflict between the two countries in the future.

Role Reversal

The starting point for any discussion of contemporary Sino-Russian geopolitics is recognizing and assessing the new standing of the parties vis-a-vis each other. The first fundamental change concerns the position that Russia and China hold in Asia.

Most Russians lamenting the passing of the Soviet Union usually compare their country's decline with the apparent new omnipotence and omnipresence of their erstwhile global rival, the United States. Still, the change of fortunes between Russia and China is only slightly less dramatic. In 1989, when President Gorbachev came to Beijing to repair the 30-year old Sino-Soviet rift, the USSR still included the five Central Asian republics; Mongolia was a loyal Moscow ally, and home to some 75,000 Soviet military personnel; so was Vietnam, with its strategic naval and air facilities. Laos and Cambodia were Soviet clients. India was a quasi-ally, under the 1971 treaty. In Afghanistan, even after the Soviet withdrawal, a pro-Moscow Najibulla regime continued to hold Kabul. As long as Soviet aid flowed, Moscow retained a measure of influence in Pyongyang.

Ten years later, along the former Soviet border, China has four neighbours, and Russia is only one of them. The others, Kazakstan, Kyrgyzstan, and Tajikistan, the new Moslem states, are engaged in a careful balancing act between Russia, China and the West. The Commonwealth of Independent States (CIS), a most useful framework for the dismantlement of the Soviet

Union, has turned out to be virtually useless as a tool for post-Soviet integration. Mongolia, having shaken off Moscow's tutelage, has for the first time in its recent history adopted an independent foreign policy posture. Vietnam and its neighbours in Indochina have gravitated toward the ASEAN.

Ironically, Russia was constrained to become a supporter of the Afghan coalition which had ousted Najibulla, but the coalition has been defeated by the Taleban forces which now control at least three quarters of the country, including the capital. In 1997, many Russian political leaders and top military commanders sincerely feared that the Taleban would march across the former Soviet border and take over the entire region up to the Volga delta. These fears have since been proven false, but even without the Taleban, Russia finds it increasingly difficult to help maintain stability in the once dormant Central Asia. To add insult to injury, Moscow has found itself excluded from both the Korean nuclear energy (KEDO) project and the Korea peace talks. The ties to India have grown stale and deteriorated. In short, Russia has ceased to be a political superpower in Asia and it faces a hard task of asserting itself even as a major regional player.

China, by contrast, has gone some way to becoming a regional power in Asia-Pacific. The „gathering of Chinese lands" has achieved important results. In 1997, Beijing achieved a historic reunification with Hong Kong, to be followed by reabsorption of Macau at the end of 1999. After this, only Taiwan will remain on Beijing's reunification agenda. China's claims to the South China Sea have been repeatedly reasserted. Beijing's diplomatic stature has also grown. From Kashmir to Korea, its influence is acutely felt and often sought by the local and regional forces. Whether it is nuclear proliferation in South Asia or the stand-off on the Korean Peninsula, Beijing is a key outside player. In Central Asia, it is quietly supplanting Russia's waning influence as it moves to diversify its sources of energy supply and to protect its rear. Beijing diplomats have been issuing statements on the conflicts in the Persian Gulf and the Balkans. In a symbolic recognition of its new role, China has evidently become the single most important country from the perspective of the world's only superpower, the United States.

The change in the relative economic weight between Russia and China is equally, if not more drastic. In 1989, the U.S.S.R. was still the world's third largest economy, after the U.S. and Japan. It produced substantially more goods and services than China. Ten years later, Russia has been demoted to the 16th place, in terms of its GDP. By contrast, China, due to its phenomenal growth rate since the start of Deng Xiaoping's reforms, has been able to surpass its former mentor several times over. Even if Russia starts to grow again at a decent annual rate of 3-4%, which is not yet in sight, its relative decline vis-a-vis China will continue. By 2010, the margin of difference between them can be tenfold. Even in per capita GDP terms the gap is fast closing. Thirty years ago the Soviet Union dominated China in this respect by approximately seven to one. Currently, China accounts for about 60% of Russia's level, and some of its coastal provinces have surpassed Russia's national average. Russia's technological lead over „backward China", historically the source of Moscow's pride, is also becoming history.

In 1989, the Soviet army was the most potent military force in both Europe and Asia. In the following years, it has gone through unprecedented decline. In 1997, e.g., it was officially admitted that the Russian military did not possess a single army division that was combat-ready. The quantity and quality of the forces deployed in the Far East have gone down significantly. Their power projection capabilities have been drastically reduced, and problems with the discipline abound, as weapons arsenals catch fire and blow up, and conscripts take to the taiga to escape hazing. The defeat of Moscow's attempt to subdue rebellious Chechnya by military force has become an emblem of a thoroughly new phenomenon – Russia's military weakness. By and large, Russia has missed on the revolution in military affairs. As a result, many have become convinced that, in any hypothetical major military conflict Russia would probably lose if the war remained conventional. Consequently, reliance on nuclear weapons for national defence has never been more pronounced in the Russian military doctrine and strategy. Clearly, this has implications not only for the West, but for the East-i.e. China – as well. Some Russian military officers privately admit that in a conflict with China the main Russian defenses along the border, including all the principal cities, will be overrun in a matter of days, leaving the General Staff with few options other than going nuclear.

China, for its part, has been steadily, if slowly modernizing its vast, although still primitive armed forces. Since 1992, it has been able to do this with the help of steady Russian transfers of arms and military technology, at the average annual rate of about $1 billion. In a pathetic symbol of the changed fortunes of the two states in the defence area, Russian military enterprises have been constrained to sell their products to China – or face closure. Recently, the People's Liberation Army has been buying more Russian-made combat aircraft than the Russian Air Force itself. Even in the nuclear field, there are projections that China may get even with Russia in the next 10-15 years if the latter continues on its path of decline and Beijing adopts an ambitious nuclear build-up policy.

In 1989, the last year of the Soviet census, the country's population reached 282 million, which made it the world's third largest. In 1999, when Russian census was cancelled due to the lack of funding, the country's population dropped to 146 million – two million less than when the USSR was dismantled. This figure roughly equals the combined population of China's three northeastern provinces which border on the Russian Far East.

As to the Far East itself, its population has been declining faster than the national average, about 9% in the last decade of this century. Across the Amur and the Ussuri rivers, some 5 million Russians are facing around 130 million Chinese.

Even if the entire population of Russia were resettled along the Chinese border, that would redress the imbalance with North-East China only temporarily. The population decline in Russia will continue unabated, and the country may lose as much as 10% of its current population in the next three or four decades.

China's population will continue to grow from the current 1.2 billion, and Beijing's family planning policy will only moderate that growth, not arrest it. It has become commonplace in Moscow and Vladivostok to refer to the huge Chinese demographic „overhang" in the border area as a prime security concern.

Thus, the collapse of the Soviet Union, which itself was a result of a quarter of a century long decline, has dramatically reversed the geopolitical dynamics of Eurasia as a whole. Long an assertive and expanding centre, Russia has been on the defensive all around, losing ground to the historical rivals and to the new states which for centuries were its provinces. It strives to project an image of a still great power, to win time and restore the status quo, but it has found this increasingly difficult.

China, by contrast, is not a status quo power. In the past 150 years it has suffered from too much humiliation at the hands of Europeans, including the Russians.

It is now looking forward to coming back to the world stage as a strong independent force to be reckoned with. In the Sino-Russian relationship, roles have been reversed.

Never since the two countries have established permanent contacts three hundred years ago, has Russia been the weaker, the less dynamic and the less confident of the two. This new distribution of power and influence, this newly prevailing „wind from the East" is more than a passing phenomenon.

Even assuming that Russia's economic crisis will be eventually overcome, and allowing for inevitable and increasing difficulties in China as its transformation deepens, it is unlikely that the traditional geopolitical relationship between the two countries – i.e., Russia's preponderance – will be restored.

Russia's relative decline vis-a-vis China will probably continue well into the 21st century. This change in stature has wide-ranging implications for both countries, and for the outside world. For the time being, however, the reversal of roles has helped to establish a more equitable relationship from which both Russia and China have been able to draw important benefits.

Positive Gains

It would be absolutely wrong to argue that the new geopolitical environment in Asia, in the short to medium term, is inherently inimical, or even threatening to Russia. The end of the 25-year-long cold war between Moscow and Beijing has brought both countries important benefits. This concerns above all the 4,400-kilometer long common border, once the scene of bloody armed clashes. Since 1991, a series of agreements have been signed which led to the delimitation, demarcation and the partial demilitarization of the border. Of its entire length, only three river islands currently controlled by Russia remain contested. Beijing is no longer raising claims to some 1.5 million square km of territory annexed in the 19th century by Czarist Russia through „unequal treaties". The border which for three decades had been a source of tension and a likely site for large-scale conflagration has become a zone of tranquillity.

Both governments have felt confident enough to decrease and dealert their military forces facing each other. Confidence-building measures are in place. The nightmare of a Sino-Russian conflict has become remote. In fact, both countries' General Staffs have designated different risks and opportunities. Beijing's main axes of strategic interest run to the south and southeast; Moscow feels the pressure of NATO enlargement and NATO interventionism in the west and the heat of instability in the south. Instead of confronting each other face to face, as they did in the past, Russia and China are actually standing now back to back to each other and feel so much more secure.

What is more, the border agreements and the military detente have been extended to the three former Soviet republics in Central Asia. Together with Mongolia, from which all Russian forces were withdrawn in 1992, they now form a huge buffer zone between Russia and China in Inner Asia, limiting their direct contact to Chinese Manchuria and the Russian Far East. The rise of the new states lowers the prospect for the resumption of a Cold-War type confrontation, though it could revive the traditional schemes of the struggle for the zones of influence. For the time being, however, both China and Russia abstain from this kind of competition. Beijing and Moscow are concentrated on the domestic needs rather than outward expansion.

Another major change is linked to the emergence of regionalism in both Russia and China. For the first time in 500 years, centralized political control in Russia is no longer absolute. Popularly elected provincial governors, legislators and city mayors are wielding real power and occasionally challenge the federal authorities. In a parallel development, China's provinces have been becoming more assertive vis-a-vis Beijing, eager to preserve their particular interests. As on the Russian side, these interests have much more to do with gaining (or preserving) economic advantages than with power politics.

Thus, although this may appear paradoxical, the dramatic reversal of geopolitical roles between Russia and China has resulted in a more peaceful and equitable relationship which is mutually satisfying and valued by both. Whether this relationship will continue depends on how the longer-term interests of the two countries will interact.

Convergence of Interests and Its Limitations

In their rhetoric, Moscow and Beijing employ many like-sounding formulae. However, a geopolitical tour d'horizon allows one to see both convergence of interest and important differences which limit cooperation and may even point to conflict.

Multipolar world

Both Russian and Chinese leaders use the concept of multipolarity as the shorthand for the desired state of international relations in the post-Cold War era. Yet, taken on its own merit, the concept in the longer term can probably suit Beijing much more than Moscow. China is on the way to become a regional power, whereas Russia's fortunes continue to decline. Having ceased to be for the first time in history a self-contained and self-sustained universe, Russia will soon discover that its territory falls within the zones of attraction of several power centres, and, moreover, that some of Russia's own regions start to gravitate in different directions. The North-West from Kaliningrad to Karelia to Kola, e.g., would move to „meet" the European Union, whereas Khabarovsk and Primorie would become part of China's „near abroad". It will require more than an average effort on behalf of the Russian leadership to respond to this new challenge creatively, and work out a new geopolitical model for the Russian state-both in terms of its domestic structural organization and its relation to the outside world.

This, however, is yet a task for the future. For the time being, Moscow and Beijing continue to use the rhetoric of multipolarity as a code word for their opposition to what they see as the domination of the world arena by the United States. This reminds one of the anti-hegemony platform that Washington and Beijing used to characterize their alignment in the late 1970s-1980s, when both perceived the Soviet Union as an adversary.

The United States

The Cold War-era triangular relationship has undergone a fundamental change, both in structure (with the diminishing of Russia's role) and in meaning (America no longer has a better relationship with China and Russia than these two have between themselves). In the early 1990s, when it briefly appeared that Moscow could become Washington's strategic ally, the Chinese grew concerned – for such a change would have meant, to them, a U.S. – engineered encirclement of the People's Republic. The failure of the Russo-American strategic partnership, which became evident in the dispute over NATO enlargement, brought relief to the Chinese government. By the mid-1990s, Sino-Russian relations reached the level of public cordiality which is no longer present in the U.S.-Russian case. In 1996, Moscow and Beijing agreed on a formula for a long-time partnership.

Having started with verbal expressions of opposition to „hegemonism", Russia and China have found it useful to work together on specific issues, such as Iraq, the Balkans and theatre missile defenses, in an attempt to contain U.S. assertiveness, or at least to get some leverage vis-a-vis Washington. In general, this has not worked, but has increased the self-confidence of both governments. After the Kosovo crisis, both countries' militaries have come to see themselves on the receiving end of American-led international interventionism. The NATO operation against Yugoslavia has resulted in the intensification of political and military contacts between Moscow and Beijing. The UN Security Council has become de-facto split with China and Russia routinely teaming up against the United States and its allies.

Still, all this cooperation, or even strategic alignment is likely to fall far short of an anti-American bloc. China, by culture and tradition, prefers to act alone; Russia would probably reject the role of a junior partner that it would be offered in any hypothetical coalition; most important, both countries, whatever their current differences with the United States and their opposition to the „unipolar world", need good relations with America for a host of economic, financial and other reasons. For Moscow, the most vital foreign policy issue is debt restructuring and relations with the international financial institutions, where Washington plays a paramount role. Russia's economic development is doomed without access to Western technology and capital investment. For Beijing, suffice it to mention that China's trade with America is worth ten times its trade with Russia.

Japan

It is still too early to speak about a „triangle" with Beijing, Moscow and Tokyo as its three corners: the level of mutual dependency among the three is far too low. However, from the Russian point of view a solid relationship with Japan is a necessary second pillar of Moscow's Asian policy, which otherwise would be too slanted toward China – to Russia's disadvantage. No meaningful economic integration of Russia into Asia-Pacific is possible without Japanese participation in the development of the Russian Far East. As for Japan, the rise of China is displacing it from the long-held position as the number one nation in Asia. From Tokyo's perspective, an active and successful policy of engagement toward Russia would serve as a hedge against a too dominant China.

Russia finds itself in a situation where the natural Sino-Japanese rivalry presents Moscow with an opening. It needn't make a choice between the two; rather, developing ties with one would strengthen its position with respect to the other, and vice versa.

Even though both Beijing and Moscow remain suspicious of a resurgent Japan, China's fear is much stronger. Even though Russia and China expressed concern over the expansion of Japan's role in the bilateral defence relationship with the United States, China is more worried. Russia, by contrast, has acknowledged the stabilizing effect of the U.S.-Japan security relationship which effectively places Japan's defence policy under American control– something which the Chinese are yet to recognize.

Moscow and Beijing have voiced their objection to the U.S.-driven plans for a theatre missile defence system in East Asia, but Beijing's interests are more directly implicated than Moscow's. Interestingly, however, China shares the Japanese view on the status of the Kurile islands – a vestige of the times when the USSR was regarded its chief adversary.

Korea

China and Russia, no less than America and Japan, are clearly interested in the successful management of the situation on the Korean Peninsula – both the stand-off between South and North Korea and the incipient crisis within the North. The two countries, however, are able to exercise very different degrees of influence on the situation on the Peninsula. Whereas Beijing is the only international player with a real access to the Pyongyang leadership, Russia can only watch the situation from the sidelines. China, unlike Russia, is also party to the Korea peace talks – by virtue of the 1953 armistice agreement. Moscow's pleas to broaden the talks to include itself (and Japan) have fallen on deaf ears in Washington as well as in Beijing. China is reluctant to give up its exclusive position as one of the two outside powers – alongside with the U.S. – involved in the peace process. The Chinese hope that Korea, which historically used to gravitate toward China, will once again assume this familiar posture. In the future, however, a reunified Korea may indeed see its ties with Russia, the weakest major power in North-East Asia, as a natural and relatively benign counterweight to the domination by the two regional hegemons and historical overlords, China and Japan. If this happens, Moscow's relations with Beijing will become more delicate.

Central and Inner Asia

On their flanks, Russia and China border on a potentially very unstable region of the former Soviet Central Asia. Potentially, this is an immense powder keg. Ethnic and religious conflicts in that part of the world can spill over both to the north and the east. The new states in the region are all too fragile, with the post-Soviet regimes remaining vulnerable to domestic unrest inspired by political Islam. Faute de mieux, Beijing even prefers that for the time being Russia exercise a leading role in the region, through elite contacts, limited military presence and even the moribund institutes of the CIS. Interestingly, the post-Soviet border treaty, the confidence building agreement and the force reduction accord were negotiated and signed by China with the three Central Asian states and Russia simultaneously, as multilateral documents.

Russia, however, no longer has sufficient leverage with its southern neighbours. Like Beijing, Moscow sees the growth of Western influence at elite level and the spread of political Islam and Turkic nationalism at grassroots level in Central Asia as a cause for concern or even a threat (in the latter case). The Western presence in Central Asia is overwhelmingly of economic nature and is of private character. However, the Central Asians' participation in the NATO Partnership for Peace program, including the staging of joint exercises, and Uzbekistan's membership in GUUAM, a U.S.-backed loose association of former Soviet republics, is being read as a sign of growing American and European political and security attention given to the region. This Western geopolitical „trespassing", however, pales in comparison to the threat of domestic conflict, intra-state rivalry, and the spread of political extremism, coupled with the exponential growth of drugs trafficking from Central Asia.

Much like the West, China sees Central Asia primarily as a source of energy supplies for its growing economy. Ever since 1991, Beijing has been successfully cultivating ties with the governments in the region, winning their support for the Chinese pipeline projects. So far, Russian and Chinese interests in Central Asia do not collide. In the future, they might, especially if both governments continue to espouse the traditional form of geopolitical thinking with its emphasis on zero-sum gaming.

Since 1990-1991, Mongolia has been enjoying true independence – due in large part to the benign neglect simultaneously demonstrated toward it by China and Russia, each preoccupied with its domestic problems. On the other hand, pan-Mongolism, initially feared in both Russia– because of the two ethnically close republics – Buryatia and Tuva (of which the latter was an independent state between 1921 and 1944), and in China – due to the existence of the autonomous region of Inner Mongolia, has remained dormant and non-provocative.

If Mongolia manages to use this pause to construct a viable market economy and a durable system of political institutions, which would win it international recognition in America, Europe and Japan, it can become an anchor of stability in Inner Asia, a useful transit corridor and a meeting place for Russia and China. If, on the other hand, Mongolia fails to get on its feet, it will be a source of tension, likely to solicit both Russian and Chinese response. In the worst-case scenario, Mongolia may come under the domination of China, or turn into an area of competition between China and Russia.

The two other areas of Inner Asia worth mentioning are Xinjiang and Tibet. Both have an indigenous population which is distinctly non-Chinese, both have been subjected to a policy of Sinicization, both have political movements aiming at separation from China. Moscow, currently a champion of territorial integrity, gives moral support to Beijing. It professes little sympathy for the Turkic independence activists in Xinjiang and has no interest in interfering with Beijing over the human rights situation in Tibet. The domestic pressure in Russia in support of the Dalai Lama is very light, producing virtually no impact on the government's policy course.

Taiwan

Moscow's official view that Taiwan is part of China ruled from Beijing has remained unchanged during the decades of Sino-Soviet confrontation. Since then, Russia's ties with Taiwan have been carefully confined to economic, cultural and other non-political issues, never provoking a protest from Beijing. Throughout the 1990s, Beijing's support of the Russian position on Chechnya, including during the 1994-1996 war, can be regarded as a downpayment for Russia's understanding of any action the PRC may take with respect to Taiwan. At the end of the decade, in the wake of the crisis over Kosovo, both Moscow and Beijing strongly advocate non-interference in the internal affairs of states over secession issues.

Moscow is actually content that Beijing's strategic activism is directed at Taiwan, where Russia does not have any significant interests which could be affected by a crisis. Thus, China is likely to continue concentrating its military resources at a significant distance from the Russian border and for a very special kind of mission. The Taiwan issue, Moscow appreciates, is a permanent source of tension and mutual suspicions in Sino-American relations, preventing too close a collaboration between those two countries. Russia is happily providing China with arms and equipment which Beijing has been purchasing with an eye for the evolving situation across the Taiwan Strait. A continued stand-off in the area works to increase China's dependency on Russian military supplies. Still, if and when push comes to shove, and Beijing resorts to military measures against Taipei, leading to U.S. involvement in whatever form, Moscow will face a hard choice, for openly becoming China's ally and military supply base will irreparably damage its relations with America and Japan.

South Asia

There is little justification at present for the new idea of an emerging Sino-Russo-Indian „triangle". All three countries are important players in Eurasia, and relations among them will help shape the future of the continent, but in the foreseeable future the specter of the strategic triangle will remain a figment of wishful thinking of those who would do anything to upset the „unipolar world".

It is important to note, however, that here, too, the Cold War confrontation lines have recently become relaxed. There is no longer a situation where two of the three countries were engaged in parallel stand-off with the third, China. Moscow and Beijing are no longer maintaining exclusive client relationships with New Delhi and Islamabad. India has normalized relations with China, and Russia has warmed up to Pakistan. Indeed, nuclear proliferation in South Asia warrants cooperation among America, China and Russia with the aim of preventing a nuclear war between India and Pakistan and helping the two countries to stabilize their strategic relationship.

The Russian Far East

Still, it is the Russian Far East, and not some third country, which may become a prime factor in the future Sino-Russian relationship. Unless Russia wants to de-facto lose the region, already semi-detached from the rest of the country, it will need to seriously develop it. Developing the Far East calls for a much more intimate relationship with China than heretofore – in particular where it concerns the import of Chinese labour. While at present there are few Chinese residents in the Russian Far East – 20.000 or so in Primorie, most of them temporary, their number is likely to grow, and not only east of the Urals. Even now, the number of Chinese semi-permanent residents in Moscow is roughly estimated to be around 50.000. Some projections assume that by mid-21st century the Chinese diaspora in Russia may reach 7 million, which will make them the second largest ethnic group in the country after the Russians themselves. A failure to construct a mutually satisfying relationship under such conditions could result in a conflict with ethnic and even racial overtones which in turn could lead to a full-fledged Russo-Chinese confrontation. This danger is very remote now, but it shouldn't be overlooked.

SINO-RUSSIAN RELATIONS AFTER THE COLD WAR

The period from March 1999 to September 2001 was marked by new, hitherto unseen challenges in the international environment for Moscow, Beijing, and Washington alike. During this period, China and Russia had the strongest common interests and the greatest need for cooperation (Cheng, 2009: 152). Accordingly, two crucial factors paved the way for the Sino-Russian rapprochement at the beginning of the new millennium: (1) U.S. aggressive foreign policy and (2) political change in Russia. First, U.S. military strikes against Iraq and increasing American presence in the Central Asia; plans for creation of U.S.-Japanese Theatre Missile Defence (TMD) and National Missile Defence (NMD); NATO expansion into the Baltics; and, ultimately, bombing of Yugoslavia, during which the Chinese embassy in Belgrade had been destroyed. All these developments reflected Moscow and Beijing's concerns over growing American influence, inasmuch as many of the above-mentioned events directly affected Russia and China's spheres of national interest. Second, Russia's new leader, former Prime Minister Vladimir Putin, started to pursue a course aimed, *inter alia*, at working towards a multipolar system of international relations and creating a favourable environment for Russia's economic development upon assuming the presidency in 2000. One of the main tenets of Putin's foreign policy, delineated in the Foreign Policy Concept of June 28, 2000, was maintaining good-neighbourly relations with the country's neighbours, and Russia's relationship with China (on a par with India) was defined as "one of the most important" directions of Russian foreign policy in Asia (Leksyutina, 2010).

In July 2000, Vladimir Putin paid his first official visit to Beijing, where Russian President and his Chinese counterpart issued a joint communiqué, "the Beijing Declaration," on the

Anti-Ballistic Missile problem. In light of Washington's plans of withdrawing from the ABM Treaty signed between the United States and the Soviet Union in 1972, Vladimir Putin and Jiang Zemin China confirmed their strong opposition to the U.S. plans of deploying missile systems and agreed upon the essence of the U.S. National Missile Defence and Theatre Missile Defence programs, which, according to the parties, was to seek "unilateral military and security advantages" (Wilson, 2004: 161). One year later, during Jiang Zemin's visit to Moscow in July 2001, Russia and China signed a historical agreement, the "Treaty for Good Neighborliness, Friendship and Cooperation," under which Moscow and Beijing agreed to develop long-term relations of friendship and equal partnership. Furthermore, the Treaty prioritized strengthening confidence in the military area and enhancing security between countries, while providing framework for moving towards a more stable regional and international environment. Under the pact, Moscow and Beijing expressed their will to uphold the strict observance of generally recognized principles and norms of international law against any actions aimed at exerting pressure or meddling in the internal affairs of the sovereign states. In addition, Russia and China agreed to develop mutually beneficial cooperation in trade, military, energy, transportation, scientific and technical spheres, and other fields. Ultimately, the parties to the Treaty voiced their determination to fight terrorism, separatism, extremism, organized crime, drug trafficking, and illegal migration in the following twenty years.

Another significant achievement in Sino-Russian relations during this period was the establishment of the Shanghai Cooperation Organization, in June 2001. Building upon the Shanghai agreement of 1996, China, Russia, Kazakhstan, Tajikistan, Kyrgyzstan along with the new member, Uzbekistan, further consolidated their relations by setting up the Shanghai Cooperation Organization with the declared objectives of strengthening mutual trust and good-neighbourly friendship among the member states; encouraging effective cooperation among the member states in political, economic and trade, scientific and technological, cultural, educational, energy, communications, environment and other fields; devoting themselves jointly to preserving and safeguarding regional peace, security and stability; and establishing a democratic, fair and rational new international political and economic order (Bailes et al., 2007).

Despite increasing cooperation between Moscow and Beijing resulting in the new Sino-Russian Treaty and the establishment of the Shanghai Cooperation Organization, both agreements lost their tremendous significance, albeit for a short period of time, in the wake of the post-9/11 realignment in global politics (Kutchins, 2010: 41). After the collision of U.S. and Chinese planes in April 2001, increased arms sales to Taiwan, and U.S. President George W. Bush's remarks about defending Taiwan by all means, Sino-U.S. relations reached their nadir prior to the 9/11 events. Likewise, U.S.-Russian relations exacerbated after the "espionage" scandal in early 2001, and were further damaged by plans of the NATO enlargement and U.S. withdrawal from the ABM treaty. For these reasons, the improvement of relations with the United States was on top of China and Russia's foreign policy agendas in the aftermath of the terrorist attacks on the United States. Accordingly, both countries sought to take advantage of the momentum in order to improve their relations with Washington during this period, but Russia even more so.

After Vladimir Putin supported the United States in its efforts to combat the Taliban in Afghanistan, Russia's President expected Washington to provide more room for negotiation on such divisive issues in bilateral relations as the second round of NATO expansion and termination of the ABM Treaty. However, just like at the beginning of the 1990s, Russia's "honeymoon" with the United States appeared to be short-lived: the Bush Administration provided too little in return for the Kremlin's support. China, for its part, also sought to resuscitate its relations with the United States after September 11. During the informal summit of the Asia Pacific Economic Cooperation (APEC) in Shanghai in October 2001, President George W. Bush and Jiang Zemin reiterated that both countries attached great importance to Sino-U.S. ties, vowed to work together to build a constructive relationship, and agreed to establish long and medium-term mechanisms for combating terrorism (Mao, 2003: 85). Nonetheless, the U.S. invasion in Iraq in 2003, spread of the "color revolutions" into the post-Soviet states, and the third round of NATO expansion in Europe made Moscow rethink its approach to relations with the United States and focus on further developing of the "strategic relationship" with China.

During Vladimir Putin's visit to Beijing in October 2004, Russia and China concluded the supplementary agreement on the Eastern section of the Sino-Russian border, which was subsequently ratified by the countries' parliaments in 2005. Furthermore, during this summit, Vladimir Putin and Hu Jintao approved the implementation guidelines of the Sino-Russian Treaty of 2001 for the next four years (Cheng, 2009: 161). Subsequently, in July 2005, the Chinese and Russian leaders issued a joint communiqué on the "International Order in the 21st Century," which reaffirmed the common goals of working toward a multipolar world previously stated by Moscow and Beijing.

During the Shanghai Cooperation Organization's Astana summit in 2005, Russia and China along with four Central Asian states released a declaration, which declared that "a rational and just world order must be based upon consolidation of mutual trust and good-neighbourly relations with no pretense to monopoly and domination in international affairs" (Bailes et al., 2007). Russia and China participated in joint military exercises under the SCO's Peace Missions in 2005 and 2007, which were aimed at combining efforts at preventing a possible ethnic conflict in a third country and countering terrorism (Wishnick, 2009: 20). However, in light of the Georgian crisis and ensuing split of Abkhazia and South Ossetia in 2008, China did not express support for Russian policy toward Georgia due to dangerous ramifications of the of the republics' cessation. During the presidential meeting in Dushanbe following the Russian-Georgian conflict, China's Hu Jintao expressed his concern to Russia's President Dmitri Medvedev about the conflict and voiced his hope that the disputing parties would be able to resolve the conflict through dialogue and consultation (Yuan, 2011: 12). Nonetheless, Moscow's recognition of the breakaway regions was not welcomed by Beijing due to its concerns over the Taiwan issue and separatist movement in Xinjiang.

DISRUPTION OF THE POWER BALANCE: SINO-RUSSIAN RELATIONS IN THE 1990S-2000S

The looming collapse of the Soviet Union was greeted with alarm in Beijing. The Chinese leadership grew increasingly cautious of the political transformation in the Soviet Union, and reacted with criticism to the plans of restoring capitalism in the former communist country. Moreover, China was openly supportive of the putschists (the KGB generals), who attempted to preserve at least the core of the Soviet Union by carrying out a coup in August 1991. After Boris Yeltsin quelled the *putsch*, Beijing accused Russia's new leader of dismantling the socialist system, damaging nascent Sino-Russian relations (Wishnick, 2001a: 122). Yet, in spite of mounting ideological differences between China and the Soviet Union, relations between countries were expanding in 1990 and 1991.

During the Chinese Prime Minister Li Peng's visit to Moscow in April 1990, the Soviet Union and China signed a number of agreements on mutual cooperation in the spheres of border security, economics, science and technology, and peaceful use and research of space (Xia, 1997: 24). The most important among them was the agreement on guiding principles of mutual and balanced force reductions and confidence-building measures along the Sino-Soviet border. According to this agreement, China and the Soviet Union expressed their commitment to reduce their troop presence to the lowest level in the area of the Sino-Soviet border, which would pave the way for good neighbourly relations based upon mutual security (Yuan, 1998: 8). Further, during Jiang Zemin's visit to Moscow in May 1991, Moscow and Beijing made significant progress on border issues. Mikhail Gorbachev and Jiang Zemin signed an agreement on the "Eastern Section of the Sino-Soviet Border," which settled 98 per cent of the 7,400 km border stretching from Russia's Vladivostok to Eastern Tajikistan in the Central Asia (Moltz, 1995: 516). Under this agreement, China also received once fought for Zhenbao (Damansky) Island and was allowed free navigation on the Amur River. However, further progress on border-related issues was disrupted by the dissolution of the Soviet Union following the signing of the Belavezha accords in December 1991.

The new leadership of Russia became more focused on forging closer ties with the West, and with the United States in particular, rather than with authoritarian China or the former Soviet Republics, which Russia nevertheless considered its exclusive sphere of interests. Russian foreign policy thus prioritised Moscow's adherence to democratic values, pluralist institutions, and respect for human rights. This Western-centrism in Russian foreign policy making pioneered by Minister of Foreign Affairs Andrei Kozyrev in the first part of the 1990s could be defined as quixotic, for it expected Russia to be accepted as an equal by Western countries (despite its lack of geopolitical power) and deemed emphasis on relations with China tantamount to the rejection of Western values and identities (Lo, 2002: 23). Although Wilson (2004: 192) argued that Russia's new political elite was largely uninformed and uninterested in China, the new leadership nonetheless deemed Sino-Russian relations necessary and, therefore, did not fully discard them.

By the end of 1992, the Kremlin's pro-Western sentiment gradually began to subside in light of growing U.S. influence in global affairs, especially during the Gulf War in Iraq, and internal opposition to the Kremlin's pro-Western foreign policy. In response to the above-mentioned concerns, during his first visit to China in December 1992, President Boris Yeltsin proclaimed that Russia was seeking balanced relations in both Europe and Asia, admitted common interests between Moscow and Beijing, and also noted that the Taiwan issue was primarily China's internal affair (Rozman, 1998: 400). For its part, China sought to establish better relations with Russia due to the growing diplomatic isolation and sanctions levied against Beijing in the aftermath of the Tiananmen upheaval. Furthermore, China considered the Sino-Russian relationship a counterweight to American influence and a partnership, which would subsequently give way to a multipolar world (Wishnick, 2001b: 800). Thus, the desire to shape a new international order based on multipolarity as opposed to U.S. hegemonism resonated with Beijing and Moscow alike. In his 1994 article in *Foreign Affairs*, Russian Foreign Minister Andrei Kozyrev accordingly maintained: "The international order in the 21st century will not be a *Pax Americana* or any other version of unipolar or bipolar dominance. The United States does not have the capability to rule alone ... the nature of modern international problems calls for solutions on a multilateral basis" (Kozyrev, 1994).

During Jiang Zemin's visit to Moscow in September 1994, Russia and China signed a joint communiqué, which defined the Sino-Russian relationship as a new "constructive partnership" based on the principles of peaceful coexistence, equality, good-neighborliness, friendship, mutually beneficial cooperation, and nonalignment. Further, the 1994 communiqué reaffirmed the parties' commitment to the United Nations as a mechanism for creating a multipolar world order; their mutual respect for each other as major powers; their intolerance for expansionism; and ultimately, their opposition to hegemony, power politics, and the establishment of antagonistic political, military, and economic blocs (Wilson, 2004: 147). This joint declaration reflected Moscow and Beijing's shared concerns over the expansion of the North Atlantic Treaty Organization (NATO) eastwards in particular, and the U.S. role as a global hegemon in general. During the summit in 1994, the two presidents also signed an agreement on the demarcation of the Western part of the Sino-Russian border and expressed their willingness to increase interregional economic cooperation. In June 1995, China's Premier Li Peng attended the second Sino-Russian summit in Moscow, where the Chinese Prime Minister and his Russian counterpart Viktor Chernomyrdin confirmed their mutual support, commitment to maintaining regional stability and cooperating in global affairs. This meeting coincided with deterioration of Russia and China's relations with the United States caused by Taiwanese President Lee Tenghui's visit to the United States and Western criticism of the military intervention in Chechnya (Wishnick, 2001a: 128).

Thus, once again, a power shift in the strategic triangle caused by the U.S. aggressive foreign policy brought China and Russia together in the second half of the 1990s. This period saw a dramatic change in Russian foreign policy and Sino-Russian relations alike. In January 1996, Evgenii Primakov was appointed as Russia's new Minister of Foreign Affairs. This decision was widely perceived as a reorientation of Russian foreign policy toward the East, and namely China and India (Pant, 2004: 21). Unlike his pro-Western predecessor Kozyrev, Yevgenii Primakov, a geopolitically savvy adherent of orientalism and Eurasianism, held that Russia must reassert its interests in Asia and in the Middle East and focus more on developing multilateral cooperation with the former Soviet Republics (Wishnick, 2001a: 800). Like Chinese leaders, Yevgenii Primakov was a staunch advocate for a multipolar world, in which, according to his vision, no country would play a dominant role. The second half of the decade was marked by Russia's reassessment of its geopolitical role in the world, which policymakers in the Kremlin started to associate more with the East rather than West after Moscow's failed rapprochement with the United States.

In April 1996, Russian president Boris Yeltsin and his Chinese counterpart, Jiang Zemin, signed a joint communiqué, which proclaimed a "strategic partnership" between Russia and China and marked a new stage of partnership between Moscow and Beijing directed towards strategic cooperation in the 21st century. The two presidents reiterated their determination to seek a multipolar world and stressed that the new partnership would not be aimed at any third country. Nonetheless, given U.S. assertive policy toward the Taiwan issue and NATO expansion, Moscow and Beijing considered this "strategic relationship" an effective mechanism to counter U.S. power in the world. Furthermore, during the summit, Chinese and Russian leaders announced an ultimate goal of increasing trade toward $20 billion by the end of the century and identified energy, nuclear power, and large-scale construction as priorities for both sides (Garnett, 2001: 46). Besides, in April 1996, China, Russia, Kazakhstan, Kyrgyzstan, and Tajikistan signed the Shanghai agreement, which addressed such issues as confidence-building measures along the shared borders between states, and exchange of information on military exercises. A year later, significant progress was made on the reduction of troops along China's border with the former Soviet countries after the signing of a five-party agreement in April 1997.

During the 1997 Sino-Russian summit in Moscow, Boris Yeltsin and Jiang Zemin again emphasized their shared goal of establishing a multipolar world in a "Joint Declaration on a Multipolar World and the Formation of a New International Order" (Buszynski, 2010: 266). However, rhetoric aside, as China's prospects for cooperation with the United States increased, Beijing's reasons for strengthening relations with Moscow reached their limit (Rozman, 1998: 404). Moreover, economic relations between China and Russia, lagged far behind political achievements. Despite pledges to achieve the level of $20 billion in bilateral trade, both countries fell significantly short of attaining this objective (level of $20 billion was surpassed only in 2004). Accordingly, in 1997, only 5 per cent of Russia's exports flowed to China, and only 2.5 per cent of Chinese exports went to Russia. The prospects of joint Sino-Russian energy projects were overshadowed by the economic crisis in Russia as late of 1998. By the end of the 1990s, bilateral trade between Russia and China was in a steady decline.

CHINA, RUSSIA, AND WORLD ORDER

In 1996, China and Russia proclaimed a strategic cooperative partnership, which was subsequently anchored in the Treaty for Good Neigh-borliness, Friendship, and Cooperation signed in 2001. In 2008, both countries ratified an action plan to implement the treaty. In 2011, the nature of the relationship was raised to a "comprehensive strategic and cooperative partnership," the highest level of cooperation from China's perspective. Since the 2001 treaty, Chinese and Russian leaders have signed more than 50 additional bilateral agreements. When Russian president Dmitry Medvedev attended the Shanghai Expo in 2009, he proclaimed that Russian-Chinese relations had achieved their "highest point in history." This partnership has been characterized by frequent visits between high-level leaders, growing cooperation in energy, expanding trade, Russian arms sales to China, expanded people-to-people contacts, and some level of diplomatic cooperation over the Middle East and other issues.

The partnership between China and Russia is motivated by two broad factors: common views on what they object to in the contemporary world order and practical concerns. Regarding world order, both countries hope to end what they have seen as US hegemony and institute a more multipolar system. This would involve a stronger role for the United Nations Security Council (UNSC), where Russia and China both have a veto, in dealing with pressing security issues. There is, of course, some irony in the fact that the "liberal" United States has reservations regarding the United Nations while China and Russia embrace this institution. A more multipolar world order where China and Russia had greater influence would raise their status and better protect states that raise the ire of the West but where China and/or Russia have important interests, such as Iran, Syria, and North Korea. In March 2014, Russia used its veto in the UNSC to defeat a draft resolution condemning the referendum by which residents of Crimea voted to join Russia.

Another element of the current world order that China and Russia wish to undermine is the liberal emphasis on human rights and minority self-determination and the resulting erosion of sovereignty that these entail. Russia and China believe that human rights are primarily an issue for state governments, not the world community. This view stems in large part from domestic politics. Russia wants freedom to do what it sees as necessary with Chechnya, the Caucasus, and most recently,

Ukraine. China is determined to suppress all dissent in Tibet, Xinjiang, and other restive regions, as well as recover Taiwan. Moreover, both China and Russia believe in maintaining geographic spheres of influence. For Russia, this means having decisive influence in the foreign policy of the states of the "near abroad," or republics of the former Soviet Union. For China, this means a privileged position for its territorial claims in the South China Sea and the maintenance of a friendly government in North Korea. For both China and Russia, preventing revolutions in Central Asia or other former Soviet republics that would bring democratic, pro-Western governments into power is a priority.

Another relevant world order issue for Russia and China is reform of international institutions. Interestingly, this does not include the UNSC. Neither country is eager to see an expansion of the Security Council or loss of its veto power there. However, it does include reforms to financial institutions such as the World Bank and International Monetary Fund (IMF), giving a greater share of authority in those institutions to non-Western states. It also includes the development of multilateral organizations that exclude the West, such as the BRICS (Brazil, Russia, India, China, and South Africa) and the Shanghai Cooperation Organization (SCO).

Nevertheless, Russian and Chinese views on world order diverge in important respects as well. It is unclear what kind of world order China ultimately will seek, but there are numerous voices on foreign policy being heard in China today with multiple views on the proper direction of foreign policy. While Hu Jintao insisted that China's development is peaceful, recent aggressive policies in the East and South China Seas lead China's neighbours to doubt these assurances. Some in China, including some People's Liberation Army (PLA) officers, push for a triumphalist foreign policy that seeks Chinese hegemony. Other thinkers envision a return to an "all under heaven" system consisting of a hierarchical world order led by a benevolent Chinese imperialism. Most of these views of world order envision a more powerful international position for China that could undermine important Russian interests.

Putin's view of world order is more limited, but also challenges the status quo. Putin demands that Russia be treated as a great power. While attempting to build closer ties with Europe, Russia still insists on keeping the former Soviet republics in its orbit, a policy some compare to the Monroe Doctrine and others describe as imperialism. While this has mainly disrupted the international system in Europe, with Russian military force used in Ukraine and Georgia, it also confronts Chinese interests in Central Asia.

The Chinese-Russian relationship is also built on very practical issues. The first is economics. Both Russia and China place a high priority on domestic economic development. One result is that mutual trade and investment are important to both sides. As Russia has an abundance of oil and other natural resources while China is an importer of such products, the energy trade is a practical way in which both sides benefit. In addition, the Russian Far East (RFE) has an undeveloped economy that Moscow cannot afford to expand alone. Economic growth in the RFE has been a goal of Russian-Chinese cooperation, although one that has been less successful. Overall, the levels of trade and investment outside the energy sector have been disappointing.

Security is another important issue. Threats and border clashes led perilously close to war in the late 1960s and early 1970s. By the 1980s, both China and Russia were absorbed with domestic concerns. A secure Russian-Chinese border was imperative for both sides. After a series of negotiations, the last border dispute was resolved in 2008 and the border demilitarized. In addition, throughout the 1990s and early 2000s, the Russian defence industry was desperate for orders and cash. China wanted advanced weapons systems, and both sides benefited from Russian weapons sales to China, including fighter planes and submarines.

In politics, economics, and security, the Sino-Russia "comprehensive strategic and cooperative partnership" is driven by mutual interests, not mutual affection. Dmitri Trenin, a well-regarded analyst of Russian politics, observes, "There has never been a spirit of camaraderie about Russo-Chinese summits. The leaders do not take off their ties or use first names. And there have been few truly strategic conversations. But the summits are invariably business-like and results-orientated."

In a similar vein, Andrew Kuchins asserts that Russia has "profound ambivalence" toward China, but acts in a pragmatic fashion. Trenin's conclusion from his study of Chinese-Russian relations is that "while both countries need each other and would benefit from a stable political relationship and close economic ties, both Moscow and Beijing lack the long-term strategies to create such a bond."

The foundations of the Sino-Russian partnership may not be stable for the long term. As China rises in power, its conception of the ideal world order is likely to diverge from Russia's viewpoint. For example, Leszek Buszynski argues that Russia has been eclipsed by China in the Asia-Pacific region. Russia is being marginalized, and its partnership with China has not been in Russia's best interests. Moreover, there may be increasing conflict between China and Russia over spheres of influence that overlap, especially in Central Asia. In sum, world order is driven by values but also power, and as China's power increases relative to Russia's, there will be a divergence of views on such an order.

Even practical issues change character over time. Growing Chinese military capabilities may make Russia rethink its border security. Russian concerns about being primarily a provider of resources to China may dampen economic ties, as may Russian fears about Chinese dominating the RFE. Thus, it is worth exploring issue areas to understand where China and Russia cooperate and where they have conflicts.

Russia's annexation of Crimea in March 2014 illustrated tensions between the Chinese and Russian worldviews which also affect practical issues. Russia's move put China in an uncomfortable position. China's foreign policy declarations (if not always its actions) have long rejected outside interference in the internal affairs of any state. China has often criticized the United States for violating this principle, and Russia clearly violated the noninterference principle in Ukraine. Moreover, China has important interests in Ukraine. It imports Ukrainian weapons and military technology, it has agricultural interests in Ukraine, and Ukraine is the linchpin for Chinese investment plans in Eastern Europe. Most seriously, the Crimean referendum provides an unwanted precedent that residents of Taiwan, Tibet, or Xinjiang might refer to in calling for similar referenda.

On the other hand, Russia is an important strategic partner of China, and Putin clearly counts on Chinese support. The Chinese government saw advantages in a Western setback, while the Chinese press went further in praising Putin for being strong and poking the West in the eye.

Moreover, China had much to gain in a confrontation between Putin and the West that make Russia more dependent on China for energy purchases and economic growth.

In the end, China refused to commit to either side. It abstained on a UNSC draft resolution condemning the Crimean referendum. It issued bland statements that were fairly noncommittal and tried to muddle through in a way that would not offend Ukraine or Russia. However, clearly practical considerations and realpolitik overrode a firm stance on principles.

CHINA-RUSSIA SPECIFIC INTERACTION

As noted, a number of very practical issues affect the Chinese-Russian relationship in various ways. Most significant among these are economics, security, and shared and/or competing interests in Central Asia.

Economics

The most important economic exchange between Russia and China involves energy. Russia is a major energy exporter, while China's imports grow each year. Moreover, China has become a profitable market for Russian oil. Nevertheless, creating the necessary energy infrastructure and reaching concrete agreements on energy supplies and pricing has not gone smoothly, exacerbated by infighting among Russian energy companies and mutual mistrust and misunderstanding between China and Russia. This has led to frustration, especially in China.

After years of negotiations and Russian efforts to play off China against Japan, in January 2011, Russia began shipping oil to China through the East Siberia–Pacific Ocean (ESPO) pipeline. This was enabled by a 2009 agreement that provided a $25 billion Chinese loan to Russia's oil and pipeline companies, Rosneft and Transneft, with an agreement for Russia to provide China with 300 million tons of crude oil over a 30-year period. However, in the first two months of the pipeline's operations, Russians charged the Chinese National Petroleum Corporation (CNPC) with underpaying for oil by $100 million. The dispute was settled the next year. Moreover, when Chinese president Xi Jinping visited Moscow in June 2013, China and Russia signed an additional crude oil deal worth $270 billion.

Natural gas, however, has yet to flow from Russia to China, in spite of a 2006 memorandum between Gazprom and CNPC that pledged 30 billion cubic meters of gas to China via a western route and 38 billion cubic meters across a route in the east, as well as an additional 2009 agreement. Russia and China have been sharply divided on the price of gas, and as a result, the necessary pipelines have not been built. This is due, in part, to issues in Chinese politics related to CNPC. Some analysts speculated that a loan deal with Gazprom would eventually lead to a resolution, similar to the oil deal.

However, it seems that gas exports will no longer be a monopoly of Gazprom. Rosneft now has plans to sell liquid natural gas (LNG) to Japanese companies from a terminal on Sakhalin, while Novatek, an independent gas producer, has partnered with CNPC to sell China LNG from the Arctic. Finally, at the May 2014 summit between Vladimir Putin and Xi Jinping, China and Russia agreed to a 30-year gas deal that will begin delivering gas from Russia to China in 2018 after the necessary infrastructure is completed. The price of that gas is referred to as a "commercial secret."

In a related issue, Russia has clear economic and political interests in further developing the RFE, where it needs to reassert its control over the region and form a stronger basis for international influence in the Asia-Pacific region. Energy plays a role in these goals, but there are other aspects to this challenge as well. After the fall of the Soviet Union, the RFE was virtually ignored while the new leaders of Russia attempted to put the state back together. Since 1991, the population in the area has shrunk by 20 percent, to 6.28 million, and is projected to drop further to 4.7 million by 2025.[24] However, in recent years Russia has paid new attention to the RFE, due in part to the growth of China and dimming prospects for economic growth based on European trade and investment. Thus, in 2009 the Russian government approved the "Strategy for Socio-Economic Development of the Far East and the Baikal Region until 2025 (Strategy 2025)" to promote the development of its eastern regions. The 2012 Asia-Pacific Economic Cooperation (APEC) summit in Vladivostok also served as a catalyst for Moscow's attention, with the Russian government reportedly spending over $20 billion to upgrade Vladivostok's infrastructure.

Russia has a dilemma in developing the RFE. On the one hand, it needs the assistance of China and other Asia-Pacific powers to spur economic growth. The Russian government does not have the resources itself, and corruption and bureaucratic inefficiency stymie much of its efforts. On the other hand, Russia does not want the RFE to become an appendage of China. It is uncertain if Russia will be able to successfully walk this line. In August of 2013, the Chinese State Development Bank announced that it may spend $5 billion in the RFE to finance Russian development programs. Moreover, Chinese workers reportedly now farm 40 percent of arable land in the Jewish Autonomous Region of the RFE, while Chinese farmers grew 90 percent of vegetables sold in the RFE in 2012.[26] In sum, the RFE provides numerous opportunities for economic cooperation that would benefit Chinese and Russians. However, these opportunities also provide a potential liability to the Russian state as it seeks to establish a firm grip on its eastern regions. China and Russia are also finding areas of cooperation on trade and investment. In 2010, China became Russia's biggest trade partner, and Russia's Micex exchange began trading the yuan and ruble as China and Russia sought to reduce dependence on the dollar in international trade. Nevertheless, Russia's place in China's overall trade is still modest. According to Chinese data published by the IMF, Chinese exports to Russia rose from $13.21 billion in 2005 to $44.07 billion in 2012, more than tripling. Nevertheless, calculations show that Chinese exports to Russia as a percentage of total exports only rose from 1.7 percent in 2005 to 2.2 percent in 2012. For sake of comparison, Chinese exports to Russia in 2012 were only 12.5 percent of Chinese exports to the United States. From 2005 to 2012, Chinese imports from Russia rose from $15.89 billion to $43.95 billion, although the percentage of total imports remained at 2.4 percent.

Russian data provided to the IMF shows that Russian exports to China grew from 5.4 percent of its total in 2005 to 6.8 percent in 2012. Russian exports to the United States in 2012 were only 36 percent of exports to China. Russian imports from China grew more than fivefold from 2005 to 2011, rising from 5.2 percent of the total in 2005 to 14 percent of the total in 2012.27 Thus, Russia is more dependent on mutual trade than China. In 2013, total trade rose only 2 percent from the previous year to $90 billion.

While increasing trade is beneficial for both states, the nature of trade is of concern to Russia. Russia fears becoming a provider of natural resources to China and little else, and in 2006 Putin made a political issue of unbalanced trade. Chinese observers tend to complain of structural issues. For example, writer Qiu Huafei notes that Sino-Russian trade is largely focused on the needs of border communities, involving too few advanced technological goods. Qiu also points out that trade is hindered by contract violations, lack of institutionalized channels for resolving disputes, poor treatment of Chinese business personnel in Russia, the prevalence of a "China threat" mentality in Russia, and unsettled Russian debts. Other Chinese analysts, however, are more optimistic, pointing to the potential for Russian high-technology exports to China and foreseeing a Chinese move toward more of a domestic consumption-based economy that will provide greater export opportunities for Russia.

Security

Following armed clashes in 1969,[31] both sides' desire for border security became a major factor leading to rapprochement in the late 1980s and early 1990s and continues to be a key issue. Russia looks defensively at the United States and NATO and also sees a major contemporary threat in terrorism coming from its south. At the same time, China is embroiled in disputes with Japan and Southeast Asia and seeks to suppress minority unrest within its borders. Each side needs assurance that their joint border will not create problems.

One fascinating aspect of the security relationship is the recent change in relative power positions. During the Cold War, the Soviet Union was the dominant power in the political, economic, and military arenas. Today, apart from nuclear forces and the technological sophistication of some major weapons systems, China is ascendant in the relationship. In fact, the rapid buildup of the PLA might lead one to expect that Russia would shift to a more defensive posture toward China.

There is some evidence that this is occurring, although for the most part, Russia does not see China as a major security threat at this point. China's rise makes the world more multipolar, giving space to Russia. Moreover, Russia sees China as focused on its east and south and understands that China has many domestic problems that take up resources and the attention of its leaders. For Russia, good ties with China are important for Russian security. From China's perspective, strong ties with Russia help prevent closer Russian ties with NATO in a manner that would isolate China. Likewise, Russia's annexation of Crimea was seen by many in China as a welcome defeat of the West. Taking various factors into consideration, one Chinese analyst suggests that the United States, Russia, and China are all hedging against each other. Arms sales are one important component in the Sino-Russian security relationship. China has been engaged in a sustained, long-term buildup of high-tech arms since the 1990s. With the United States and Europe refusing to sell China most types of military equipment since 1989, Russia has been China's most important source of foreign weapons. From 2006 to 2010, 84 percent of Chinese arms imports came from Russia.

From the Russian perspective, the period since the collapse of the Soviet Union has been marked by severe economic difficulties, moderated now by energy exports. As a result, military sales to China have been a welcome and at times industry-saving source of funds, and Russia has sold China a large variety of weapons. These include Su-27 and Su-30 fighter aircraft, surface to air missile (SAM) systems, *Sovremenny*-class destroyers, helicopters, transport aircraft, antiship missiles, torpedoes, radars, and jet engines. Nevertheless, Russian arms sales to China peaked in 2005 and have declined since then. Sales have dropped from \$3.13 billion in 2005 (in constant 1990 prices) to \$679 million in 2012. While sales to China comprised 60 percent of Russian arms exports in 2005, by 2012 the figure had fallen to only 8 percent. Most major weapon system deliveries from Russia to China were completed by 2009, and since 2006, major arms exports have been limited to jet engines, fire control radars, transport aircraft, and helicopters.

There are a variety of explanations for this drop in arms sales. From China's perspective, its own defence industries are capable of producing many of the weapons previously purchased from Russia. Additionally, there was some dissatisfaction with Russian arms sales.

Russia often refused to sell China its highest-technology equipment, even though it was willing to sell more-advanced items to India. This has been an irritant to China. China hoped for more licensed production of systems within China and technology transfers, and was unhappy with delivery delays and the quality of Russian arms. The Russian perspective is more complex. On the one hand, there is consternation about China reverse-engineering Russian technology and then using it in its own weapons exports, beating Russia on price in the process. Russians claim the Chinese J-11B fighter plane is a copy of the Su-27, while China is heavily marketing the JF-17 fighter, developed with Pakistan. In 2011, the Russian government commissioned a report entitled "The Strategies and Tactics of Chinese Exporters of Arms and Military Equipment," and the head of the Mikoyan (MiG) and Sukhoi design bureau sent a letter to Roxoboronexport asking that it not sell large numbers of RD-93 engines to China because the MiG-29 competes against the JF-17 for export sales and the JF-17 uses that engine.

Various Russian officials are also concerned about the strategic implications of China's growing military power. In this regard, there are differing opinions among Russian elites. Kevin Ryan notes that "the view from Moscow of military relations with China varies depending on the organizational viewpoint of the individual." Arms manufacturers have a different perspective from strategic planners. Russia faces the conundrum that China wants more and more sophisticated weapons, which might decisively affect the balance of power in the Asia-Pacific region (alienating the United States), as well as the balance of power between China and Russia itself.

The arms sales relationship between Beijing and Moscow will require careful observation as a barometer of their defence cooperation. Recently, there has been discussion of renewed Russian arms sales to China, especially the 400-kilometer-range S-400 SAM system and the Su-35S fighter, Russia's most advanced weapons. In December 2012, *Jane's 360* reported that Russia will also sell four *Lada*-class diesel submarines to China. Nevertheless, these deals are not firm. Another indicator of Sino-Russian defence ties is joint military exercises. The first military exercises were Peace Mission 2005, held under the auspices of the SCO with the publicly stated aim of combating terrorism. This exercise was conducted in the RFE and China's Shandong province and involved naval and amphibious operations. Ten thousand troops participated, as well as submarines and strategic bombers. This led to speculation that the exercises were about much more than terrorism, with China hoping that they would be seen as simulating an invasion of Taiwan. Various other Peace Mission exercises have been held as well. However, the level of actual coordination in such exercises is usually low.

Recent naval manoeuvres demonstrated greater coordination in military cooperation. From 5 to 12 July 2013, Russia and China conducted joint naval exercises of unprecedented size, named Joint Sea 2013. China sent seven naval vessels, including a guided-missile destroyer and frigates, while Russia provided 11 warships, including the Pacific fleet's flagship *Varyag*, a guided-missile cruiser, and a Kilo-class submarine. The exercises focused on surface warfare, antisubmarine warfare, air defence, and the rescue of a kidnapped vessel. Apart from the military aspects of the drills, the political message was also important. China would like the exercises to be seen as a warning to the United States and Japan, with an implication that Russia stands beside China in its various maritime disputes, especially the Diaoyu/Senkaku Islands. Russia, however, has taken a neutral position in these disputes, thus the exercises may misrepresent Russia's actual position.

As if to balance these exercises, shortly after the Chinese departed, Russia began its own unilateral military drills. In the largest military exercise since the fall of the Soviet Union, it reportedly conducted manoeuvres involving 160,000 troops, 500 tanks, 130 combat aircraft, and ships from the Pacific fleet. The exercise involved the rapid reaction of Russian forces deployed to the RFE. It was designed to demonstrate the power of the Russian military to its Asian neighbours and its ability to quickly move forces to defend its eastern domains. Thus, while the naval exercises in early July showed tight cooperation with the Chinese military, the exercises later in the month demonstrated Russian independence and the ability of Russia to defend itself against any potential Chinese encroachment.

Central Asia

Central Asia (defined here as Kazakhstan, Kyrgyzstan, Tajikistan, Uzbekistan, and Turkmenistan) is an arena of relatively weak states with small populations attempting to govern vast areas. The region has large energy reserves and is strategically located between China, Russia, and the Middle East. Moreover, it can contribute to stability in Afghanistan but is also vulnerable to radical ideology and violence spilling over Afghanistan's borders. Thus, it is a region where Russia, China, the United States, India, Pakistan, Iran, and Turkey all seek influence. The Central Asians themselves, of course, strive for autonomy and room to maneuver, playing the various powers against each other. They also have squabbles with each other. In this setting, Russia and China engage in both conflict and cooperation. So far, their common interest in regional stability and keeping US influence out of the area has led the cooperative element of the relationship to dominate. Charles Ziegler notes, "Surprisingly, these two powers have found their interests coincide remarkably well in Central Asia, at least in the short term."

Zbigniew Brzezinski noted in 1997 that Russia's dilemma in Central Asia is that it is too weak to dominate the area politically and too weak economically to develop the region. This still holds true today. Central Asia is part of Russia's "near abroad," a strategic part of the former Soviet Union. Russia sees Central Asia as being within its sphere of influence. The security of Central Asian states, and the form of government they adopt, is particularly important to Russia. However, it also has economic interests. Russia has attempted to control the energy infrastructure of Central Asia, purchasing energy at cheap prices and then reexporting it to Europe at a profit. It further uses its influence to protect ethnic Russians left in the area after the disintegration of the Soviet Union.

China has three major interrelated goals in Central Asia. The first is to ensure stability in its northwestern Xinjiang Uyghur Autonomous Region. China does not want Central Asia to be used as a base for promoting separatism in Xinjiang. Second, China desires closer overall economic and infrastructure linkages with Central Asia. This will further its overall goal of rapid economic development and, in Beijing's view, stabilize

Xinjiang. Third, China strives to increase energy imports from Central Asia by winning energy contracts and developing the infrastructure to deliver oil and gas to China. China sees this as an essential part of an energy diversification strategy. Moreover, it sees pipeline routes across Central Asia as more secure than sea lanes from the Middle East that are susceptible to disruption by the US Navy.

Russia and China both want to eliminate the "three evils" of "terrorism, separatism, and religious extremism" from the region. They work to reduce as much as possible the influence of the United States in Central Asia by seeking to limit US military basing in the region and preventing new "colour revolutions" that might bring stronger democratic governance to the states of the area.

China has been active in developing infrastructure in Central Asia. For example, the China Road and Bridge Company won a contract to build a road from Osh in Kyrgyzstan to the Irkeshtam Pass with China, funded in part by the Chinese government. China is developing rail links to connect Xinjiang with Afghanistan via Tajikistan, while Chinese telecom and internet companies are tying the region together electronically. China has been active in the Asian Development Bank's (ADB) Central Asia Regional Economic Cooperation (CAREC) program, designed to accelerate economic growth and reduce poverty. Moreover, China is systematically attempting to increase its soft power and "people to people" understanding in Central Asia through Confucius Institutes, government-funded organizations that promote Chinese language and culture outside China. Russia has lost ground to China here, although there is still suspicion of the latter among residents of the region due to China's size and potential influence.

Chinese president Xi Jinping's visit to Central Asian states in September 2013 illustrated the success of China's strategy when he sealed economic deals in what he called the "Silk Road Economic Zone." President Xi visited Turkmenistan, Uzbekistan, Kyrgyzstan, and Kazakhstan. In Kazakhstan, Xi and Kazakh president Nursultan Nazarbayev signed $30 billion worth of agreements and symbolically opened a 700-mile gas pipeline that, in conjunction with other pipelines, will take gas from the Caspian Sea to the Chinese coast. China, through CNPC, also purchased an 8.4 percent stake in Kazakhstan's Kashagan oil field in the Caspian Sea, joining a consortium of international oil companies. In Turkmenistan, Xi opened the world's second biggest gas field, Galkynysh, which will lead to a tripling of Chinese gas imports from that country. In Uzbekistan, he signed $15 billion in energy deals.

With China's major economic investments in the region and establishment of new "strategic partnerships," Russian deputy foreign minister Igor Morgulov felt it necessary to assert, in a not entirely convincing manner, "Our Chinese friends recognize the traditional role our country continues to play in this region, so we do not see any regional rivalry problems."

The institutional body that ties Russia and China together on Central Asian issues is the SCO. The SCO consists of China, Russia, Kazakhstan, Kyrgyzstan, Tajikistan, and Uzbekistan.

Established in 2001 with a history rooted in successful border negotiations, the SCO provides a mechanism for Russia and China to cooperate on issues relevant to Central Asia, and, as mentioned earlier, is the institution through which China and Russia conduct military exercises. The SCO is a unique organization for China in that China took the initiative in its founding and considers itself a leader of the organization. Chinese analysts proudly point to the SCO as a key example of China's "new diplomacy" based on trust, equality, respect for diversity, and an emphasis on development.

In some ways, the SCO has been very successful from the perspective of its founders. One Chinese analyst notes that the SCO has been able to maintain stability through the world economic crisis that began in 2008, and there was no "Arab Spring" in the region. There have been no major terrorist attacks in the area, Chinese and Russian relations are good, and the Central Asian states are cooperating. Moreover, other regional actors have been eager to join the SCO as observers.

However, Russia and China do have differences over the SCO. Russia demonstrates some ambiguity toward the organization. It would prefer that the Collective Security Treaty Organization or the Eurasian Economic Community, both of which Russia dominates and do not include China, take the lead security and economic roles in Central Asia.

Moreover, Russia prefers that the SCO primarily focus on security cooperation and strategic issues, while China's emphasis is on economic cooperation. From a Chinese perspective, Russia is not very active in cooperating with China in the SCO but does not block Chinese initiatives. There has been disagreement on additional members, too. One Chinese analyst claims that while Moscow has reportedly supported the membership of Iran, India, and Pakistan, China believes that this would move the focus away from Central Asia and give the SCO an anti-Western character, which China does not want. Furthermore, the SCO has challenges in actually implementing its cooperative agreements, due in part to the lack of capacity in Central Asian member states. Yet, in spite of these differences, the SCO remains a relevant organization in structuring ties between Beijing and Moscow.

Implications for the United States

The United States does not and should not oppose good relations between Russia and China. A peaceful relationship between these two nuclear powers leads to stability in Eurasia. The time period in the 1960s and 1970s when China and the Soviet Union were close to war was very dangerous. Washington also views closer ties between Russia and China as helpful to US interests in a variety of areas. For example, energy cooperation between Russia and China can, in the long run, make China less dependent on Iranian oil supplies, possibly loosening China's ties with Iran's government. Chinese and Russian cooperation is useful in developing Central Asia while preventing any one power from dominating the region, while greater coordination between Russia and China may help in efforts to stabilize Afghanistan after the US withdrawal.

Nevertheless, the relationship between the United States, Russia, and China also has a competitive, triangular aspect to it, with each side adapting hedging strategies. One analyst in Beijing explicitly stated that, despite much of the rhetoric coming out of Beijing to the contrary, the US pivot to China is a hedging strategy rather than a containment strategy. China, similarly, is hedging against the United States through its relationship with Russia. Russia hedges against both China and the West. Each state worries about the other two countries getting too close, although arguably the United States is less susceptible to this worry than China or Russia. For example, Russia strongly objects to the concept of a G2 between the United States and China, as this would deny Russia a seat at the table in making decisions on world order. In fact, Russia is overshadowed by more powerful states in most multilateral forums, including the G8 and BRICS gatherings. Similarly, China is worried about the potential for closer Russian ties with NATO, and in particular does not want to see joint missile defence cooperation between the two sides. At the same time, China does not want the United States to believe that it has entered an alliance with Russia that would threaten US interests. Similarly, Russia looks to the West for modernization and development and does not want a relationship with China that would isolate it from Europe or the United States.

How can the United States best manage this foreign policy triangle? First, it needs to understand the dynamics of this triangle and consider how policy decisions on issues important to Russia or China affect the triangle. When the United States supports policies that Russia and China oppose or commits to policies targeted at China or Russia, it drives those two states closer together. This does not mean the United States cannot oppose Russia and China on any given issue, but it must understand that closer Russian-Chinese cooperation on world order issues will result. One example is Syria. We can debate whether the US decision to back away from a military strike on Syria was correct in terms of Middle East policy. However, the decision to compromise with Russia did defuse a world order question that was pushing Russia and China closer to each other and further from the United States. Another example is the Ukraine conflict. Recent Western economic sanctions on Russia have created stronger economic links between China and Russia. Policymakers should assess regional policies both in light of their regional impact and a broader strategic perspective.

Second, Russia wants to again be an important player in the Asia-Pacific region. The historic US interest has been to ensure that no single country dominates the region. A stronger Russian role in Pacific affairs, bolstered by a more prosperous RFE, can be good for the United States once the Ukrainian crisis is resolved. Therefore, the United States should in the long run encourage better relations between Japan and Russia and between South Korea and Russia. This means encouraging energy exports from Russia to South Korea and Japan and encouraging a resolution of the dispute between Japan and Russia over the Kurile Islands.

The United States should provide incentives for US companies to invest in the RFE to the extent it is profitable. The US Pacific Command has engaged Russia through port calls and Russian participation in RIM-PAC exercises, but more might be done to develop military-to-military cooperation.

Third, the time may soon come to press for three-way nuclear negotiations. China's historic policy has been to maintain a small nuclear deterrent whose numbers are a tightly controlled secret, claiming that the United States and Russia must substantially reduce their forces before China will enter into arms control negotiations. However, the United States and Russia have reduced their deployed nuclear weapons, while China has been presumably increasing its weapons. Thus, Alexi Arbatov and Vladimir Dvorkin assert that "it can be speculated that the real motives behind China's complete secrecy about its nuclear forces lie not in their 'weakness' and 'small size' but in the much larger strength of China's actual nuclear arsenal than can be construed from observing the weapons deployed on its surface. In addition, China's economic and technical potential would allow it to build up its nuclear arms rapidly."

This is more threatening to Russia than the United States because of Russia's greater reliance on nuclear weapons for defence. Thus, it may finally be time to push for trilateral arms control negotiations, although at this point there are still serious obstacles to such negotiations. These include new strains in US-Russian ties, continued Chinese secrecy over the size of its arsenal and its nuclear doctrine, as well as Chinese insistence that Russia and the United States further disarm before China engages in meaningful nuclear reduction talks.

Fourth, the US withdrawal from Afghanistan opens new possibilities for three-way cooperation to work for stability in Afghanistan and all of Central Asia. While the United States was criticized by both Russia and China for having troops in Afghanistan, they now fear the results of a US withdrawal. China feels it lacks the resources to deal with Afghanistan, and many Chinese analysts feel the Afghan government will fall after 2014 when Washington withdraws combat troops. China, which is heavily concerned with its own domestic stability, is worried about the implications of potential chaos in Afghanistan for what it sees as its Uyghur problem. Thus, it is clearly in the interest of all three states to have a strong Afghan government after 2014 that can minimize the level of violence within Afghanistan and prevent the spread of extremism and terror outside its borders. The United States, Russia, China, and perhaps the SCO can coordinate policies to produce an outcome that will be in the interest of every state. In other words, the struggle in Afghanistan and its environs is one of organized states against nonstate actors, and the states have incentives to cooperate.

In conclusion, the Chinese-Russian relationship is strong and has been building momentum for close to two decades. Russia and China are bound together by a desire to bring about a world order that is marked more by a concert of great powers than US hegemony, an order that is defined by classical Westphalian values as opposed to liberal concepts that degrade the sanctity of state sovereignty. The relationship is also built on practical cooperation in the realm of economics, energy, security, Central Asian issues, and the SCO. Nevertheless, this is not an anti-US alliance. For their own development goals, Russia and China need the United States and Europe. China feels that its developmental accomplishments are fragile and domestic unrest is a threat, while Russia has failed to substantially expand its economic base beyond energy production. A certain degree of cooperation between Russia and China can be in US interests. Moreover, each of the issue areas discussed in this article has arenas of conflict. If in the long run Chinese power continues to grow relative to that of Russia, these conflicts will become more intense as Moscow resists being identified as a junior partner of Beijing. With smart policies, Washington can work the strategic triangle to ensure that its core interests are maintained.

Bibliography

Ajey Lele: *Strategic Technologies for the Military : Breaking New Frontiers*, Sage, Delhi, 2009.

Alam, Aftab : *US Policy Towards South Asia: Special Reference to Indo-Russia Relations*, Raj, Delhi, 1998.

Benjamin, Joseph : *China-India Relations : Prospect and Retrospect*, Reference Press, Delhi, 2004.

Bhatia, Shyam: *India's Nuclear Bomb,* Ghaziabad: Vikas Publishing House, 1979.

Brooks, Constance : *Disaster Preparedness,* Washington, DC, Association for Research Libraries, 1993.

Buszynski, Lezsek: *The future of China-Russia relations.* Lexington: University Press of Kentucky, 2010.

Fatima, T. : *Islamic Law and Judiciary,* Deep & Deep Publications, New Delhi, 2001.

Friedman, G.: *The Future of War: Power, Technology and American World Dominance in the 21st Century*, N.Y., Random House, 1996.

Ghosh, Ajoy : *China-Russia Conflict : Threat to South Asian Security*, Reference Press, Delhi, 2003.

Goldstein, Joshua S.: *Three-way Street: Strategic Reciprocity in World Politics.* Chicago: University of Chicago Press, 1990.

Harold Glenn. *Fundamental Economic Issues in National Defense.* Washington, DC: Brookings Institution, 1941.

Haukkala, Hiski: *The EU-Russia Strategic Partnership: The limits of post-sovereignty in international relations.* Oxon: Routledge, 2010.

Heimanson, Rudolph: *Dictionary of Military,* N.Y.: Oceana Publications, 1967.

Holsti, K.: *The State, War, and the State of War,* Cambridge, Cambridge Univ. Press, 1996.

Huntington, S.P.: *The China Modernisation Military and the State*, N.Y., Vintage Books, 1964.

Ikenberry, John G.: *After Victory: Institutions, Strategic Restraint, and the Rebuilding of Order after Major Wars*. Princeton, NJ: Princeton University Press, 2001.

Imtiaz, A.: *State and Foreign Policy: India's Role in South Asia*, New Delhi, Vikas, 1993.

Janowitz, M.: *The Professional Soldier: A Social and Political Portrait,* N.Y., The Free Press, 1960.

Jones, W.H.: *The Government and Politics of Indian Military*, London, Hutchinson, 1971.

Kapur, C.K. : *Chinese Military Modernisation*, Manas, Delhi, 2003.

Kelly, John B.: *Britain and the Persian Gulf 1795-1880*, Oxford, Clarendon Press, 1968.

Pierre, Andrew J. *The Global Politics of Arms Sales*. Princeton, N.J., 1982.

Qureshi, A. Iqbal : *Islam and the Theory of Interest,* Kitab Bhavan, New Delhi, 1994.

Radhakrishna: *Military Ethics: Guidelines for Peace and War*, Sumit Enterprises, Delhi, 2009.

Rhodes, Richard, *The Making of the Atomic Bomb*, New York: Simon and Schuster, 1988.

Sivard, R L.: *World Military and Social Expenditures,* World Priorities, Washington D.C, 1993.

Smith, C.: *The Diffusion of Small Arms and Light Weapons in Pakistan and Northern India,* Centre for Defence Studies, Brassey's, London, 1993.

Thampi, Madhavi : *India and China in the Colonial World,* Social Science Press, Delhi, 2010.

Thayer, George. *The War Business.* New York, 1969.

Van de Goor, L.L.P.: *Conflict and Development: The Causes of Conflict in Developing Countries,* The Netherlands Institute of International Relations, The Hague, 1994.

Whitaker, D. J.: *The Terrorism Reader,* New York: Routledge, 2001.

Worster, Donald : *Dust Bowl: The Southern Plains in the 1930s,* New York, Oxford University Press, 1979.

Index

I

M

N

O

P

R

S

T

W

❑❑❑